THE BORDERLAND
IN THE
CIVIL WAR

THE BORDERLAND

IN THE

CIVIL WAR

BY

EDWARD CONRAD SMITH

Select Bibliographies Reprint Series

BOOKS FOR LIBRARIES PRESS
FREEPORT, NEW YORK

First Published 1927
Reprinted 1969

104490

STANDARD BOOK NUMBER:
8369-5078-X

LIBRARY OF CONGRESS CATALOG CARD NUMBER:
70-95078

PRINTED IN THE UNITED STATES OF AMERICA

ACKNOWLEDGMENT

The author is indebted to Professor Edward Channing for encouragement, advice and criticism during a great part of the period of his research; and to Dean Marshall S. Brown, who has read the manuscript and suggested a number of important revisions.

EDWARD CONRAD SMITH.

March 1, 1927.

CONTENTS

THE BORDERLAND
IN THE
CIVIL WAR

THE BORDERLAND IN THE CIVIL WAR

CHAPTER I

SOCIAL AND ECONOMIC CONDITIONS

The Civil War has usually been described as a conflict between two wholly distinct sections, abruptly divided by state boundary lines. It grew out of the controversy over slavery, it is said, and was waged on the one side by slaveholders and their misguided neighbors, while on the other side the people of the North fought to emancipate the slaves and to maintain the Union. Such a view, though a natural one, gives an incorrect impression of the character of the struggle. In the first place, the boundary between the sections, throughout most of its course, was artificial. There had been no such development of state patriotism as would make the people choose one side or the other because their public authorities told them to do so. In the second place, there was in the beginning, and there existed during the whole course of the war, a middle section in which the question of slavery was unimportant compared with other issues. Three of the Western slave States fought under the national flag because they loved the Union and hoped to keep their slave property within it. In three of the greatest free States half the people had no quarrel with slavery, and would have been glad to see it prosper. These groups, contiguous to each other, formed a third section which had little in common with the other two. It took part in

1

the war with entirely different motives from those which
actuated either the North or the South.

This section was the Borderland west of the Alleghanies, or, as I shall call it for convenience, simply "the
Borderland." It was bounded on the north by the watershed between the tributaries of the Ohio River and the
streams which flowed into the Great Lakes. This watershed, though an insignificant natural barrier, was of
extreme importance, since it marked roughly the line of
division between the settlements which had been made
from the South, and in which the culture was distinctly
Southern, from those which had been made from New
York and other parts of the North. From Indiana, the
division line ran across Illinois to the northeastern corner
of Missouri, and thence westward to the frontier. The
eastern boundary was the crest of the Alleghanies, difficult of crossing, which effectually separated the Atlantic
seaboard from the West. The southern boundary was
the line between the cotton-growing South and the region
in which the plantation system had not developed, owing
to the absence of a staple crop. Leaving out of the account
the Southern Highlands, which were separated from the
Borderland by difficulties of communication, it began in
northeastern Tennessee and ran nearly with the southern
boundary of Kentucky to the Mississippi. Then crossing
the river, it followed fairly closely the boundary between
Missouri and Arkansas. The Borderland therefore
included the southern halves of Ohio, Indiana and Illinois, all of Trans-Alleghany Virginia, and all but insignificant parts of Kentucky and Missouri.

This great homogeneous section, extending almost the
whole width of the country, had it in its power to determine the outcome of the Civil War. Its white popula-

tion was nearly as great as that of the eleven seceded States.[1] Lying between the other sections, and having some interests in common with both of them, it was debatable ground. If it cast in its lot with the South or remained neutral, as most Southern people expected it would, the division of the United States into two republics was certain. If, on the other hand, it actively supported the cause of the Union, it was only a matter of time until the secessionists would have to submit and return to their allegiance. For both the Federal and the Confederate governments the attitude of this section afforded easily the most important domestic problem of the war.

Since Maryland and Delaware have always been classified as border slave States, I feel obliged to explain why they have not been included in the Borderland. The reason is that the two sections are distinct in nearly every particular except a common hesitancy about entering the war. A glance at the map will show that they were geographically separated, the populous part of Maryland being pinched off between Virginia and Pennsylvania long before it touched the watershed of the Ohio River. Between the two sections the Alleghanies interposed a

---

[1] According to the Eighth Census, 1860, the white population of the Borderland was distributed as follows:

Kentucky	919,517
Missouri	1,063,509
Western Virginia	355,144
Southern Ohio	1,208,298
Southern Indiana	789,003
Southern Illinois	632,398
Total	4,967,869

The white population of the seceded States (excluding western Virginia) was 5,094,318.

barrier which effectually prevented a mingling of settlements or an interchange of ideas. The emigrants who went westward from Maryland usually passed through either Pennsylvania or Virginia, and arrived at their permanent homes often after a residence of considerable duration in those States. Their individuality as Marylanders was therefore forgotten. On account of the fact that the State never possessed Western lands, the emigrants became mingled with those from other sections. It was not a "mother State" for any part of the West. Its sentimental associations with the Ohio Valley were far less than those of Tidewater Virginia or Pennsylvania —or even Massachusetts, whose citizens had established several important Western colonies.

In its commercial relations with the West, Maryland had not been particularly fortunate, owing again to the barrier of the Alleghanies. The people of a part of northwestern Virginia, lacking more convenient markets, resorted to Cumberland and Baltimore for the sale of their produce and the purchase of salt, coffee, calico and other necessities. But the volume of this trade was small, and the section dependent on the eastern centers was limited, particularly after the development of the steamboat. When the Baltimore and Ohio Railroad was extended to the Ohio River a few years before the war, a much greater area was made tributary to the commercial centers of Maryland, which in turn became dependent upon the West. In 1861, however, the change had been too recently accomplished to have modified the prior diversity of interests between them.

Not merely were the two sections lacking in sentimental associations and commercial connections: they were wholly dissimilar in their habits of life, their sym-

pathies and their interests. The people of Maryland and
Delaware had belonged to the soil for generations. Their
institutions had developed farther than those of the West,
which had only recently passed beyond the frontier stage.
They had become conservative, while the West was filled
with the spirit of radical democracy. Located on the
Atlantic seaboard, they could afford to pursue their own
policies without fear of being cut off from contact with
the world. They were therefore less responsive to the
sentiment of nationality than the Borderland, which
was dependent upon all other parts of the country.
Finally, they had developed important commercial and
sentimental associations in other directions.

Without forming a separate section, Maryland and
Delaware were linked with the South in some respects,
with the North in others. They were usually classed as
Southern because they had coöperated with the South in
questions relating to the admission of new States, and
because slavery existed among them. But the institution
was not deeply rooted. Only southern Maryland had
many slaves. In other parts of the State there were a
few who worked with their masters in the fields or were
kept as household servants. Nearly everywhere slavery
appeared to be diminishing in importance on account
of voluntary manumission, which had given Maryland
a larger free negro population than any other State.
Aside from this matter, both States were identified with
the North through their important manufacturing and
commercial interests. In 1860 Baltimore stood fourth
among the cities of the United States, and had a third
of the population of Maryland. It made and sold goods
for use in the South in the same way as New York
and Philadelphia, and seems to have traded directly with

the South only a little more than those cities.[2] Its principal trade was foreign. Its business relations were mainly with the North. For that reason, if for no other, the secession of Maryland could hardly have taken place with ordinarily good political management.

There is still another reason, more important than any yet given, for the distinction between these States and the Borderland. That is the different political problem which the two sections presented to the national government. At the southern edge of Maryland was situated the national capital, one of the most important symbols of the unity of the nation. Possession of it had to be maintained at all hazards, even at the cost of alienating the people of Maryland. The Borderland had no such prize within it, but it had men in tens of thousands. In dealing with a powerful group of doubtful States or a numerous body of dissatisfied people, it is essential for public authorities to cultivate diplomacy, to use tact, and to compromise on all but those issues which are absolutely necessary to the desired result. The threat of force or an actual invasion is disastrous. The Borderland was so important a section as to make such a policy indispensable. Maryland was not. The result was that the national government moved troops across the State when it felt impelled to do so. If it had seceded, there is little doubt but that Northern troops would have compelled it to submit at once. On the other hand, the national government delayed, and conceded points to the people of the Borderland throughout most of the period of the war.

In contrast with the separateness of the Eastern and

[2] See a pamphlet by John P. Kennedy, entitled "An Appeal to Maryland."

Western border States, the different parts of the Borderland were unified through common interests and associations. The section was a geographical, social, industrial and political unit. It had within its wide territory many variations in surface, many kinds of soil, many different means of livelihood, and some differences of nationality, without losing its homogeneity. The climate was everywhere similar. The same forms of wealth were produced, which were transported to common markets over common highways of commerce. The people, everywhere of the same stock, had been further unified by habits of association in settling the common problems of expelling the Indians, obtaining an outlet for their surplus produce, developing facilities of transportation, and promoting the unity of the whole country. Where there were differences in interests and opinions, they usually appeared within comparatively small districts, and were not peculiar to any one State.

These generalizations hold true despite the fact that the Ohio River formed a western extension of the Mason and Dixon line. For the people of the North and of the South, it was a real line of division. But for the people of the Borderland, it was of far less importance than the barriers that separated them from other sections and isolated them from the world. From the very nature of their location, their outstanding problem was the maintenance of friendly relations throughout the country. They were dependent upon both the other sections, and, in case of a division of the Union, would be cut off from profitable intercourse with one of them. They were, in addition, interested in other matters, such as the opening of the Western lands to settlement and the building of a transcontinental railroad by the national government, which were more important to them than the question of slavery. Thus it happened that when an issue concerned slavery alone, the people north and south of the Ohio River held opposite opinions and took sides; but when it became complicated with other questions, as it nearly always did, they united in securing compromises and adjustments that would promote unity and harmony. Clay and Benton, who for a long period led in the movement for national solidarity, correctly represented the sentiments of the whole Borderland.

In other respects the Ohio River had a unifying influence that far outweighed the fact that it marked the limits of different States. It was a "natural boundary" only in being a possible military frontier. When settlers first entered the valley, it, with its tributaries, were the easiest routes of travel by which choice locations were reached. Floating down a southern branch in canoes or threading their way along the banks with pack horses, they met with little difficulty in crossing and moving up a northern branch. After having established their farms, they naturally resorted to the trading posts along the main stream for the sale of their surplus produce and the purchase of supplies. In the course of time the trading posts grew into cities which drew trade from the whole valley in every direction. Opposite them were satellite towns which flourished by transferring goods across the river to the main markets. Regular ferries were established at intervals. Where there were none, the crossing was easy for anyone who owned a canoe or a skiff. Visits back and forth were common, and intermarriages not infrequent. Moreover, the river was the common highway for all the people living in the valley, and as such was a unifying force of the greatest significance. The same

influences were exerted by the Missouri, which poured
its muddy flood into the Mississippi a hundred and fifty
miles north of the mouth of the Ohio. The rivers of the
Borderland drew the people, east and west, north and
south, into close association.

In its other natural features, parts of the Borderland
were different without being disunited. In western Virginia and in eastern Kentucky and Tennessee the surface
was broken by a succession of high, winding ridges and
deep valleys, which had their counterpart nowhere else
save in the Ozark highlands of Missouri. From these hilly
regions the surface sloped away in every direction with
gradually decreasing undulations. Southeastern Ohio
was a region of hills, like western Virginia except that the
elevations were not so great and the valleys were wider.
In Indiana and western Kentucky the surface was somewhat broken near the Ohio River. Only southern Illinois was a continuous level plain. But these differences
were not so significant as they appear. The chief interest
of the region in 1861 was in grazing, and the grassy
pasture lands were of nearly equal value whether they
were level or sloping. For tillage, every section had more
or less surface that could easily be plowed without danger
of having the soil washed away with every heavy rain.
Finally, the state boundary lines were drawn without
regard to natural topographical divisions. The differences between parts of the same State were often more
marked than the differences between States.

The people who settled the Borderland were as homogeneous as the region itself. Beginning in 1769, daring
pioneers from Virginia and North Carolina made their
way over the Alleghanies and established settlements in
the Monongahela, Kanawha, Kentucky and Tennessee

valleys which proved to be permanent. For a long time their numbers remained few on account of the interruptions caused by Dunmore's War and by the Indian ravages along the frontier which accompanied the British attempts to put down the Revolution. But after 1783 the tide of emigration set in with tremendous force. Thousands of frontiersmen crossed the divide and drove the Indians from the fertile sections of Kentucky and Tennessee. Following them came settlers from the Tidewater regions who completed the work of establishing new societies. Within a decade from the close of the Revolution the best lands in the Blue Grass section of Kentucky had been occupied, and settlements had been extended to the less favored adjacent regions. In 1792, Kentucky was separated from Virginia and admitted as a State.

It was inevitable that the area of settlement would soon spread to the northern bank of the Ohio River. The first important colony was established at Marietta in 1788 by emigrants from New England. A little later, people from other Northern States planted isolated settlements along the river as far west as Cincinnati. But the movement of settlers from the North was not rapid enough to occupy the intervening territory before emigrants from the South crossed the Ohio River in large numbers and spread themselves over it. Long before the Peace of Greenville assured the safety of the outlying settlements, many former soldiers of the Virginia Line took up lands that had been reserved for them in the Scioto Valley. Afterward the Southern settlers came into the region in ever increasing numbers. While Indians still roamed through the region south of Lake Erie, and while the Western Reserve of Connecticut was still a comparatively feeble settlement, they had pushed their way up the tributaries of the Ohio to their sources, and had made all of southern Ohio their own.[3] The movement of settlers into Ohio was so rapid, in fact, that it hindered the proper development of Kentucky and western Virginia. Owing to the abominable confusion of land titles that existed under various grants of the State of Virginia, many settlers left desirable locations there and moved on into the Old Northwest, where they could purchase land from the national government at a lower price, and where they could be sure of a clear title. Four of the early governors of Ohio were former residents of western Virginia,[4] and the leaders in nearly every walk of life were of Southern extraction.

The early development of Indiana was the same as that of Ohio, except that the immigration was less directly from the Southern States of the Atlantic seaboard. Most of the settlers came from Kentucky which, like ancient Miletus, doubled and tripled itself in the new colonies that it sent forth. Its frontiersmen engaged in almost constant conflicts with the Indians which often led them to make counter raids across the Ohio River, and afforded them an opportunity to appraise the desirable lands that lay beyond their settlements. With the western Virginians, they formed most of the army with which George Rogers Clark conquered the Northwest. They made up the great bulk of the armies of St. Clair and Wayne which expelled the Indians from southern Ohio and southeastern Indiana. In the Tippecanoe campaign and in the War of 1812, Kentucky regiments under William Henry Harrison finally broke the power of the

[3] Rufus King, *Ohio, First Fruits of the Ordinance of 1787*, chap. viii.
[4] Virgil A. Lewis, *History and Government of West Virginia*, p. 259.

Indians. Having done so much to conquer the Northwest, the people of Kentucky naturally considered it their own. So many of them went into Indiana as to make it an even more Southern community than Ohio. When the constitution of the State was being drafted, it was only with great difficulty that an anti-slavery clause was inserted.[5]

In Illinois, the settlement was made at a later date than that of Indiana because both of its western position and of its lack of important tributary streams. With one insignificant exception the whole area was occupied by people who came either directly or indirectly from the South. Though the first constitution prohibited the introduction of slavery, the first legislature enacted laws which nearly reduced the free negroes again to a condition of bondage. In 1824 a proposed slavery amendment was narrowly defeated.[6] Southern Illinois remained practically an appendage of Kentucky until after the Civil War.

As the course of settlement proceeded westward the amount of Southern influence tended always to increase. In Missouri, the conditions differed from those of the Old Northwest principally in that the Congress had not prohibited the ownership of slaves in the territory acquired from France. Consequently most slaveholders who wished to take their slaves with them when they left their homes in Kentucky or Tennessee went to Missouri. Many others moved into the State after having lived for a considerable period in southern Illinois. By 1830 they had settled the bottoms along the Mississippi

[5] J. P. Dunn, Jr., *Indiana, A Redemption from Slavery*, pp. 418-430.
[6] Frederic L. Paxson, *History of the American Frontier, 1763-1893*, pp. 198-199.

and Missouri rivers and were pushing toward the boundaries of the State in every direction. They occupied the whole of it before there was any important immigration from the Northern States.

In the course of time, when the Borderland had passed beyond the pioneer stage, its population was greatly augmented by the coming of Northern immigrants. The census reports of 1860 show that thousands of the people in every State had been born in the North. In Ohio, the natives of Pennsylvania alone outnumbered the natives of all the Southern States. But these figures do not by any means give a correct impression. More than a million people were shown to be natives of Ohio, of whom probably two-thirds had been born of Southern parents. Furthermore, the later comers were scattered among people who had established a Southern society and peculiarly Southern institutions, and therefore must have been influenced by them to a tremendous degree. Nearly everywhere they seem to have become merged with the people among whom they lived. Only the settlements made by New Englanders at French Creek, Virginia; Marietta and Springfield, Ohio; Evansville, Indiana; and Edwards County, Illinois, stood out like islands in a sea of Southern influence.

Among the later comers to the Borderland were nearly half a million Germans and Irishmen. The Germans were generally of a superior type, having left their native countries in consequence of their failure to achieve liberty in the revolutions of 1848. Desiring to maintain their culture in America, they were difficult of assimilation. Most of them congregated in the larger towns. By 1860, there were fifty thousand Germans in St. Louis —almost a third of the population of the city—all living

in a well defined section. In Cincinnati, the district
north of the canal was occupied so exclusively by them
that it was familiarly referred to as "beyond the Rhine."
In the smaller places, even where they did not live in
separate districts, they clung tenaciously to their Old
World customs. Recognizing their solidarity, the Republican party in Illinois began the practice, in 1856, of
nominating a German as the candidate for lieutenant-
governor. The Irish, who were about half as numerous
as the Germans, had come westward to engage in construction work on railroads, turnpikes and other public
works. On the completion of a job many of them purchased small farms in the neighborhood or gravitated to
the cities. Unlike the Germans, they quickly adopted
the customs of the people among whom they lived.[7]

The people of the Borderland were homogeneous in
their social organization to a remarkable degree. Rich
and poor there were of course, but, living in a new country, the poor were hopeful of the future and the rich
were not so wealthy as to discourage others from striving
to attain to their condition. Everywhere practically the
whole population was engaged in agriculture, which, in
the absence of a plantation system, retarded the development of class distinctions. There were no cities large
enough to present problems of rural *versus* urban interests. Cincinnati, including Covington and Newport, with
a total population of 180,000, was the largest. After it
came St. Louis with 160,000 and Louisville with 75,000
people. No others approached these three in importance.
Only twenty-seven other towns in the whole section

---

[7] The German population by States was: Missouri, 88,000; Kentucky,
27,000; Illinois, 131,000; Indiana, 67,000; Ohio, 168,000—of whom 49,000
were congregated in Cincinnati. The Irish were similarly distributed.

boasted a population of more than five thousand.[8] Most
of the county seats were merely centers of local trade,
the chief institutions being a courthouse and jail, a mill,
a tannery, several stores and blacksmith shops, and occasionally a distillery.

In their economic life the people were unified through
their common means of livelihood. Nearly all of them
were directly or indirectly dependent upon agriculture.
The principal industry was the raising of live stock. In
the hilly regions and on the great ranches of southwestern Missouri it was the only practicable means of utiliz-
ing the land. In the more level sections it appears at
first glance that tillage would be more profitable, but the
position of the Borderland with respect to markets determined otherwise. When the West was first settled, it
was possible for the frontier farmers to devote their
attention mainly to the growing of wheat for sale in the
market at New Orleans. The prices they received were
high, and the difficulties of transportation, though great,
were by no means insuperable. As the cleared area
became larger, a new problem developed. The production of grain in the Ohio Valley increased so much faster
than the demands of the Southern market that an abrupt
decline in prices took place shortly after the close of
the War of 1812, which would have been ruinous to the
Borderland if there had been no other resource. Fortunately it had been discovered that pigs and fat cattle
could be driven over the Alleghanies from points as far
distant as the Scioto Valley and Kentucky. Soon thereafter many wheatfields were turned into pastures and
cornfields, and cattle raising became an important indus-

[8] One each in Kentucky and Virginia, eleven in Ohio, six in Indiana,
three in Illinois, and five in Missouri.

try in which all the Borderland shared. The young stock were bred in Illinois and Missouri, driven eastward to Indiana, where they were kept a year or two, and finally were taken to Ohio, where they were fattened preparatory to the final journey to the Eastern markets. After the middle of the century, when the completion of the railroads to the East afforded an easier method of marketing, this process was somewhat changed. Cattle were then fattened in nearly all parts of the Borderland.[9] Many hogs were also raised to supply local demands, to be driven over the mountains, or to be killed and cured for shipment to the East or the South. Finally the wool-growing industry assumed considerable importance when the construction of canals and railroads afforded an outlet for the product.

After grazing, the growing of crops was the next most important industry. During the period from 1815 to 1860 there was a steady increase in the demand for agricultural produce in the Southern markets. At the same time the development of the steamboat made transportation cheap. These factors encouraged the farmers of the Borderland to devote considerable attention to the growing of hemp, tobacco and cereals. In 1860 more than three-fourths of the hemp produced in the United States came from Kentucky and Missouri. In the production of tobacco, Kentucky stood second among the States, with a total of 108,000,000 pounds, and Ohio and Missouri each produced more than 25,000,000 pounds.[10] Of cereals grown for other markets, 2,500,000 bushels of corn, 5,000,000 bushels of wheat and 2,000,000 barrels of flour went southward to New Orleans in 1849. Two or

[9] *Eighth Census, Report of Agriculture*, pp. cxxix-cxxxi.
[10] *Eighth Census, Report of Agriculture*, p. 185.

three years later the completion of the railroads to the East brought a new prosperity to this branch of agriculture. Thereafter it increased by leaps and bounds.

Another important industry was manufacturing, which had developed in the cities and towns to supply local demands for goods that could not easily be imported, and to convert some of the bulky products of the region into forms in which they could be shipped out with profit. The principal products were ready-made clothing, flour and meal, whiskey, lumber, pig-iron, agricultural machinery and pork. The chief center of manufacturing was Cincinnati. Upwards of ten thousand operatives were employed in the ready-made clothing industry in the city, which became the distributing point for the clothing trade throughout the West.[11] Its pork packing establishments were so important as to give it the nickname of "Porkopolis." In addition, it had important distilleries. In St. Louis, Louisville and several smaller places there were similar establishments. Every county seat had one or more flour and lumber mills which supplied local demands and shipped their surplus to more distant markets.

Some reference has already been made to the means by which the products of the Borderland were transported to outside centers of trade, but the importance of commerce warrants greater attention. For any country it is usually the greatest single external interest. Its foreign policy is mainly directed toward securing uninterrupted routes of transportation and favorable treatment for its products in the markets of other countries. The opinions of its people toward other nations are greatly influenced by the existence of tariff walls, monop-

[11] *Eighth Census, Report of Manufactures*, p. lxi.

olies, reciprocity and other commercial policies. For the Borderland, shut in as it was, commerce assumed even greater importance than it has in international affairs, shaping the attitude of the people toward the national government and toward the other sections. To a great extent it determined their course during the period of the Civil War.

The natural highways of the Borderland were the Ohio and Mississippi rivers and their tributaries. Few places were farther than twenty-five miles from a stream navigable at high water by flatboats. In the beginning it was the custom of the people of every pioneer community to build and load a flatboat every year to be taken to the Spanish port of New Orleans with the first autumn freshet. When they arrived at their destination the boats were sold for the lumber they contained, and their crews returned to the upper settlements on foot or on horseback bearing the far less bulky necessities of life. The importance of the trade was such that the people threatened to secede from the Union and make their own terms with Spain when the national government failed to secure the opening of the port of New Orleans to them. Their agitation soon resulted in the acquisition of Louisiana. But the dangers and limitations of flatboat navigation were so great as to weigh heavily against the rapid development of Western commerce. It must always have remained in a crude state if better means had not been employed. Fortunately such means were soon at hand. The first steamboat went down the river in 1811. Within a short time thereafter others had been built in sufficient numbers to supplant the flatboats altogether. Their effect was almost revolutionary, since they could bring goods up the river with far less difficulty than had formerly been encountered in carrying them down. Providing a safe, speedy and cheap means of transportation, they caused a great increase in both the exportations and importations of the Borderland. Furthermore they increased the popular feeling of dependence upon the South.

Meanwhile the leaders in public and business affairs in the East, realizing the importance of Western commerce, had started the construction of canals through the passes of the mountains. In 1784 the General Assembly of Virginia, acting on a report of General Washington, authorized a company to connect the waters of the Potomac and the Monongahela. Before the close of the century business men in both New York and Philadelphia planned similar connections through the valleys of the Mohawk and the Juniata. None of these was successful except the Erie Canal, which was opened in 1825. It secured to New York the undisputed control of the trade of the Lake district, and greatly accelerated the development of the Northwest. It also stimulated the States of the West to begin the construction of canals to serve as feeders to it. The Ohio and Miami Canal and the Sandusky-Scioto Canal connected the Ohio River with Lake Erie, and in Indiana a canal was completed between the head waters of the Maumee and the Wabash. All were used to some extent in conveying the less bulky products, such as pork and whiskey, to the East, and for the shipment of manufactured goods to the West. But their insufficient width limited their capacity, and placed the Ohio Valley at a disadvantage in competing with the Lake district.

The problem of securing an adequate means of transportation for the Borderland was first really solved when the railroads were built across the mountains. In 1851 the Erie Railroad was completed to the Lakes. The next year the Pennsylvania Railroad reached Pittsburgh. In 1853 the Baltimore and Ohio Railroad, after long delays, was opened from Baltimore to Wheeling, and five years later a branch was built to Parkersburg, then the head of summer navigation on the Ohio River. Meanwhile there had been an immense amount of railroad construction in the comparatively level region west of the Alleghanies. Beginning with eighty-nine in 1840, the total mileage increased to thirteen hundred in 1850, and to more than eleven thousand in 1860.[12] In the last named year, Cincinnati was connected with Toledo, Sandusky, Cleveland, Pittsburgh, Wheeling and Parkersburg on the north and east, and with Chicago and East St. Louis on the west. Other cities, like Louisville, St. Louis, Columbus and Indianapolis, had railroads leading in all directions. From the Ohio River lines ran northward from Portsmouth, Lawrenceburg, Evansville and Cairo, and southward from Covington and Paducah. All these, with shorter lines, formed a network of railroads throughout the Borderland. They connected the section only with the East: no lines had yet been built to any point in the South.[13]

The building of the railroads had an effect on the economic life of the Borderland comparable only to that of the introduction of the steamboat thirty years earlier. Affording a much quicker and cheaper means of transportation, they completely supplanted the canals and highways. The quantity of pork and whiskey shipped northward over the canals shrank to nearly nothing, all except purely local trade being diverted from them. The railroads assumed the burden with ease, and in addition cared

---

[12] Edward Channing, *A History of the United States*, vol. vi, p. 382.
[13] *Official Records, War of the Rebellion, War Atlas*, plates cxxv and cxl.

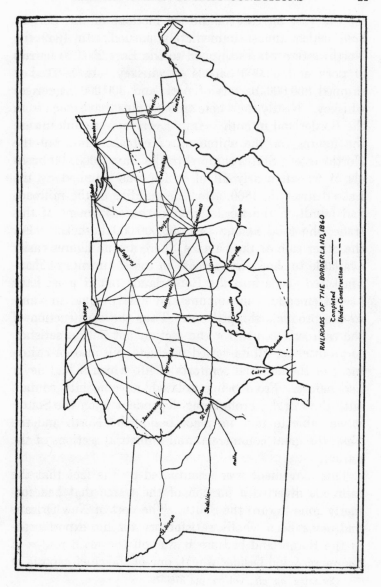

RAILROADS OF THE BORDERLAND, 1860
Completed ———
Under Construction ------

for the vast increase in the productions of the Borderland which almost immediately ensued. In 1849 the
Northwestern States shipped to the East 250,000 barrels
of pork and 63,000 barrels of whiskey. In 1860 they
shipped 860,000 barrels of pork and 300,000 barrels of
whiskey. Nearly the whole amount must have come from
the Borderland in both years. Even more significant are
the figures for the shipment of cereals. In 1849 the
Northwestern States shipped to the East 5,000,000 bushels of wheat, nearly all of which was supplied by the
Lake district; in 1860, after the building of the railroads
had admitted the Borderland to the enjoyment of this
trade, the total amount was 30,000,000 bushels.[14] For
the other side of the balance, there are no figures easily
available to show the increase in the shipments of manufactured goods into the Borderland; but it must have
been tremendous in amount and nearly equal in value
to the products shipped out. Thus the construction of
the railroads gained for the section not only a satisfactory outlet for all its varied products, but also an enjoyment of the material comforts of life which it had never
had before. From being isolated, it came into contact
with the world. From being dependent upon the South,
it was able to take its place beside the North and the
East, the great commercial and industrial sections of the
nation.

This movement was accentuated by the fact that the
railroads diverted a portion of the traffic that had formerly gone toward the South. The port of New Orleans
had never been wholly satisfactory for the export trade
of the Borderland because it was off the main routes of
commerce; and besides wheat, one of the chief exports of

[14] Channing, *op. cit.*, vol. vi, pp. 378-379.

the section, was liable to mold there while awaiting shipment. By 1860 the exports of this important article
from the port had shrunk to practically nothing, and the
exports of pork and some other products had greatly
decreased. Even some cotton from as far south as Memphis was sent up the river on the first lap of its journey
to the mills of New England.[15] The direction of the
great bulk of Western commerce was definitely turned
toward the East.

In spite of these revolutionary changes, the importance
of the Southern trade continued to bulk large in the
economic life of the Borderland. There were two reasons for this. In the first place, there existed between
the business men of the Borderland and those of the
South friendly trading relations that had been built up
over a period of years. From the standpoint of convenience it seemed better to follow in the established course
than to form new connections, even when a cheaper
means of transportation had been developed. From reasons of habit shipments continued to be made by boat
on the Missouri River from towns on the Missouri
Pacific Railroad.[16] Seven-eighths of the tobacco crop
of Kentucky was still sent down the river to New Orleans
because that city had been the great market for this
product. From New Orleans, also, nearly all the coffee
and sugar used in the Borderland continued to be shipped
up the river.[17] In the second place, the Southern con-
sumption of the products of the Borderland, which had
always been extensive, continued to increase. In the

[15] Carl Russell Fish, "The Decision of the Ohio Valley," in the
Annual Report of the American Historical Association, 1910, p. 160.

[16] Hiram M. Chittenden, *History of Early Steamboat Navigation on
the Missouri River*, vol. ii, pp. 417-418.

[17] Fish, in *Annual Report*, Am. Hist. Assn. 1910, p. 160.

five-year period from 1856 to 1860 forty per cent more flour was received at New Orleans than in the similar period from 1851 to 1855, notwithstanding the virtual cessation of the export trade. The receipts of corn and whiskey nearly doubled from 1849 to 1860. At other Southern cities the receipts of these articles must have increased in like proportion, since the plantation owners were becoming more and more dependent on outside sources for their foodstuffs, clothing and other supplies. The whole of this trade was monopolized by the Borderland on account of its location. As long as it continued to exist and to grow it was a source of great prosperity for the section, particularly Missouri, southern Illinois and western Kentucky, which could ship their products to the South by boat somewhat more cheaply than to the East by rail.

As may be inferred from the statement of facts just made, the public opinion of the Borderland concerning commercial relations with other sections was in a confused state. There can be no doubt that the railroads had diverted much trade from the steamboats and that they had released most of the people from their dependence upon Southern markets. But to the great mass of the people, living detached lives on their farms, these facts were by no means clear. They knew that an improvement in business had taken place, for they were able to produce more and to sell at higher prices than before. But they did not know the ultimate destination of their produce, nor did they care about the matter so long as they received satisfactory prices. Being slow to appreciate the significance of great economic changes, like the mass of the people everywhere, they continued to regard the commerce of the rivers as of the highest importance to them simply because they had always believed it. On the other hand the introduction of manufactured goods in large quantities and the quickened economic life of the section must have moved them profoundly, causing at least the beginning of a new economic outlook. If the final settlement of the slavery controversy could have been delayed for another decade, it is more than probable that the section would have become commercially so closely allied with the North that the South would not have dared to secede. As it was in 1860, the doubtful state of popular sentiment encouraged the Southern leaders to proceed with the secessionist movement in the belief that the Borderland was dependent upon the South.

In reality it was the South that was dependent upon the Borderland, rather than the reverse. The Borderland procured little from the South except coffee, sugar and molasses. The South, on the other hand, procured from the Borderland most of the necessities of life. As the demand for cotton increased, the plantation owners found it more profitable to divert their land to its production rather than continue on a self-sustaining basis. They therefore depended upon the farmers of the Borderland for their grain, meat and livestock. The horses and mules which drew the plows, the corn and bacon which made up the diet of the plantation hands, the flour and beef consumed by the planters and their families, and the whiskey which the planters and overseers drank, all came down the Mississippi River. The places of the slaves who were worn out by the intensive labor on the plantations were in part taken by negroes reared in Kentucky and Missouri. Even the bagging for the cotton bales was made of hemp grown in the Borderland.[18]   The Southern people first came to a sharp realization of their dependence when the war shut off their supplies and compelled them to divert the labor of their slaves to the production of foodstuffs.

A factor which helped to counterbalance the effect of racial and commercial ties between the South and the Borderland were the different social systems in the two sections.   In the beginning they seemed to have a common destiny.   Both were settled by Southern frontiersmen.   The problems of frontier life, being everywhere much the same, developed a lively sense of coöperation between them, which was strengthened by the opportunities to mingle freely in the common market city of New Orleans.   But all this was changed with the greatly increased demand for cotton.   Attracted by the rich new lands along the lower Mississippi, Southern men of wealth bought the farms of the frontiersmen and turned them into great plantations.   In the space of two or three decades the region became an extension of the Lower South, which had little in common with the Borderland.   New Orleans, which early gave promise of becoming the social and political center of the whole West, remained for the Borderland only a commercial mart.

The differences between the social organizations of the two sections were inherent in the systems of labor employed.   On the farms of the Borderland the labor was generally performed by the owner and members of his family, occasionally assisted by hired help or apprentices in the free States or by slaves in Kentucky and Missouri.   Few farms, even in these States, were large enough to justify the ownership of many slaves.   Most

[18] Col. R. M. Kelly, in *Union Regiments of Kentucky*, p. 13.

slaveholders had only three or four. Under these conditions it was natural that the system should be paternalistic, with close personal relations between master and slave. But on the great plantations of the South, where production was on a large scale, all the labor was performed by slaves. When the masters went into the fields at all, it was in a supervisory capacity. Most of them preferred to employ overseers. These, acting under instructions to obtain the utmost possible production, worked the slaves at high speed early and late, with the result that many of them were worn out after a few years. When they were no longer able to maintain the pace demanded they were discarded, and their places were filled by others, easily obtainable in the markets. It was this system and the terrible conditions which sometimes arose under it that gave point to the denunciations of the abolitionists.

For slave labor to be successful, three things were necessary. In the first place, the tasks must be simple and within the comprehension of the slave. Secondly, the supervision of the work must be thorough. And finally, there must be continuous work for nearly the whole year, since the expenses for food, clothing and medical attendance were nearly as great during periods of idleness as during the season of production.

Cotton was the crop most nearly suited to slave labor. It had a long growing season. The planting, cultivation and harvesting of the crop required almost constant manual labor. Usually the preparation of the soil was begun in February and continued until April or May, when the planting took place. Afterward, for two months or more, the crop demanded much cultivation. At midsummer in most sections the bolls began to open;

and from that time until late in the autumn the whole force of the plantation was busily engaged in gathering the crop. The picking of cotton was such a simple and easy task that it could be done by women and children, making it possible for whole slave families to be put to work. Thus there was profit in rearing negroes from the time they were able to accompany their mothers to the fields. After the crop had been gathered, the stalks had to be cut and the land prepared for plowing again. Practically the whole year, therefore, was required to grow the crop. For the greater portion of the time a large number of workers could be employed on a small area where adequate supervision was possible.

The short growing season of the Borderland made the production of cotton and other peculiarly Southern products impossible. The principal crops were wheat, corn, tobacco and hemp. For the growing of wheat slave labor was utterly unsuited, since from the period of seeding—usually only a few days in the early fall—until the harvest in June or July no labor was required. For the growing of corn it was likewise out of the question, since the crop made such a quick growth that only two or three cultivations early in the summer were thought necessary. It was usually harvested by turning hogs into the fields; but when it was to be husked, the task required a relatively slight expenditure of labor which could be spread over a considerable period. The growing of tobacco demanded the expenditure of much labor throughout the spring and summer months. Owing to its short growing season it was possible to start fields at different times, thus eliminating periods of idleness. The seed was planted in beds, and the plants were later pulled up and transplanted by hand—a process that required much effort in digging, carrying water and providing shade. Frequent cultivation was then necessary to kill weeds. Insect pests had to be combated. The tops had to be pinched off to insure a more stocky growth. The cutting, hauling, storing and curing of the crop demanded careful work that could not be postponed beyond a certain stage in the growth of the plants. There was thus plenty of work for the slaves to do during half the year, although during the winter season they spent their time in idleness, eating up the profits, as the farmers almost constantly complained. Conditions would have been better if it had not been for the low prices received, owing partly to the competition of tobacco grown by free labor, which was usually of superior quality.

The growing of hemp, like tobacco, involved a great deal of manual labor. Though little cultivation was necessary, the cutting of the crop by hand and the retting and other processes for removing the fibers consumed much time and energy. The crop was usually profitable, probably owing rather to limitation of the area of suitable land than to the superiority of slave labor. Many of the plantations of Kentucky and Missouri were devoted to the production of hemp in combination with cereals. By working their slaves in the cornfields during the early summer months, the planters were able to make their lands self-sustaining. During the winter the slaves were sometimes employed in clearing forest lands, though for the most part they remained idle. The holding of many slaves in the grazing sections was of course unprofitable.

In no part of the Borderland was slavery a controlling factor in the industrial life of the people. Missouri had

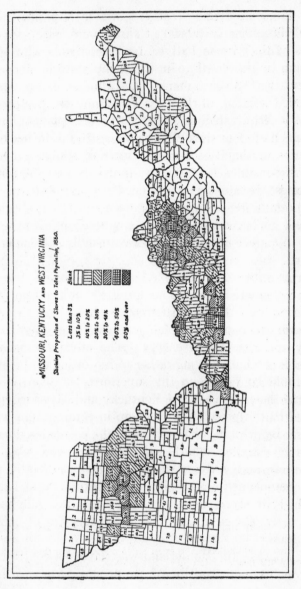

PROPORTION OF SLAVES TO TOTAL POPULATION, 1860

only 115,000 slaves in 1860 out of a total population of 1,200,000. Nearly 80,000 of them were within twenty miles of the Missouri River, far from the area of slave-holding in the South. In Kentucky the importance of slavery was much greater, the number being almost 250,000—a fifth of the total population. Woodford County, "the asparagus bed of the garden spot of the world," had more slave than white residents. A few other counties in the Blue Grass region had almost as many, and there was a large slave population along the Tennessee border, just east of the Cumberland River. In the mountainous region of eastern Kentucky the number did not make up more than two or three per cent of the total population.[19] Everywhere the slaves were well treated, the worst feature of the institution being their exportation to the Lower South. In western Virginia the number of slaves was far less than in any other part of the South. The district was totally unsuited to slavery owing to the short growing season, the rugged topography and the lack of a staple crop. In 1860 the total number of slaves in the counties now included in the State of West Virginia was 18,368. In sixteen of the fifty counties they made up less than one per cent of the total population. There were thirty-one counties in eastern Virginia, on the other hand, which had more slave than white inhabitants. The contrast indicates the difference in the economic organization of the two sections.

The people of the Borderland were naturally much less attached to slavery than those of the South. Many

[19] In Kentucky only one person owned more than 200 slaves, six owned between 100 and 200, 63 owned between 50 and 100, and 392 owned between 30 and 50. The great slave holding class therefore numbered only 462 heads of families. See *Eighth Census, Report of Agriculture*, p. 229.

thoughtful people, believing that it was more or less an economic evil, wished that all the slaves could be emancipated and sent out of the country. In 1832 the legislature of Virginia seriously considered a proposal for gradual emancipation. A substitute resolution providing for the removal of free negroes from the State was defeated by only one vote.[20] In the district west of the Blue Ridge the agitation was continued for twenty years longer.[21] In Kentucky gradual emancipation was one of the principal issues of the campaign for the election of delegates to the constitutional convention of 1849. The chief support, surprisingly enough, came from the counties which had the largest slave populations. In other counties the voters, thinking only of the possibility of a large free negro population, were apathetic. The movement was defeated chiefly through lack of organization and through the failure of its proponents to devise a satisfactory scheme for the transportation of the freedmen. From that time until the outbreak of the Civil War the free discussion of the slavery question was permitted in Kentucky to a greater extent that in any other slave State.[22] In Missouri a similar movement began as soon as the animosities aroused over the struggle for the admission of the State had died away. By 1828 a scheme for gradual emancipation had received the endorsement of leaders of both the political parties, and was in a fair way to be submitted by the legislature to a popular referendum. At this particularly favorable moment a

[20] Channing, vol. v, p. 143.
[21] In 1847, Samuel McD. Moore, John Letcher, and Henry Ruffner published a pamphlet advocating the gradual emancipation of the slaves held in the State.
[22] Asa E. Martin, *The Anti-Slavery Movement in Kentucky Prior to 1850*, pp. 134-138.

report gained circulation that a prominent anti-slavery leader in New York had recognized negroes as his social equals by entertaining them in his home. Such a storm of popular feeling was aroused against his action that it was not thought best at the time to submit the amendment. Five years later, when Lovejoy established his anti-slavery newspaper in St. Louis, a fierce controversy was precipitated which resulted finally in the definite ending of the popular movement for emancipation.[23]

The movement just described, which had an economic motive, must be distinguished from the abolitionist movement in the North, which was a moral upheaval against slavery. The people of the Borderland did not believe that the holding of slaves was immoral. Furthermore, they resented the attitude of the people of the North in trying to determine questions of morals for them. A good indication of their feeling is in the division of the Methodist Episcopal Church in 1844, which took place on the question of slaveholding by ministers. In northwestern Virginia nearly all the congregations elected to remain with the Northern church.[24] But in the Kanawha Valley and in the eastern part of the State they were gradually won over to the Methodist Episcopal Church, South. The Kentucky conference, by a vote of ninety-eight to five, decided to withdraw from the Northern church, though a few congregations near the Ohio River remained in it.[25] In Missouri five-sixths of the members seceded.

After 1850 the emancipationist movement in the bor-

[23] Lucien Carr, *Missouri, A Bone of Contention*, pp. 172-178.
[24] W. W. Sweet, *The Methodist Episcopal Church and the Civil War*, pp. 53-55.
[25] Martin, *op. cit.*, p. 81.

der slave States almost wholly died out owing to the
abolitionist agitation, which first showed great strength
when the question of extending slavery to the territory
conquered from Mexico was being debated in the Congress. The quarrel arrayed the people of all the slave
States solidly against the danger to their institutions.
Had it not been for the compromise arranged by the
greatest statesman of Kentucky and supported by the
Borderland, it is probable that the war would have
broken out in 1850. The compromise, however, only
allowed a breathing space. Neither party seemed willing
to carry out its terms in good faith. The South continued to demand the further extension of slavery, and
the North attempted to nullify the Fugitive Slave Law
by passing "personal liberty acts." Since most of the
fugitives belonged to owners in the border States, their
escape through the connivance of the people of the North
caused ill feeling. The people on the border, who had
formerly laughed at the fanatical agitation of Garrison
and Phillips, now began to take it as seriously as did the
people of rural New England. Many came to believe
that much of the wealth of their States was in danger of
being destroyed. Worse still, they were threatened with
the presence of a large free negro population—a condition which had long been dreaded, and which had been
the chief obstacle to carrying out the emancipationist
movement.

The effect of the abolitionist agitation was not merely
to inspire opposition to the North, but also to promote
the development of an aggressive pro-slavery movement.
In Missouri it was sponsored by David R. Atchison, then
a United States Senator, and by Claiborne F. Jackson,
who was to become the governor of the State in the

critical year 1861. By a combination with the advocates of paper money they succeeded in ousting Benton,
the great leader of the nationalist party in Missouri,
from his seat in the Senate in 1850.[26] A little later they
eagerly took part in the struggle for Kansas with the
object of adding another slave State to the South.[27] By
various means they sought to stir up enthusiasm for the
enterprise, but without a great deal of success. They
were wholly unable to match the colonizing activities of
the abolitionists, and so lost Kansas. But the internecine struggle along the western border, in which the people of Kansas made raids into Missouri, crystallized public opinion in their favor, and nearly resulted in turning
the people toward the complete support of the Southern
program.

In Virginia, during the same period, a movement was
begun by Governor Henry A. Wise and others to secure
a "united State with a united South." The task which
they attempted was by no means easy, since the eastern
and western sections were nearly as dissimilar as they
could well be, and from the time of the Revolution they
had been drifting farther and farther apart. The western section was a part of the Ohio Valley. Like the rest
of the Borderland, it had been settled by frontiersmen
who had little in common with the people of the Tidewater region. It had few slaves. Even more important
as bases of sectional cleavage were the facts that, from
the beginning of the existence of the State, it had had
far less than its share of members of the General Assembly, and that many of its people had been disfranchised
by a property qualification for voting. Despite insistent

[26] Theodore Roosevelt, *Thomas Hart Benton*, pp. 342-343.
[27] Eugene M. Violette, *A History of Missouri*, pp. 314-315.

demands for reforms, only a few had been granted. The basis of representation had been only slightly improved, because the eastern section was unwilling to relinquish any of its power. Universal white manhood suffrage was first achieved in 1851; but the fact that a man might vote in every precinct in which he owned land still gave the eastern section a disproportionate influence in elections. In the system of taxation equally strong reasons for discontent existed. The early reliance of the State for revenue had been upon a poll tax, which was, of course, unequal. Later it had been shifted to a general property tax which discriminated in a most unjust manner against the western section. In 1851 the delegates from this section, after a bitter struggle, succeeded in having a provision inserted in the constitution that all taxes were to be "equal and uniform." But in the very next paragraph it was stipulated that all slaves over twelve years of age were to be assessed at the uniform amount of $300 each, and that all slave children were to be exempt.[28] There was no exemption for any other class of property. Every horse, every cow, every pig, every piece of household furniture, was to be assessed uniformly with the value of land. Since the value of a mature slave was from $800 to $1200, and that of a slave child about $300, the slaveholder enjoyed an important exemption which other taxpayers did not. Small wonder that the people of the western section ascribed most of their ills to the selfishness of the eastern slaveholders. Many times in the history of the State they had muttered threats of withdrawing from political connection with eastern Virginia and setting up a separate State of their own. And their attitude on this

[28] Constitution of Virginia, 1851, art. iv, sect. 22, 23.

point had by no means been changed by the niggardly grants of reforms. The situation was really critical, if the pro-slavery leaders had but realized the fact.

Though obviously their proper course would have been to secure the removal of all the discriminations against the western section, they were either unwilling or unable to follow it. Instead, they directed their attention mainly to pushing forward works of internal improvement which would unite all sections of the State. In the Shenandoah Valley and in southwestern Virginia they constructed railroads connecting with the eastern ports, which pushed back the area of discontent from the Blue Ridge to the Alleghanies. They were unable, however, to complete either a projected canal or a railroad beyond the mountain barrier. The Trans-Alleghany section therefore received only promises of aid. In addition, the leaders engaged in propaganda to increase the sentiment of pride in the State, to which the people of the western section were extremely susceptible. Though they attained some success in this, the movement had only begun in 1861. It was in the precarious position where a mischance or a suspicion of selfish interest would cause it to fail ignobly.

In the northern portion of the Borderland the sentiment of the people on the question of slavery was not greatly unlike that in the border slave States. With the exception of the New England element, a few Quakers, and some very recent immigrants from the North, there were not a great many abolitionists. The majority were tolerant of slavery, and believed that the abolitionist movement was a wrong against the South. Several factors were responsible for their attitude. The principal one was, of course, the kinship of the people with the res-

idents of the border slave States, which led to frequent
visits back and forth. The paternalistic form of slavery
which they knew from actual observation or from the
accounts of their friends and relatives was totally different from the lurid descriptions of the abolitionist
speakers and writers. In common with the people of
Missouri and Kentucky they believed, therefore, that
the abolitionists were deliberately misrepresenting the
actual conditions under which slavery was operating.
Then too, the commercial interests of many of the people made them sympathize with the views of the Southerners to a greater extent than they were willing to
admit. Finally, many of the political leaders were
closely connected with slaveholding families. The wife
of Stephen A. Douglas was a former resident of North
Carolina. John A. Logan married into a family which
had strong pro-slavery leanings. Clement L. Vallandigham had married a resident of Maryland, and for several
years had lived on the plantation of his father-in-law.
From his own personal knowledge he was certain that
the abolitionists had exaggerated the conditions which
they attempted to describe. Senator Jesse D. Bright of
Indiana owned a plantation in Kentucky, and was,
besides, on intimate terms with most of the radical pro-
slavery leaders. And there were others with like interests and connections. Considering all the factors which
tended to influence their opinions in favor of slavery,
it was only natural that the people of southern Ohio,
Indiana and Illinois would oppose vehemently the agitation of a question which had in it so much of danger
to the peace of the country. Through their control of
the legislatures, the residents of the Ohio Valley prevented the abolitionists of the Lake region from accom-

plishing anything beyond propaganda until after the middle of the century.

At the beginning of the Civil War the attitude of the Borderland was extremely doubtful. Though its most important commercial relations were with the North, the fact was not realized by the majority of the people. Though it was Southern in origin, it was yet not a part of the South because of its different system of labor. At the same time, it stood with the South in opposition to the abolitionist agitation. Only two things were fairly certain: that it would make every reasonable concession to insure the maintenance of the Union; and that, whatever decision it made, it would be united.

CHAPTER II

THE ELECTION OF 1860

At the beginning of a great national crisis some event usually occurs to which later writers may point, saying, "If the full significance of this had been understood at the time, the course of history would have been changed." The election of 1860 was such an event. After forty years of bitterness the controversy over slavery had frayed the bonds of national unity almost to the breaking point. The two national parties had each been divided into two branches; and in the extreme sections of the country public opinion had reached the point where sectional advantage seemed more important than national interests. In the Lower South, the pro-slavery group, weary of compromises, boldly threatened to disrupt the Union if they were to be denied the right to take their slaves into the territories on the same basis as other property. The abolitionists on the other hand, regarding slavery as a purely moral question, refused to yield an inch or to compromise in the slightest degree with evil. They pursued their prejudiced way, wholly unmindful of the dangers to the future existence of the Union which lurked in the controversy. Between these extreme groups were the great body of people in the Borderland and some others in both the North and the South who deprecated the bitterness of the struggle as inimical to the best interests of the country. These

40

citizens, upon whom the future unity of the country depended, seem to have thought, in a vague sort of way, that the difficulties could again be smoothed over by compromises arranged in the halls of Congress. They failed utterly to realize how terribly in earnest the Southern leaders were in their threats of secession. If they had grasped the seriousness of the situation they would certainly have abandoned their existing party organizations and united in a great national party which could easily have prevented the success of either extreme group.

There had been previous campaigns in which important sectional divisions had occurred. There had been occasions also when a minority had threatened to refuse their assent to the legally constituted measures of the government. But never before 1860 had these manifestations assumed such proportions as to imperil the nation. The development of sectional factions in the place of national parties was in itself sufficient to alarm the friends of constitutional government. What made the situation critical was the fact that nearly every other nationalizing influence had been broken down. The feeling of commercial solidarity had been disrupted by the tariff controversy of the 'twenties and 'thirties. Free intercourse between the sections had practically ceased. Southern men rarely sent their sons to be educated in Northern colleges. Even the churches had been divided. But in spite of these divisions the politicians, by sedulously avoiding the issue of slavery in popular elections and by diverting attention to the tariff, the banking system and the disposal of public lands, had managed to preserve the national parties intact. As long as slavery remained a question of state politics—or at most of interstate relations—it was not impossible for the party leaders to hold their followers. When, however, it became a national question, that is, when it concerned the status of slavery in the territories or in the District of Columbia, the cohesive force of the parties was first impaired, and then finally destroyed altogether.

The Whigs were the first to feel the disintegrating influence of the slavery question. The membership of the party included a more intelligent and substantial body of citizens than the opposition, since it had developed as a protest against the excesses of Jacksonian democracy. In the North its advocacy of a protective tariff and of sound financial policies had obtained the support of the commercial classes. In the South most of the planters supported it because their interests in state politics were opposed to those of the small landholders, who were generally Democrats. The party had made no embarrassing record on the question of slavery. In 1849 it came into power with hopes of being able to make its tenure permanent—hopes that were dimmed only by the problem of fixing the status of the territory acquired from Mexico, which it had inherited from the preceding Democratic administration. In spite of all that the leaders could do, the controversy over this question soon became so acute that the disruption of the Union seemed not improbable. Fortunately they were national in their point of view. By conciliation on the part of Webster and by an involved set of compromise measures sponsored by Clay and supported by President Taylor, the immediate problem was solved. The Union was preserved for the time being. But out of this struggle the Whig party emerged with little contemporary credit, losing much of its popular support. Many of its members in both sections, being dissatisfied with the details of the compromise, left the party and caused its defeat at the following election by so overwhelming a majority that all hope of reviving it was lost.

Many Whig leaders then turned to the Know-Nothings, an anti-foreign secret society, which seemed to have considerable strength, and which had no record of failure on the question of slavery. In the elections of 1854 it carried Massachusetts and made an excellent showing in New York and Pennsylvania. Much was expected of it in the presidential election of 1856. With the assistance of the Whig leaders, its organization was rapidly extended to all sections of the country. It attained great strength in the border States, in spite of the comparatively small foreign population there. In the South, however, it failed to hold all the former Whigs, both because of the almost total absence of foreigners, and because the protection of slavery was regarded as of primary importance. In the Northwest it likewise had a disappointing reception, since it did not advance a definite program for the disposal of the unsettled lands that lay to the west. The Know-Nothings suffered equally with the Whigs from the injection of the slavery question into politics. Their issue of prejudice against foreigners was inadequate to divert popular attention from the great problem of the day.

Meanwhile the Democratic party had also begun to feel the destructive effect of the slavery controversy. By 1854, many moderate Northern leaders, from a variety of motives, felt impelled to grant further concessions to the South. Senator Douglas, supported by others, pushed through the Congress the Kansas-Nebraska bill, which permitted slavery in territory made free by the

Missouri Compromise. It further provided that the inhabitants of new States created in the region might have the option of being admitted with, or without, slavery. From the standpoint of practical politics the bill is significant as an attempt, not merely to conciliate the South, but also, through the invention of the doctrine of popular sovereignty, to remove the slavery controversy from the sphere of national affairs. Unfortunately it proved to be unacceptable to the people of the North. Members of Congress who had supported it were derided as "Northern men with Southern principles," and in the elections of 1854 many of them were retired in favor of "anti-Nebraska" Democrats, who thenceforth formed an active part of the opposition.

After the storm of the slavery controversy had thus cast thousands of voters adrift from their political moorings, it was almost inevitable that a new anti-slavery party would arise. In 1854, while the Kansas-Nebraska bill was being debated in the Congress, a spontaneous popular movement began in the West which resulted in the formation of the Republican party. It quickly gained adherents in the region around the Lakes; then spreading to the East, it was joined by nearly all the anti-Nebraska Democrats and by most of the former Whigs, who found its principles more satisfactory than those of the Know-Nothings. Leadership came with numbers. Many astute politicians of both the old political parties, sensing the popular strength of the movement, lost no time in placing themselves at its head. By the opening of the campaign of 1856, it was the dominant political group in New England, New York and the Northwest.

In this period of uncertainty all the parties made nominations that were calculated to appeal to the mass of doubtful voters. The Democrats chose James Buchanan, the minister to Great Britain, probably because he was the only prominent member of the party who had taken no active part in the discussion of the Kansas-Nebraska bill. The Know-Nothings nominated Fillmore, whose support of the Compromise of 1850 commended him to voters of conciliatory views. Even the Republicans preferred an "available" candidate rather than jeopardize their chances of success by nominating a man of outspoken views on the subject of slavery. A small group of politicians, whose leader was Francis P. Blair, hit upon John C. Fremont, a "pathfinder" of the Far West and popularly well known. The fact that he was the son-in-law of Senator Benton identified him with the nationalist group of the Democratic party and made it likely that he would attract votes from among that important element. The further fact that he had never committed himself on the subject of slavery made him an excellent candidate, regardless of his lack of qualifications for the office.

The canvass resulted in favor of the Democrats. Buchanan received the electoral votes of the Lower South and of all the States on each side of the border, with the exceptions of Maryland and Ohio. In Pennsylvania, New Jersey and California he had overwhelming pluralities. In Indiana and Illinois the great Democratic pluralities in the section south of the National Road overcame the Republican pluralities to the north of it. The Republicans were successful in the extreme Northern

States and in Ohio, which was turned toward them by the almost solid anti-slavery vote of the Western Reserve.[1] The Know-Nothings made a respectable showing in all the slave States, carrying Maryland, and narrowly missing pluralities in Kentucky and Louisiana.

Buchanan's administration was an interlude between the political and military struggles over slavery. No opportunity was presented for a decisive contest between the sections. There were, however, three events which, in the excited state of public opinion, were important in increasing the feeling of bitterness. The first was the effort of Chief Justice Taney and some other members of the Supreme Court to settle the controversy by the decision in the case of Dred Scott. They upheld the right of the slaveowners to take their property into the territories, thus strengthening the position of the Southerners and of Douglas and other Northern Democrats. Unfortunately their opinions were so poorly reasoned out that the anti-slavery men could pick flaws in the arguments of nearly every paragraph. The court itself was divided, the Northern justices delivering dissenting opinions which furnished a basis for disputes on the constitutional questions involved. Far from allaying the controversy, as the court had hoped, the decision of the case only extended it. The second event was the attempt of the Southerners to secure the admission of Kansas as a slave State without complying with all the provisions of the Kansas-Nebraska act. The colonizing efforts of the North had far surpassed those of the South, and the application of the doctrine of popular sovereignty would certainly have made Kansas free. In trying to secure it by

[1] Buchanan carried southern Ohio by 8,800, an increase of 5,000 over Pierce's majority in 1852.

underhand means, the Southerners caused the reopening
of a wound that had almost healed. The third event,
though it appears now to have been only an incident, was
the attack of John Brown upon Harper's Ferry. There can
be little doubt that Brown was an irresponsible fanatic;
but Governor Wise of Virginia chose to make political
capital of the affair, with the result that many Northern
people believed Brown to have been a martyr.[2]

In both sections every event was magnified and dis-
torted, every phase of the controversy was exposed with
all the force that imagination and rhetoric could give.
At the North, Wendell Phillips and William Lloyd Garrison so bitterly attacked slavery that the dormant principle of sectionalism was awakened and the sentiment
of nationality was obscured. At the South, the "fire-
eaters" were equally as rabid and dangerous as the
fanatical abolitionists. The greatest and most persistent
of them was William L. Yancey of Alabama. He boldly
told the Southern people that they must either leave
the Union or be destroyed—there was no other choice,
since dependence upon compromises was illusory. In
his opinion, Douglas and the nationalists were the worst
enemies of the South because they were luring it on
with concessions until such a time as the North was ready
to destroy the foundations of its economic prosperity.[3] Nor was Yancey "throwing a solitary somerset,"
as some Northern men believed. His reiterated appeals,
falling among people who had been sadly disillusioned
by the results of popular sovereignty, at last found general acceptance. Furthermore, an organization was at

[2] *Correspondence of R. M. T. Hunter,* pp. 278-286.
[3] William Garrot Brown, *The Lower South in American History,*
pp. 115-141.

hand to promote his cause. The pro-slavery element had obtained control of the Democratic party, and through it were able to shape the course of public affairs in their own section. When the election campaign of 1860 opened, they were prepared to receive an unconditional surrender, but not to yield a single concession, even to their party associates in the Northern States.

The people of the Borderland, with few exceptions, were free from the taint of extreme sectionalism. It could not exist among them from the nature of things. Located between the contesting sections, they were able to take a calm, objective view of the situation. They could not be misled by the exaggerations of orators and editors, since they knew more or less of the problems and interests of both the North and the South. Isolated and dependent as they were, they were truly national in their point of view. Though they may have favored separation in the late seventeen hundreds, it was inconceivable for them in 1860 to consider seriously a proposal for the disruption of the Union, such as had met with approval in the Lower South. Their attitude was naturally to favor the main-tenance of the *status quo;* and this attitude determined the course of all the parties—Northern and Southern Democrats, Republicans and Constitutional Unionists— in the campaign of 1860.

A close presidential election is always decided by a comparatively small number of independent voters in the so-called doubtful States. The electoral votes of States which may be depended upon to give large majorities for a party hardly count in the considerations of campaign managers. In 1860 the Southern Democratic party might have been in absolute control in the Lower South, and still have fallen far short of the number of electoral votes needed for success. The Republicans might have received the solid electoral vote of New England, New York and the Northwest, yet they could not hope to win without the support of at least two States in the Borderland. It was necessary, then, for the leaders of the two extreme parties to so modify their platforms that they could make an effective appeal to the independent voters of the Borderland. It was equally necessary for the two moderate parties to nominate candidates with the greatest possible strength in the Borderland, and to combat sectionalism with all their power, if they were to succeed even in creating a deadlock. That they had any further expectation than to throw the election into the House of Representatives can hardly be maintained. If they had done so, indeed, they might have secured the election of one of their number; for in a deliberative body the chances were against the election of a candidate who represented one of the extreme groups. Let us see how the nominations and the platforms were worked out to fit these conditions.

When the Democratic national convention met at Charleston in April, 1860, it became evident almost immediately that extremely bitter feeling existed between delegates representing different sections of the country. Those from the South openly charged the Northern Democrats with having abetted the abolitionist agitation by their refusal to take a determined stand in defense of Southern rights. Hating Douglas and his scheme of popular sovereignty which had raised their hopes only to dash them cruelly to the ground, they demanded the adoption of a resolution that the national government should protect slave property in the territories, or wherever it should be taken. In urging it, Yancey declared that if the Northern Democrats were sincere, they should state openly their belief that slavery was not wrong. This was a statement which they could not make, nor could they recognize the principle by indirection. Such a concession would have resulted in the defection of thousands of voters in their own section and insured, beyond possibility of retrieval, the defeat of the party in the election. Besides, the adoption of the resolution would be a repudiation of Douglas's doctrine of popular sovereignty; and Douglas was preferred by the Northern delegates above any other candidate. After long debates the resolution was rejected. Immediately afterward the delegates from the Gulf States withdrew from the convention. The others, after vainly attempting to agree upon a solution of the problem, adjourned to meet in Baltimore. When they reassembled they nominated Douglas and adopted a platform in accordance with his views.[4]

Though Douglas was possibly not the best choice under the circumstances, his candidacy contained many important elements of strength. He was the idol of the Northern Democrats, possessing greater personal popularity than any other leader. He represented the prevailing tendencies among conservative men; and by popularizing the idea of self-determination for the territories he had given them a workable political principle to justify their position. In the senatorial campaign of 1858 he had carried the pivotal State of Illinois, and it was believed that he had a better chance to secure the electoral votes of other doubtful States along the border than any other candidate the party could have chosen.

[4] James Ford Rhodes, *History of the United States from the Compromise of 1850*, vol. ii, pp. 445-451; 473-475.

The nomination of Herschel V. Johnson of Georgia for the vice-presidency was doubtless made to strengthen the ticket in the South, where the leaders still had hopes of appealing successfully to the Union men.

The delegates who had withdrawn from the convention met at Baltimore, June 28th, and nominated John C. Breckinridge of Kentucky and Joseph Lane of Oregon. Both were regarded as conservatives, and therefore their candidacy was calculated to appeal to voters of moderate views. The choice of Breckinridge is significant as an attempt to extend the influence of the pro-slavery element over the Borderland. The platform, aside from its pronouncements on the question of slavery, was devoted chiefly to advocating the rights of States within the Union.

The former Whigs and Know-Nothings heeded the lessons of the campaign of 1856 when they carried only Maryland. It was recognized that the anti-foreign issue would not attract many voters in the Borderland or among the Union men of the South. In view of the sectional divisions among the voters, the leaders determined to substitute a new issue which would appeal to nationalist voters everywhere. Minimizing the question of slavery, they expressed the whole purpose of the party in the slogan, "the Union, the Constitution and the enforcement of the laws." The nominees were John Bell of Tennessee and Edward Everett of Massachusetts, both men of wide experience in public life and of apparently greater ability than the candidates of any other party. Bell had the further advantages of being the leader of the Whig party in Tennessee and of having a wide acquaintance throughout the Borderland.

The position of the Republicans at the beginning of

104490

the campaign was extremely favorable. They had secured a plurality in the House of Representatives in 1858, and they seemed to have at least a plurality in most of the free States. The Republican party in 1860 did not, however, form the well integrated organization which characterizes a political party to-day. It was rather a mass of diverse elements loosely cemented together by a common purpose to stop the spread of slavery. There were former Democrats and former Whigs; former Know-Nothings and immigrants from Germany; old free-soilers and ultra-abolitionists. There was, too, a sectional difference between the Northwest, which wanted to prohibit the further extension of slavery, and the Northeast, which opposed the institution wherever it existed. There were even a few advocates of gradual emancipation living in the border slave States, whose numbers might be greatly increased if the people could be shown that the object of the party was to prevent the spread of slavery into the territories and not to interfere with it where it existed. Extremely wise political management was necessary to hold these inharmonious elements together and gain the additional voting strength necessary to win the election.

There was no lack of political leaders, representing every one of the diverse elements of the party, who offered themselves as candidates for the presidency. The most prominent was William H. Seward of New York, a former United States Senator and in 1860 the governor of the State. He was regarded as the ablest man in the Republican party. He was also the acknowledged leader of the Whig element. There were, however, important weaknesses in his candidacy. During his long and active political career he had made many hasty statements

reflecting upon the principles and leaders of the Democratic party, which, being still remembered, served to
alienate large numbers of voters. His connection with
Thurlow Weed and the corrupt machine at Albany made
his candidacy distasteful to the influential group of
thoroughgoing Republicans who stood for reform.
Finally, his radical expressions of opinion on the subject
of slavery, though commending him to the rank and
file of the party, made many leaders doubtful of his
ability to win the votes of independent citizens. Diametrically opposed to Seward in the minds of most men
was Salmon P. Chase of Ohio, who had been a senator
and was then also a governor. He was a favorite candidate of the former Democrats, and he had a distinct
advantage in that he resided in one of the doubtful
States of the Ohio Valley. His friends believed that his
nomination would appeal to conservative voters. Other
prominent candidates were Nathaniel P. Banks of
Massachusetts, Simon Cameron of Pennsylvania, Caleb
B. Smith of Indiana, and Abraham Lincoln of Illinois,
all of whom had strong local support.

While these candidates were engaged in securing the
pledges of delegates, a movement developed among the
Republicans of the border slave States to obtain the
nomination for one of their number. It was led by
Francis P. Blair, "the Nestor of American politics," and
one of the outstanding figures of the Jacksonian period.
In his early life he had been the editor of an influential
newspaper in Kentucky which had ardently championed
the presidential aspirations of Henry Clay. In 1824,
however, he turned to Jackson and helped to elect him
in the following campaign. His reward was the editorship of the *Globe,* the organ of the administration. In

this position, and as a member of Jackson's "kitchen cabinet," he consistently and ably promoted the cause of the nationalist wing of the Democratic party. Following the party revolution of 1844, in which the Southern leaders gained the ascendancy, he was retired to private life. Thereafter he remained quietly at his home at Silver Spring, just outside the District of Columbia, until the rise of the Republican party again afforded him an opportunity to exercise an influence in politics. As we have already seen, he had an important share in the nomination of Fremont in 1856. His two sons, Montgomery, of Maryland, and Francis P., Jr., of St. Louis, were also prominently identified with public affairs. Both were natives of Kentucky, and both had moved to St. Louis where they had practiced law and engaged in politics under the patronage of Benton. Montgomery had been the chief counsel for Dred Scott, and Francis P., Jr., had succeeded to Benton's leadership of the free-soil, hard-money faction of the Democratic party in Missouri. He was elected to the House of Representatives in 1856, was narrowly defeated in 1858 through the candidacy of a Know-Nothing, and was an avowed candidate for the seat in 1860.[5]

When the Blairs entered the Republican party they retained their nationalist ideas. They desired, as far as possible, to remove from the party all taints of sectionalism, both to insure its future success and to combat the pro-slavery movement. Realizing that this movement derived much of its strength from the popular belief that the Republicans intended to abolish slavery where it existed, they planned to prove to the people

[5] John McElroy, *The Struggle for Missouri*, p. 19; John G. Nicolay and John Hay, *Abraham Lincoln, A History*, vol. iv, p. 206.

of the border slave States that the party had no such object in view, but was, on the contrary, anxious to help them solve their peculiar problems. If they were successful, the pro-slavery movement would be confined to the Lower South, and the danger of disunion which was inherent in the controversy would be reduced. One of the means upon which they relied to accomplish their purpose was newspaper publicity, in which they naturally had great faith. At a conference between Francis P. Blair, Jr., and Lincoln—then the obscure leader of the Republicans in Illinois—it was arranged that the Missouri *Democrat,* in which Blair had an interest, should announce its conversion to Republican principles on January 1, 1860. Simultaneously the Louisville *Journal* and some paper in Virginia were also to become Republican.[6] A second means by which they planned to increase the membership of the party—and this was by far the more important—was to secure the presidential nomination for a man who would have the confidence of the slaveholders as well as of conservative men who owned no slaves.

Edward Bates of St. Louis was the man whom the Blairs proposed for the honor, and they worked hard for his success. He had the reputation of being the ablest lawyer of the St. Louis bar. He was in favor of protection, and therefore would appeal to business men in New England and Pennsylvania. He was a former Whig, who would obtain support from Whig centers everywhere, while the influence of the Blairs would go far toward conciliating the former Democrats. He had presided at a Whig convention in 1856 which had endorsed the

6 Walter B. Stevens, "Lincoln and Missouri," in the *Missouri Historical Review,* vol. x, p. 65.

Know-Nothing ticket. He had been a slaveholder, and therefore understood the problems of other slaveholders. He had favored the extension of free soil, and would therefore be acceptable to the moderate Republicans.[7] In short, he appeared to be an ideal candidate. The Blairs believed that the election of a former slaveholder who had never taken part in the anti-slavery movement would not give the South sufficient grounds for secession. He would therefore be an ideal President for such a troubled period.

The Blairs, being crafty managers, succeeded in obtaining support for Bates in many parts of the North. Nearly everywhere the opposition to Seward seemed about to be concentrated in his favor. But fatal weaknesses were soon apparent in his candidacy. In the first place, he failed to obtain the pledges of delegates from all the border slave States. The Republican organization in Kentucky, which was controlled by Cassius M. Clay, refused to accept him. According to Clay's statement, the elder Blair invited him to Silver Spring for a conference at some time prior to the meeting of the convention and offered him the post of secretary of war in return for his support.[8] But apparently the old feud between the Blairs and the Clays was still too fresh in the mind of Clay for him to accept the offer. Secondly, Bates failed to secure the support of any delegates from Illinois. One of the strong points in his candidacy was supposed to be his great popularity among the former Whigs in the southern part of the State, many of whom seemed on the point of becoming Democrats. The

[7] See an article by Charles Gibson in the *Collections* of the Missouri Historical Society, January, 1900, pp. 52-56.

[8] C. M. Clay, *Life, Memoirs, Writings and Speeches*, p. 244.

candidacy of Lincoln deprived him of support which he otherwise would probably have had. A third circumstance would have been fatal to his candidacy without the others. This was the evident impossibility of his carrying his own State.

When the convention assembled at Chicago on May 16, 1860, Seward was regarded as the probable nominee. His friends were noisily confident. He had the solid support of New York, and had received the pledges of nearly all the delegates from New England and of many from the border slave States. The weakest point in his candidacy was the fact that in the West few delegates had been instructed to vote for him. He could not count upon the support of a single delegate from the free States of the Borderland which it was absolutely necessary for the Republicans to carry if they were to be successful at the polls. If Seward were nominated, it was felt that he could not be elected.[9] The extensive opposition to his candidacy, having failed to unite upon Bates, turned to Justice McLean of Ohio; but his advanced years told against him. Shortly after the opening of the convention the attention of the delegates was attracted to Lincoln, hitherto almost entirely neglected,[10] through the novel methods of his campaign managers. A tremendous roar of cheering followed the presentation of his name. Other great demonstrations occurred several times in the course of the convention, and shouts for Lincoln frequently drowned the applause given to other candidates. When the delegates examined his qualifications they found them particularly strong.

[9] Horace White, *The Life of Lyman Trumbull*, pp. 103-104.
[10] Just before the convention *Harper's Weekly* had placed Lincoln's name last in the list of eleven possible candidates.

Lincoln was even more available than Bates as a compromise candidate. He had the support of the delegates from the doubtful State of Illinois, and no other candidate could be stronger there, especially in the section south of Springfield. As a political speaker he had proved more than a match for Douglas in the senatorial contest of 1858. His friends claimed that he had obtained a plurality of the popular vote, and had failed of election only because the northern part of the State, where most of the Republican voters lived, was under-represented in the legislature. It was thought that he would again be successful over Douglas in Illinois. This was an extremely important point in his favor; for although the Democratic nomination had not yet been made, it was practically certain that Douglas would be the candidate. Furthermore, Lincoln, like Seward and Bates, was a former Whig, who would probably receive as many votes from this element of the party as either of his rivals. His views on the question of slavery, though soundly Republican, were sufficiently unknown to be regarded as conservative. He could therefore be expected to receive many more votes than Seward. One of the first steps toward his nomination is said to have been taken by Cassius M. Clay, who asked the convention to choose him as a concession to the Republicans of the border States. They had confidence in him, Clay said, because he had been born in Kentucky, and he understood the people of the South; his election would furthermore disai... the States' Rights party, who were already talking of secession.[11] In all, Lincoln's strength as a candidate was so great that his managers easily obtained the support of the delegates from Indiana and Pennsyl-

[11] W. B. Stevens, in the *Missouri Historical Review*, vol. x, pp. 70-71.

vania by promising cabinet positions to Smith and Cameron. He was nominated on the third ballot. The border slave States indicated their preference for him on the first ballot when he received twenty votes, to sixteen for Seward. On later ballots his vote increased to twenty-nine and then to forty-two, while Seward's remained stationary.[12]

The platform of the party, like the candidate, was intended to appeal to voters in the doubtful sections. A clause favoring the enactment of a protective tariff law was inserted to make sure of the support of Pennsylvania. Another clause in favor of homesteads was designed to obtain doubtful votes in the West. On the question of slavery there was much evasion. The power of the Congress to exclude it from the territories was not affirmed, and the provisions relating to popular sovereignty were non-committal. There was no denunciation of the Fugitive Slave Law or of the continued existence of slavery in the District of Columbia, as might reasonably have been expected.[13] On the whole it seemed that the Republican party, which had begun as a result of the moral upheaval against slavery, had definitely passed under the control of the politicians.

The popular canvass that followed the nominations was conducted with unusual thoroughness by all the parties. Naturally the arguments used by campaign writers and speakers varied a great deal to suit the audiences to which they were addressed. In New England and other parts of the North the Republicans emphasized the evils of slavery, moral and economic, and promised to check its spread. In the Lower South the Breckinridge Demo-

[12] Nicolay and Hay, vol. ii, pp. 273-275, notes.
[13] Emerson D. Fite, *The Presidential Campaign of 1860*, pp. 124-125.

crats, appealing mostly to sectional prejudice, urged the people to rise in defense of their rights, and spoke of the possibility of disrupting the Union in order to preserve them. From these extreme, uncompromising positions both parties receded gradually until they reached the dividing line of the Ohio River. In the Borderland the Republicans based their arguments chiefly upon the economic principles contained in their platform, and the Breckinridge Democrats emphasized the necessity of preserving the rights of people and of States within the Union. The campaign was conducted so skillfully by both parties that the people of this nationalistic section did not realize that the continued existence of the Union was imperiled. Many voters gave them their support who would not have done so if they had understood the real character of the struggle between them.

The two other parties were in an unfortunate position. Neither possessed attractive economic issues which would divert attention from the question of slavery; and on this question neither could take a positive stand that would win votes. The Douglas Democrats were obliged to wage a purely defensive campaign, trying to prove that their compromising solution was better for the North and for the South than the thoroughgoing proposals of the Republicans and of the Breckinridge Democrats. The Constitutional Unionists, with no constructive plan to offer, had to content themselves with vague suggestions of compromises. Both parties therefore based their campaigns upon the necessity of restoring harmony in order that the Union might be preserved. From our knowledge after the fact, it seems that they should have succeeded; but the issue was an almost complete failure.

In the North and in the South the people were so much
engrossed in their sectional interests that the question
of national solidarity remained a secondary one. In the
Borderland the people were lulled into a sense of false
security by the campaign arguments of the other parties.
The position of the "nationalist" parties was further
weakened by the patent fact that neither of them was
truly national. The Constitutional Unionists were simply the Southern Whigs who had been left alone by the
incorporation of the Northern Whigs into the Republican party. The Douglas Democrats were mainly confined to the Northern States. The only slave State
they carried was Missouri. Though they cast a considerable vote in other Southern States, their influence
was sufficient only to throw the electoral votes of Virginia, Kentucky and Tennessee from Breckinridge to
Bell.

A further word needs to be said as to the character of
the Constitutional Union party, which has erroneously
been regarded as a body of true Union men in the South.
In point of fact, the principal extent of their unionist
sentiments seems to have been their unwillingness to
coöperate with their former rivals, the Democrats. A
close examination of the returns from the border States
shows that the people voted generally in accordance with
their former allegiances. In the sections where the
Whigs had always been in a majority—where politics
was dominated by the slaveholding and commercial
classes—the voters favored the Constitutional Union
party. On the other hand, the poorer districts, true to
their Jacksonian antecedents, supported Breckinridge. A
change in the popular alignment occurred only after the

secession of South Carolina. At that time the rank and file of the Constitutional Union party in the Borderland were about as likely to choose the side of the South as were the Breckinridge Democrats.

A presentation of the results of the election by States will confirm the general opinions which have just been expressed.

In Virginia the principal vote for Bell and Everett was in the "black belt" along the North Carolina border, and in a broad strip of counties extending through the Kanawha Valley to the Ohio River. There is no reason to believe that arguments in favor of the Union had much effect on the result, since this section was afterward one of the chief strongholds of the secessionist movement. The explanation lies in the fact that it had been consistently Whig for a generation. To the northward the Breckinridge Democrats were generally more numerous than their rivals. Tremendous pluralities were heaped up for their ticket in northwestern Virginia, a rather thickly settled grazing district where popular sentiment was almost solidly for the Union. Even in the Panhandle, where an important movement in favor of emancipation had developed, they had a large vote, carrying Brooke County and dividing Hancock County almost evenly with the Republicans. All of this section had exercised a great influence in the councils of the party, frequently compelling the eastern politicians to take into account its position on the question of slavery. In the gubernatorial election of 1859 it had forced the nomination of John Letcher, formerly an active advocate of emancipation, over a representative of the slavocracy. After a campaign which turned largely on the question of slavery it had secured his election over an eastern

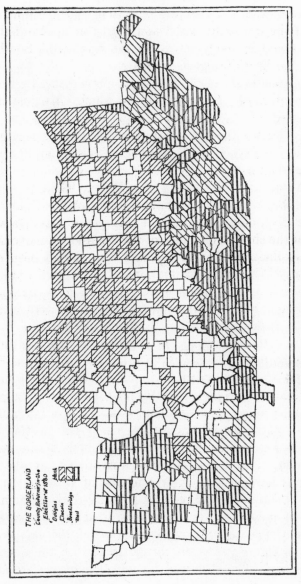

THE BORDERLAND
County Returns in the
Election of 1860
Douglas
Lincoln
Breckinridge
Bell

COUNTY RETURNS AIN THE ELECTION OF 1860

Know-Nothing.[14]   The people now generally supported
Breckinridge because his friends had obtained complete
control of the regular Democratic organization; though
a number of independent voters, believing that Douglas
represented the true Union branch of the party, cast
their ballots for him. On account of this defection the
Constitutional Union party received the electoral votes
of Virginia by a small plurality. The Republicans cast
slightly less than two thousand votes, nearly all of them
in the Panhandle.

The State of Kentucky was divided between Bell and
Breckinridge practically along the lines which had formerly separated Whigs and Democrats. Through the
disruption of the Democratic party and the transference
of some votes from Douglas to Bell, the Constitutional
Union party carried the State by a plurality of 13,000.
It was strongest in the sections dominated by the slaveholding and commercial interests, that is, in central Kentucky, in the tobacco growing district of the lower Cumberland Valley and along the Ohio River. All but seven
of the counties on the northern border were carried by
Bell, Louisville giving him a large plurality. The people
here were in contact with free territory, and they were
also somewhat dependent upon commerce with the North.
Their votes may therefore have been due partly to a
desire to preserve the Union. In the mountainous region
of eastern Kentucky where the people later showed themselves to be most devoted to the Union, they cast their
ballots for Breckinridge and Lane almost to a man. They
believed thoroughly in the rights of States within the
Union. They had been identified with the Democratic

[14] Charles H. Ambler, *Sectionalism in Virginia from 1776 to 1861*,
pp. 320-325.

party since the time of Jackson, and they could now
see little reason either for leaving it or for casting their
votes for Douglas. There were two other centers of
Southern Democratic strength—the extreme western part
of the State and the counties to the north of the Blue
Grass region. Like the mountainous district, both had
traditionally supported the Democratic ticket. There
is little evidence to justify a contention that the large
vote for Breckinridge was due to a secessionist conspiracy
among the slaveholders.

The Douglas Democrats, here as in western Virginia
the most uncompromising of all in favor of the Union,
carried in all only five counties. Much of their vote was
due to local, rather than to national, causes. A group of
four counties in the central part of the State returned
pluralities for Douglas, partly because of the unwillingness of the people to unite with their former rivals, the
Whigs, partly because some local politicians refused to
coöperate with the regular party organization. The
other county carried by Douglas was Campbell, including
the city of Newport. In the adjoining county of Ken-
ton, where there was a large German population in the
city of Covington, the Republicans were evenly matched
with the Constitutional Union party for first place. Less
than two thousand votes, however, were cast for Lincoln
in the whole State. Most of them were concentrated in
Louisville and in the three counties opposite Cincinnati.
The totals for the three leading candidates were: for
Bell, 66,016; for Breckinridge, 52,836; and for Douglas,
25,644.

In Missouri the presidential campaign was greatly
complicated by a bitter factional struggle for the control of the Democratic party, and by a gubernatorial

election which occurred coincidently. The solidarity of
the party had suffered severely from the contest between
Benton and those who favored the extension of slave
territory, with the result that it had been forced temporarily to yield the administration of the state government to the Whigs. In the beginning of the contest
the pro-slavery leaders had been successful in gaining
control of the party. In 1858, however, Francis P.
Blair, Jr., had wrested it from them and had turned it
toward Douglas and the Northern wing.[15] Two years
later the pro-slavery leaders again got the upper hand,
dominating the state convention and forcing the nomination of Claiborne F. Jackson, one of the most active
of their number, for the office of governor. The leaders
of the Northern wing acquiesced somewhat ungracefully
in the nomination; but they absolutely refused to be led
into supporting Breckinridge. It was generally understood at the time that a declaration of the convention in
his favor would have resulted in the establishment of a
separate party organization to further the interests of
Douglas's candidacy. Such a contingency was not
desired by the office-hungry Democrats. Jackson himself was one of the first to realize the situation, and after
attempting vainly for a while to balance himself between
the factions he announced that he would support Douglas. Thereupon a few leaders called another convention
which repudiated the nominations of Jackson and of all
others who had become Northern Democrats, and proceeded to place another ticket in the field.[16] In spite
of their defection, the choice of Jackson was amply

[15] Gustave Koerner, *Memoirs,* vol. ii, p. 88.
[16] J. F. Snyder, "The Democratic State Convention in Missouri in
1860," in the *Missouri Historical Review,* vol. ii, p. 124.

justified, for he was easily elected. The national ticket of the Northern Democrats, however, narrowly escaped defeat. Douglas carried the State by a plurality of less than five hundred, his vote being 58,801 against 58,372 for Bell. Breckinridge was a poor third, with 31,317; and Lincoln was last, with 17,028.

The sectional distribution of the vote showed many features in common with western Virginia and Kentucky. In the Ozark highlands Breckinridge received a great plurality, as he had in other mountainous sections. He also received considerable support in most other parts of the State. In the districts where slaves were most numerous the people turned against him, every one of the counties along the Missouri River giving pluralities for either Bell or Douglas. The counties in which the Northern Democratic party showed the greatest strength fall into three distinct sections. The first was along the border of Iowa and in the Platte Purchase in the extreme northwestern part of the State, where contact with free soil doubtless had much to do with the result. The second was a group of counties about St. Louis, where there had been a considerable industrial development. The third was along the old Santa Fe trail in southwestern Missouri, where the people were generally attached to the Union. The counties which were carried by the Constitutional Union party were mainly in the northern part of the State. In nearly every other county, however, it was second. The uniform distribution of its vote indicates that the former Whig party had held together. In the county and city of St. Louis the Republicans had a plurality, as had been expected. The party included a few voters who had been identified with the free-soil democracy of Benton, some recent immigrants from the free States and the whole German population. Besides St. Louis, the Republicans carried Osage and Gasconade counties in the interior, in both of which the Germans exercised a decisive influence. Some scattering votes were cast for the party in most of the other counties.

It was recognized from the beginning that the election would be decided in the northern part of the Ohio Valley. The Republicans could be sure of large majorities in the Lake district, but they must secure much support from the more populous section south of the National Road in order to gain the votes of Ohio, Indiana and Illinois in the electoral college. The problem of the Northern Democrats, on the other hand, was to hold the allegiance of their followers in this district. The canvass of both parties was thorough.

In Illinois the trial of strength between Lincoln and Douglas in 1858 had shown that the southern part of the State was extremely hostile to the Republicans, the vote in some counties being ten or twenty to one against their ticket. The state leaders now determined to make an additional appeal to the voters in this section by nominating for governor a man whose record on the question of slavery was not at all indicative of radical tendencies. The choice fell upon Richard Yates, a former Whig, an able lawyer, and one of the most popular citizens of the State. He had been in the Congress during the controversy over Kansas, when he had supported the Kansas-Nebraska bill. Like Lincoln, he was a native of Kentucky and a resident of Springfield.[17] A vigorous campaign was carried on, supported by speakers and funds from all parts of the country. By dexterous management

[17] L. U. Reavis, pamphlet "Life of Richard Yates," p. 18.

the leaders succeeded in obtaining a full vote in the
northern section by anti-slavery arguments, while at
the same time winning converts in the Democratic centers by emphasizing their public land policies. The
Republicans carried the State by a plurality of not quite
twelve thousand. As in previous elections, there was a
pronounced sectional distribution of the vote. North of
Peoria Lincoln had a majority in every county, and he
also carried a broad belt of counties on the eastern bor-
der of the State extending as far south as the National
Road. But in southern Illinois only four counties—St.
Clair, Madison, Bond and Edwards—were Republican.
The first three, located opposite St. Louis, had a large
German population. The fourth, which touched the
Indiana border in the extreme southeastern part of the
State, had been settled largely by emigrants from New
England. In the whole of southern Illinois the vote for
Lincoln showed a fourfold increase over that for Fremont in 1856; and this fact practically determined the
result. It is interesting to note that the candidates of
the two Southern parties received considerable support
in the counties along the southern border, where the
social and economic life of the people was similar to
that of their neighbors in Kentucky and Missouri. Bell
received more than five per cent of the total vote in a
dozen counties. Breckinridge had eight per cent of the
total in Alexander County, twelve per cent in Pulaski
County and forty per cent in Union County.

In Indiana the problems of the campaign were somewhat more difficult. The State had returned a Democratic plurality of 24,000 in 1856, and it was regarded as
more doubtful than any other in the Ohio Valley group.

The northern section, having no port on the Lakes, had not been filled up by emigrants from the free States, as the others had, but had remained open for occupancy by residents of the adjoining regions, who included people of Southern, as well as of Northern, extraction. It was still somewhat sparsely settled. The Republicans could not, therefore, depend upon a tremendous anti-slavery majority which would overcome the vote of the southern part of the State, but must carry a vigorous campaign into the territory naturally belonging to the opposition. From their point of view, it was fortunate that the society in southern Indiana had existed longer, and that the people had been more influenced by residence on free soil than in Illinois. They could not otherwise have hoped for success.

As in Illinois, the campaign was complicated by the election of state officers. The Republican leaders determined to place before the electorate as strong a ticket as possible, both to gain control of the state administration and the senatorship and to aid the national ticket. By far the ablest man in the party was Oliver P. Morton, a descendant of the Throckmorton who helped Roger Williams found his colony at Providence. He was born at Salisbury, Indiana, in 1823. After fitting himself for the practice of law at Miami University and the Cincinnati Law School, he entered upon a successful professional career. In politics he adhered to the Democratic party until he became dissatisfied with its attitude on the Kansas-Nebraska bill, when he became one of the founders of the Republican party. In common with most of the other members of the party in the West, he opposed the extension of slavery to the territories; but he went much farther than his associates in denouncing the institution.[18] On account of his oft-expressed uncompromising opinions it seemed inadvisable for the nominating convention to place his name at the head of the ticket. The honor was accordingly given to Henry S. Lane, a former Whig, whose membership in the party had resulted from the fact that the disruption of the Whigs had left him with no other opportunity to exercise an influence in politics, and not from any particularly strong convictions on the subject of slavery. Morton was nominated for the office of lieutenant-governor with the understanding that if the Republicans were completely successful, the legislature would elect Lane to the United States Senate, whereupon Morton would succeed to the governorship.[19]

In the popular canvass the itineraries of the candidates were carefully arranged so as to take them into districts where they would win votes without alienating doubtful voters. To Lane was assigned the task of speaking in southern Indiana, where his liberal views on the question of slavery might convince the people that the success of the Republicans would not endanger the continued existence of the Union. It was noticeable during his tour that the intensity of his opinions varied in inverse ratio with the distance he traveled south of the National Road. In Scott County he declared that slavery must not be interfered with in the States, though it should not be extended to the territories. At New Albany, on the Ohio River, he paid a high tribute to Henry Clay's services in arranging compromises, and

[18] William D. Foulke, *Life of Oliver P. Morton*, vol. i, pp. 36-80, *passim*.

[19] Logan Esarey, *A History of Indiana from 1850 to the Present*, p. 659.

declared himself to be a Whig of the old school.[20]   At
the same time Morton was touring the Republican counties, where his fiery anti-slavery utterances were calculated to bring out the whole vote of the party.

The Democratic state ticket was led by Thomas A.
Hendricks, a well known politician, with David Turpie, a
brilliant young lawyer, as the nominee for lieutenant-
governor. They conducted a vigorous campaign, making
speeches in all parts of the State, which apparently
deserved more popular attention than they were accorded.
As in other States, the Democratic ticket was greatly
handicapped by the defection of the office-holders, who
controlled the regular organization. Douglas, with his
unfortunate faculty for making enemies, had aroused the
rancor of the two Democratic United States senators by
voting against seating them in 1858 when their places
were contested by Republicans. From that time both
bent their efforts to encompass the defeat of his presidential aspirations.[21]   Having secured control of the
Democratic organization, they used it in support of
Breckinridge, realizing that every vote he obtained would
injure Douglas's chances. Their campaign against him
was extremely bitter, especially in the fourth congressional district in southeastern Indiana. A considerable
number of the rank and file of the party fell in with the
wishes of the leaders. Douglas was unable wholly to
make up his losses from among the pro-slavery Whigs,
since the most extreme group gave their votes for Bell.

Under the circumstances, the Republican victory in
Indiana doubtless occasioned little surprise. Lincoln

[20] Charles Kettleborough, "Indiana on the Eve of the Civil War," in
the *Proceedings* of the Ohio Valley Historical Association, 1916, pp.
176-177.

[21] *Idem*, pp. 148-149.

received 139,000 votes to 115,000 for Douglas, 12,000 for Breckinridge, and 5,000 for Bell. The Republicans thus had a clear majority of the popular vote. As had been expected, most of their strength was in northern and central Indiana. In the section south of the National Road they made important gains, carrying most of the counties of the third and fourth congressional districts, together with Vanderburg, Spencer and Perry counties on the Ohio River. In these three counties the plurality was probably due to the numerous voters of New England and German antecedents. The Democrats carried in all nine counties north of the National Road, most of them being located within a district which had only lately been developed.

In Ohio the Republicans were successful by a plurality of 34,000. As in the other States of this section, their greatest strength was in the section north of the National Road. They carried the Western Reserve by a vote of eight to one. In Toledo, also, they had a tremendous majority. There was a partial offset, however, in the Sandusky and Maumee valleys where the Democrats carried several counties. In the Ohio Valley the usual Democratic plurality was diminished, Douglas receiving only three hundred more votes than Lincoln. Considering the Southern origin of the people, the result is surprising in comparison with the returns from southern Illinois and Indiana; but it may be accounted for from the facts that most of the people had been born on free soil and that they had formerly supported the Whig party.[22] Even in the counties along the river the actual

---

[22] David C. Shilling, "The Relation of Southern Ohio to the South During the Decade Preceding the Civil War," in vol. viii of the *Quarterly Publications* of the Historical and Philosophical Society of Ohio.

contact of the people with slavery had slight influence. Only Monroe County, on the Virginia border, and Adams, Brown and Clermont counties, opposite Kentucky, were carried by Douglas. The result here was due partly to the presence of the New England element, partly to the lukewarm attitude of the people of western Virginia toward slavery. In Cincinnati the business men, who deplored the abolitionist agitation on account of its disturbing influence upon commercial relations, were outvoted by the Germans and other opponents of slavery.

The vote received by the two Southern candidates— only about 12,000 for each—was apparently too small to have had any effect on the result. If it had been given to Douglas, he would still have failed to carry the State. But the influence of the Southern Democratic party cannot be measured wholly by its numerical strength. Most of its leaders were Federal office-holders and personal enemies of Douglas, who were actuated by a desire to secure his defeat, rather than to promote the candidacy of Breckinridge. In several strongly Democratic districts they nominated separate congressional candidates with the hope of weakening the whole Northern ticket. Their activities must have resulted in turning many Democrats to the support of Lincoln. Breckinridge's largest popular vote was not in the region where the most aggressive campaign in his favor was carried on, but in the Western Reserve, where the conservatives doubtless wished to express, in the strongest possible manner, their disapproval of the abolitionist fanaticism of the region.[23] The vote for Bell was principally confined to Cincinnati.

[23] George H. Porter, *Ohio Politics During the Civil War Period*, pp. 44-49.

Viewing the results of the election in the Borderland as a whole, two facts stand out with great distinctness. The first was the relatively slight change that took place in the former party alignments, which indicates in itself that the issue of union or separatism was not popularly regarded as the chief one of the campaign. The second was the conservative attitude of the voters. In practically every section of the Borderland they expressed their preferences for Douglas or Bell, the two candidates who emphasized in their appeals for support the necessity of continuing the policies of compromise and conciliation in settling sectional differences. When they voted for Breckinridge or Lincoln they did so for reasons other than those that animated the people of the extreme sections. Certainly the large vote cast for the Southern Democratic party in the mountainous districts did not indicate such a devotion to the cause of slavery as would impel the people to leave the Union if its extension to the territories should no longer be possible. Neither was the vote of the Republicans wholly due to a desire to restrict it unconditionally. The people seem to have regarded the election as an opportunity simply for the expression of opinion on the transient issues of the day. There is little evidence to show that they generally thought of it as the final political contest between the sections.

CHAPTER III

THE DEFEAT OF PROPOSED COMPROMISES

Immediately after the close of the campaign it became evident that the political leaders of the South were fully prepared to carry out their threats of secession. The legislature of South Carolina was in session on election day for the purpose of choosing presidential electors. Contrary to its usual custom it did not adjourn, but continued the session. When the returns left no doubt that Lincoln had been elected, it unanimously passed a resolution providing for the popular election of a "sovereignty" convention, which should determine the future relation of the State to the national government. Within seven weeks the election had been held, the convention had met, and a declaration had been passed that the union between South Carolina and the United States was at an end. At the same time the Gulf States were far advanced toward similar action. Though many people in all of them strongly opposed secession, they were won over by the argument that they could make better terms out of the Union than in it; and once out, they became so identified with the policies of the majority that they quickly ceased to be objectors.

The news of the secessionist movement profoundly influenced the opinions of all the political parties, but none more than the Northern Democrats. Having felt the uncompromising temper of the South in their own

national convention, the leaders had become convinced
that a Republican victory would lead to an attempt at
secession; and they had done their utmost to impress
the danger upon the country. When the results of several state elections in October indicated that Lincoln
would be elected, Douglas gave over his speaking tour
in the North, where alone he had a chance to gain votes
in the electoral college, and went into the South in a
desperate effort to combat the spirit of sectionalism and
win back the people to support the Union.[1]   For the
first time in his career he ceased to be a candidate for
office and became a patriot and statesman. He spoke at
the principal points from Norfolk to the Mississippi
River, continuing his campaign even after the election
had taken place.[2]   When he finally left the South it was
only in order that he might prepare himself for the
approaching session of the Congress, in which he determined to devote his efforts to secure the restoration of
harmony. Other leaders were in complete accord with
his views, and the whole party stood united behind them
in demanding the adoption of concessions and compromises which would check the secessionist movement.

Among those who had voted the Republican ticket,
the secession of South Carolina was received with varying feelings. Many recent adherents of the party came
to a sharp realization that the anti-slavery movement
had gone too far. They would have been willing to
grant concessions, and would probably have done so if
they had had leaders and the means of making their
influence felt. The great body of Republicans, having

[1] Lewis Howland, *Stephen A. Douglas*, p. 354.
[2] Allen Johnson, *Stephen A. Douglas, A Study in American Politics*,
p. 439.

just gone through a difficult campaign, were not disposed to think kindly of proposals of compromise, which were likely to deprive them of the fruits of victory. The most extreme group welcomed the dissolution of the unnatural union between themselves and the slaveholders because they would no longer have to bear the reproach of being accessories to slavery. Horace Greeley's expression, "Let the erring sisters depart in peace," exactly suited their sentiments. They had nothing to offer to save the Union.

While the dominant element in the North was thus divided and lacking in the sentiment of genuine national patriotism, the Borderland was noticeably the center of true Union feeling, the nucleus around which a new nationalist movement gathered. With the exception of a few radicals who shared the views of the extreme sections, the people held the opinion that their future wellbeing depended upon the continued solidarity of the country. Everyone knew, of course, the importance of the Southern trade, and looked askance at the possibility of customs barriers and other impediments to free intercourse. Having learned from their fathers' experience of the evils which arose when a foreign power owned the mouth of the Mississippi River, they were fearful lest the rise of an independent Southern confederacy would accomplish their ruin. Even at the beginning of the secessionist movement the uncertainty of future commercial relations had caused business to be prostrated.[3] Moreover, the position of the Borderland between the

---

[3] In a speech in the Senate, December 20, 1860, Senator Pugh of Cincinnati said: "All our energies are paralyzed. Laboring men find no employers; merchants have no customers; and property of every description is depreciated almost beyond example." *Globe*, 36th Congress, 2nd session, Appendix, p. 29.

two other sections was one of great danger. Nothing was known as to the attitude that the national government would take toward the South. In 1832, President Jackson had threatened to send an armed force to Charleston to insure the collection of the revenues. If Buchanan took the same course, it was extremely likely that other States would go to the aid of South Carolina. In such a case, war would be inevitable; and war would bring almost intolerable suffering to the Borderland. It was almost certain to be fought on their own fields. Besides, it was likely that communities and even members of the same household would be divided, since there was no geographical line which marked the actual boundary between Northern and Southern sympathies. No wonder that the people watched, with terrified anticipations, the toppling of the pillars of the Union which seemed to foretoken the collapse of the edifice.

The nationalist sentiment of the Borderland by no means indicated a popular desire to join with the North in coercing the Southern States to remain in the Union; nor did it indicate a desire for a sectional administration of public affairs. What the people wanted was the old Union, the Union in which every section had an equal right and an equal opportunity. Both north and south of the Ohio River they denounced the abolitionists for having compelled the people of the South to take extreme measures for the protection of their property; and then they turned about and, with equal vehemence, denounced the people of South Carolina for having seceded before the necessities of the situation justified the action. As far as there was a preference between the two, the prevalent feeling was admiration for the slaveholders because they had asserted their rights. Admiration, however, is a weak sentiment; and, in the absence of a stronger tie binding them to one of the other sections, the people came to a fuller realization than ever before of the solidarity and power of their own section. As if by a previous understanding, they turned to concerted action by all the border States as a means of smoothing over the difficulties. Various proposals were made for closer coöperation, including one for the establishment of a "united West" which, by taking an independent stand, might prevent hostilities and afford time for the development of a new nationalist spirit in both the other sections.

In promoting the movement for the maintenance of the Union, it was only natural that the expressions of public opinion should lean heavily toward the South, since the reconciliation of that section seemed the most important object to be accomplished. Even in the free States many citizens went out of their way to show that they were friendly toward the pro-slavery group and not at all in sympathy with the abolitionists. In Cincinnati a large audience respectfully listened to Yancey through a long and bitter tirade against the North; but at about the same time a mob drove Wendell Phillips from the stage in Pike's Opera House and then sought for him in the streets, carrying a rope with which to hang him. White hoodlums made frequent attacks against the negro quarter of the city, afterward destroying a radical anti-slavery newspaper as a finishing touch to their activities.[4] Even Republican newspapers like the Cincinnati *Commercial*, the *Ohio State Journal* and the Cincinnati *Press* expressed opinions favorable to secession, though their attitude

[4] Henry Howe, *Historical Collections of Ohio* (edition of 1891), vol. ii. p. 42.

was not altogether conciliatory.[5] In Illinois, the Belleville *Democrat* declared that, since the North was hopelessly abolitionized, there was nothing for the South to do but to submit or to secede. And there was nothing in the Southern character, it said, that indicated inglorious submission. On December 6th, the Cairo *Gazette* stated that the sympathies of the people of southern Illinois were mainly with the South.[6] As we shall see hereafter, a great deal of this opinion represented a real sympathy with the secessionist movement, as well as a desire to save the Union.

Strange as it may seem, the only section of the Borderland which from the beginning took a determined stand against the policies of the Southern leaders was northwestern Virginia. On November 12th the citizens of Preston County, in a great mass meeting, unanimously denounced secession as treason.[7] Two weeks later a similar meeting in Monongalia County declared that the success of the Republican ticket did not constitute a justification for any State to leave the Union. In Wheeling the citizens passed a resolution deploring the election of Lincoln as likely to impair the harmony of the nation, but declaring that it was not in itself a sufficient excuse for the extreme course of South Carolina.[8] In other communities, the press, the pulpit and mass meetings took a similar position, leaving no doubt concerning the militant Union sentiment of the people.

In Kentucky, on the other hand, the state of public

[5] Porter, *op. cit.*, pp. 50-52.
[6] A. C. Cole, *The Era of the Civil War, 1848-1870* (volume III of the *Centennial History of Illinois*), p. 253.
[7] Thomas C. Miller and Hu Maxwell, *West Virginia and Its People*, vol. i, p. 314.
[8] *Idem*, p. 315.

opinion was more sympathetic toward the secessionist movement. A small group who had imbibed the opinions of the Southern "fire-eaters" was determined that the State should secede at once. They scoffed at the possibility of war, asserting that the North, "a nation of shopkeepers," would not fight. But even if there was a war, they declared that the Southern troops would soon be able to dictate the terms of peace. As may be inferred from their extreme statements, most of the active secessionists in Kentucky were young men who seem to have been inspired by the idea that they might have a share in the establishment of a great independent nation. Naturally enough, their loudly expressed opinions were not influential in determining the course of public sentiment; nor were their motives such as would affect the opinions of older and more conservative citizens. The great mass of the people waited in hopeful expectation for compromises to be made which would satisfy the people of the South. Nearly everyone seems to have believed that secession was merely a political maneuver, to be met by political arrangement.[9] They did not, therefore, feel obliged to make an immediate decision. If they had, at the beginning of 1861, it is probable that they would have gone with the South, on account of their extreme disapproval of the position which had been assumed by the abolitionists.[10]

This latent secessionist feeling complicated the problem of another group within the State who, at the beginning of the crisis, set themselves the task of keeping Kentucky in the Union at all hazards. Being men of

[9] Colonel R. M. Kelly, in *Union Regiments of Kentucky*, p. 15.

[10] For an excellent discussion of the division of sentiment, see an article by A. C. Quisenberry in the *Register* of the Kentucky Historical Society, January, 1917, pp. 9-21.

experience in politics, they refrained from making attacks on the South, bending their efforts instead to the
encouragement of nationalist sentiment. They seem to
have spoken often of the probability of concessions and
compromises and of the necessity of gaining time for the
existing excitement to cool. It is somewhat difficult,
therefore, to distinguish their activities from those of
other citizens who sought merely to postpone secession
until after every other alternative had been found impracticable. Afterward, they were charged with having
disguised their true sentiments even to the point of
promising to advocate withdrawal from political unity
with the North whenever it should be evident that the
Union was permanently broken.[11] The accusation may,
or may not, have been true; but at any rate, their circumspect attitude was justified by its results. The secessionist party, being unable to identify the advocacy of
the Union with Northern abolitionism, were completely
disarmed; and the patriotism of the great body of the
people was stimulated.

In point of fact, there was no reason for the unconditional Union men to adopt a policy different from that of
practically every other prominent leader. Everyone
remembered that Kentucky was the home of Henry Clay,
the author of the compromises of 1820 and 1850; and in
this, the third great crisis of the nation's history, they
believed it their duty to carry on the tradition which he
had established. On November 16th Governor Beriah
Magoffin addressed an open letter to the editor of the
Yeoman which was at once a proclamation of the attitude of the state government and an appeal for the

[11] George W. Johnson to Jefferson Davis, Nov. 21, 1861, *Official Records, War of the Rebellion,* Series IV, vol. i, p. 745.

preservation of the Union. He pointed out the dangers which might follow the secession of the Lower South, and declared forcefully that the Southern States ought to stay in the Union and fight side by side with the border slave States for the common interests of the whole section. If they deserted the border States at this juncture and failed in their duties to the whole country, no one could see the result. "Let passion be allayed," he said, "let moderation, forbearance and wisdom guide our counsels, and the country may yet be saved." [12] Shortly afterward, in a letter to other Southern governors, he presented a program of reforms which he thought the South should demand as a basis of settlement. First on the list was the repeal of the personal liberty acts passed by several Northern States, and the thorough enforcement of the fugitive slave laws. Next came a proposal that the territories should be divided between the sections on some parallel of latitude, say thirty-seven degrees, the settlers to have the option of forming their own constitutions and determining whether or not they wanted slavery. Lastly, he advocated the passing of a constitutional amendment which would give the Southern representatives sufficient power to prevent the enactment of oppressive legislation relating to slavery. [13] These propositions were the utmost that a Kentucky slaveholder and advocate of States' rights considered necessary to satisfy the South and bring peace between the sections. When later the seceded States sent representatives to urge the secession of Kentucky, the gov-

[12] Reprinted in the *Journal* of the House of Representatives of Kentucky, called session, January, 1861, pp. 12-18.

[13] *Idem,* p. 19.

ernor unflinchingly maintained his position. On December 28th he informed the commissioner from Alabama that his State desired to act within the Union to secure a redress of grievances.[14] He was willing, however, to meet representatives of the seceded States at Nashville, or any other place, and attempt to formulate a set of reasonable guarantees which would be acceptable to the North.

Magoffin's efforts to secure a proper basis of reconciliation have been almost forgotten among the mass of compromise measures that were proposed by men of greater national reputations. They are nevertheless important as an authoritative expression of the feeling in Kentucky, and indeed throughout the Borderland. They indicate a great attachment to the Union and an abiding faith that a practicable means might be found to preserve it. Realizing that the problem was of such a nature that it could be settled only by the joint action of all sections, the people centered their attention upon the officers of the national government. A great deal depended upon the policies adopted by President Buchanan. And much was expected from the coming session of the Congress.

The attitude of President Buchanan may be described as one of helpless watching. He was long past the age when men are apt to take decided action. His cabinet was divided. And he had no assurance that the people of the North as a whole would support him in an effort to preserve the Union by force. A contemporary says that in this crisis he was in the habit of throwing his arms about strangers who came to the White House and,

[14] Magoffin to S. F. Hale, *Official Records*, Series IV, vol. i, p. 14.

with tears in his eyes, imploring them to do something to save the Union.[15] The two Northern members of the cabinet, with Joseph Holt of Kentucky, advised him to send troops to important points in the Southern States and overawe the secessionists as Jackson had overawed the nullifiers. The three Southern members opposed this policy because they thought it would provoke resistance. In view of this division among his immediate advisers, it is not strange that a man of conservative temperament should hesitate to use force. There was, in fact, little likelihood that he could accomplish anything by this policy, for the whole regular army at this time numbered only 16,367 men, of whom nine-tenths were stationed on the frontier and hence were not immediately available.[16] If he had sent the inadequate force at his disposal into the South, the result would almost certainly have been to strengthen and extend the secessionist movement. The first conflict with the militia of South Carolina would have driven the Union men of the South into the ranks of the separatist party; and with all hope of the maintenance of the Union being then lost, it is probable that the border slave States would have seceded. It was extremely important, as later events showed, that every effort to save the Union by compromise and conciliation should be exhausted, and that the South should be placed in the position of having rejected the reasonable concessions offered by the people of the Borderland. The future therefore depended upon the action of the legislative branch of the government.

[15] L. E. Chittenden, *Recollections of President Lincoln and His Administration*, p. 33.

[16] Emory Upton, *The Military Policy of the United States*, p. 225. Of the 198 companies into which the army was divided, 183 were on the frontier.

The session of the Congress held in the winter of 1860-61 is noteworthy chiefly for the tremendous efforts made by the representatives of the conservative sections to effect a compromise. More than fifty different measures were proposed in the Senate alone, each designed by its authors to reassure the South. The great leaders of the moderate parties—Douglas of Illinois, Pugh of Ohio, Crittenden and Powell of Kentucky and Andrew Johnson of Tennessee—were indefatigable in their efforts to bring about an agreement. They strove for no personal or sectional aggrandizement, from no selfish or partisan motives, only sincerely and patriotically for the preservation of the Union. Would that the representatives of other sections had had similar motives!

The principal compromise measure was the one introduced by John J. Crittenden of Kentucky, the successor to Henry Clay in the Senate. It was exceedingly complex, consisting both of proposed laws and of proposed constitutional amendments. The first amendment would have restored the line of the Missouri Compromise to the eastern boundary of California. All the territories south of the line were to be open to slavery, and all north of the line were to be free. It was further provided that when new States were to be formed the people of the territories should have the option of admitting or excluding slavery as they pleased. Another amendment would have withdrawn from the Congress the power to abolish slavery in any military reservation, customs house, etc., owned by the United States in a slave State. A third would have limited its power to abolish slavery in the District of Columbia by requiring a referendum to the residents of the District, the consent of the legislatures of Maryland and Virginia, and the payment of full compensation. A fourth would have removed the transportation of slaves into the territories from the scope of the commerce powers of the Congress. Lastly, it was proposed that slaveholders should be reimbursed out of the Federal treasury when their fugitive slaves were rescued by citizens. The proposed amendments to the Constitution, together with the three-fifths rule for representation, were to be irrepealable. And no future amendment might be added which would empower the Congress to interfere with slavery in the States. The proposed laws were concerned chiefly with improving the fugitive slave acts so as to make them more acceptable to both sections. The slaveholders were to be given additional guarantees that their slaves would be returned; and the features of the existing laws that were most objectionable to the North— the requirement of the *posse comitatus* and the allowance of different fees when an apprehended fugitive was discharged and when he was returned to his master— were to be repealed.[17]

Taken as a whole, the provisions of the Crittenden compromise seem wise and fair enough to have won acceptance from any body of men who were truly desirous of preserving the Union. They did not satisfy the full demands of either section—no compromise could have done that—but they gave guarantees on every point that was practically essential and asked for concessions only on matters of minor importance. The South was asked to relinquish the right to take slaves into the northern territories; but, since the chief advantage derived from this right was that slave States might be

[17] Mrs. Chapman Coleman, *Life of John J. Crittenden,* vol. ii, pp. 224-227.

created to balance the power of the North, and thus
prevent interference with slavery in the States, it would
become relatively unimportant with the passing of the
other proposed amendments. Similarly, the Republicans
were asked to content themselves with a little less than
the full measure of victory, in that New Mexico was
still to remain a slave territory; but considering the
unfitness of that arid region for slavery, the concession
was slight. To the Borderland the Crittenden compromise was satisfactory, as any other proposal would have
been that gave promise of preserving the Union. Douglas and Pugh were especially conspicuous in supporting
it. In the Lower South the friends of the Union pinned
all their hopes upon it, or upon a similar adjustment.
Even among the Republicans there is evidence to indicate that a marked reaction from their former inflexible
attitude had occurred. Shortly after the election, Thurlow Weed, the manager of the party in New York, suggested that the line of the Missouri Compromise should
be restored, and that the owners of rescued slaves should
be reimbursed by the counties in which the rescues took
place.[18] Later on, Seward, still the recognized national
leader of the party, proposed, with Charles Francis
Adams, that the Republicans should conciliate the border slave States and hold them in the Union. If the cotton States then refused to accede to proposals of conciliation, they thought it possible, by isolating them, to
compel them to seek readmittance into the Union.[19] In
two or more of the Northern States the legislatures requested the Congress to submit the proposed amendments for ratification.

[18] Rhodes, *op. cit.*, vol. iii, p. 145.
[19] Charles Francis Adams, *Autobiography*, p. 73.

In spite of the general approval which the compromise received from conservative citizens, it was soon evident that it was unacceptable to the extreme elements who were in the majority. Various considerations prevented the moderate Republican leaders from giving it their wholehearted support. There was, in the first place, a practical objection to the form in which the measures were cast, since the passing of constitutional amendments was designed to remove the question of slavery from politics.[20] The attainment of this result would deprive the Republicans of their issue and reduce their ill-assorted organization to the position of the Know-Nothings in 1856. Whether such a narrowly partisan motive had much to do with the final decision is somewhat doubtful. A really important influence, in the minds of many leaders, was the feeling that if the North gave way at this time, its action would only encourage the South to demand further concessions—"to repeat the experiment upon us [of extorting compromises] *ad libitum"*—as Lincoln phrased it. He believed that the only constitutional amendment that could be effective would be one prohibiting the further acquisition of territory.[21] A reading of his correspondence during this period leads almost unescapably to the conclusion that he thought a determined stand necessary sooner or later. Other leaders agreed, and the majority of the Republicans were only too ready to fall in with this view. Regarding slavery as a purely moral question, they were convinced that any further recognition or extension of the institution, be it ever so little, would be a compro-

[20] Speech of Douglas, Jan. 3, 1861, *Globe,* 36th Congress, second session, Appendix, p. 41.

[21] Confidential letter to John T. Hale, Jan. 11, 1861, *Complete Works* (two volume edition, ed. by Nicolay and Hay) vol. i, p. 664.

mise with evil, hardly less reprehensible than a complete
surrender. It is easy to understand and appreciate this
feeling, though one cannot but wish it had not existed;
for it helped to defeat all plans for a peaceful solution
of the difficulties.

The Republicans were not alone in their disinclination
to accept the compromise. Equally strong reasons for
disapproval existed among the leaders from the Lower
South. At the time the measure was advanced, only the
members of the Congress from South Carolina had left
their seats. The others remained in Washington carefully guarding the interests of their section. They took
part in the debates, they served on committees which
considered the proposals, and they expressed their readiness to accept any measure that would receive the approval of their constituents. But at the same time they
were probably planning concerted action when the secessionist program should be completed. Some of them
seem to have been engaged in abetting and directing the
movement in their own States. Naturally, therefore,
they had little interest in promoting a settlement.[22] It
is even possible that they had a political motive in holding out encouragement of eventual adjustment, since
they would be in a better position to secure the coöperation of the Union party in all the slave States if they
could place the Republicans in the wrong.

In this party struggle the Southern leaders were vic-
torious. The Crittenden compromise was defeated in the
Senate Committee of Thirteen, which reported on
December 28th that it had been unable to reach an

[22] Edward A. Pollard, *Life of Jefferson Davis*, p. 68. The author
believes there was a secessionist conspiracy which had its origin in the
United States Senate.

agreement on the measure. This committee was composed of five Republicans, two Douglas Democrats, four senators from the border States, and two from the Lower South, Davis and Toombs. On the first and most important article the vote was seven to six against adoption, the representatives of the two extreme elements combining to make up the majority. It is probable that if the Republicans had accepted the measure, the two Southern senators would likewise have done so.[23] But the attitude of the one party enabled the other to take a similar position without loss of prestige. The Southern leaders, arguing that it was impossible to secure guarantees of their rights from the North, were soon successful in justifying secession and in breaking down the opposition of the Union men in the South. Within a few weeks all the Gulf States left the Union, and the secessionist movement was spread to the borders of free territory.[24] In a way, the pro-slavery party was aided at this juncture by the well meant efforts of Douglas to shame the Republicans out of their position. He placed upon them the sole responsibility for defeating the compromise, and made it appear that their decision was the result of partisan schemes concocted in the secrecy of the party caucus. He demanded that they submit other proposals if they would not agree to the ones set forth, for they owed a duty to the whole country. The people, he said, had voted for Lincoln, not for the dissolution of the Union.[25]

[23] Rhodes, *op. cit.*, vol. iii, p. 154.
[24] Toombs devoted his efforts to securing the secession of Georgia after the failure of the Crittenden compromise. Consult I. M. Avery, *History of Georgia*, p. 154.
[25] Speech on the state of the Union, Jan. 3, 1861, *Globe*, 36th Congress, 2nd session, Appendix, p. 41.

In the House of Representatives action was delayed longer than in the other chamber, the final proposal being submitted late in February. It was the work of a committee of thirty-three, consisting of one member from each State. The recommendations were, in general, more favorable to the South than the Crittenden compromise. Chief among them were the following: (1) The question of slavery in New Mexico, instead of being left for determination under the principle of popular sovereignty, was to be settled by the immediate admission of the territory as a slave State. (2) The fugitive slave laws were to be made more effective by placing their enforcement under the exclusive jurisdiction of the Federal courts, and by making requisitions *prima facie* evidence against the accused. (3) An amendment was to be made to the Constitution providing that no later amendment should interfere with slavery in the States unless it originated in a slave State and was ratified by all the state legislatures.²⁶ Upon being considered in the House, the first two proposals were rejected. The third was submitted to the States for ratification.

In the time intervening between the secession of the Gulf States and the advancement of the House proposals, public opinion, now somewhat disillusioned concerning the efficacy of legislative action, turned to a scheme for diplomatic adjustment which was brought forward by Virginia and supported by executives and legislatures in other border slave States. Basically the plan rested on the principle of state sovereignty. Its proponents virtually recognized the right of secession and the existence of a group of independent States in the South with

²⁶ Edward McPherson, *The Political History of the United States of America During the Great Rebellion*, pp. 58-62.

an international character similar to that of the national government. Assuming that their own States had independent powers, they proposed to take a neutral position between the sections and employ mediation to settle the differences between them.

In January the legislature of Virginia requested all the other States to send delegates to a "Peace Conference" at Washington on February 4th. The invitation was accepted by nearly all the States which still remained in the Union, but not a single delegate came from any of the seceded States. The answer of the Southern leaders was to establish a government of the Confederate States of America on the day the Peace Conference assembled. It was thus a meeting of the mediators with only one of the possible belligerents. The delegates from the North were placed in a false position. They might offer concessions to the South, but there was little hope of their being accepted, and no prospect of obtaining guarantees in return. The Republican leaders soon came to regard the conference as a danger to party solidarity. At one time the delegations from Ohio, Indiana and Rhode Island seemed to be on the point of favoring the extension of slavery to the territories, and those from Illinois were not far behind them.[27] After awaiting vainly for some weeks the coming of representatives from the seceded States, the sessions came to an end with declarations of undying attachment to the Union and the recommendation of a compromise less liberal to the South than the congressional proposals. It probably did some harm in that it gave an incorrect impression of the state of pub-

[27] Zechariah Chandler to the governor of Michigan, Feb. 11, 1861, quoted by Beverley B. Munford, *Virginia's Attitude Toward Slavery and Secession*, p. 254.

lic opinion in Virginia. On the other hand, it was of
some service in making evident the stubborn unreason-
ableness of the Lower South.

In spite of the fact that the proposals of compromise
and mediation produced none of the immediate results
that had been intended, their ultimate effect was exceedingly favorable to the cause of the Union. In the first
place, the early secessionist movement was limited to
the Lower South, leaving eight of the fifteen slave States
in the Union at the time of Lincoln's inauguration. If
there had been no prospect of a settlement most of these
States might have seceded at once. In the second place,
the solidarity of sentiment which was developed throughout the Borderland immensely strengthened the position
of the national government. The coöperation between
free and slave States made the latter less inclined to
welcome secession, and at the same time toned down the
anti-slavery sentiment in the former to the point where
it was completely secondary to the general desire to save
the Union. In Ohio, Indiana and Illinois, the Republican state officials, by supporting the measures which all
the Union men desired, were able in a great measure to
divert attention from the sectional character of their
party. They were therefore in a better position to carry
the people with them when aggressive measures against
the South became necessary. Finally—and most important of all—the protracted period of discussion gave the
people of the North time for sober reflection, and thus
contributed powerfully to the development of unionist
sentiment there.

CHAPTER IV

THE EARLY SECESSIONIST MOVEMENT ON THE BORDER

With the defeat of the Crittenden compromise in the Senate committee and the almost immediate secession of nearly all the Gulf States, public opinion in the Borderland entered a new phase. The feeling of devotion to the Union continued without diminution, but the popular faith that it could be maintained as before was greatly shaken. The rapid spread of the secessionist movement throughout the Lower South and the enthusiasm shown by the Southern people for independence convinced the people of the Borderland that the movement was more than a maneuver to extort concessions from the North. When proposal after proposal of conciliation and mediation had been rejected by one or the other of the extreme sections, the people were compelled to face the possibility that the Union might be permanently broken into two separate nations between which they would have to choose. The realization of this eventuality opened the way for the discussion of secession in all the border slave States. From being mere spectators of the tragedy of dissolution many people of the Borderland felt obliged to become participants. The situation was critical, for in the existing state of uncertainty, public opinion became particularly liable to be swayed by prejudices and to make important decisions on the spur of the moment.

The leaders of both the Union and the secessionist parties, quickly sensing the change in the conditions which influenced public opinion, prepared for a struggle. The friends of the Union turned their attention from ways and means of restoring the seceded States to the more pressing problem of holding their own States to their allegiance. On the other hand, the secessionists strove to secure immediate action favorable to their cause by boldly proclaiming that the Union was already destroyed, and that the time had come for the people of the border States to decide whether they would remain with the abolitionist North or take their rightful places in the councils of their sister States which had resisted the aggressions of the anti-slavery faction even to the point of leaving the Union. Both parties looked to their friends in the extreme sections to aid them.

The South was the first to seize upon the opportunity. Nearly all the people undoubtedly believed that the border slave States must sooner or later cast in their lots with them. Did not their section furnish the market for the surplus slaves of the border States, without which slavery could hardly have existed there? Did it not control the mouth of the Mississippi River? Did it not consume much of the surplus produce of the farms of the West? Realizing their strong economic position, the leaders dissipated the fears of timid opponents of secession in their own States by assuring them that the border States—indeed the whole Northwest—must either join with them or remain neutral in any conflict with the abolitionists. This opinion was intensified and made well-nigh certain through their interpretation of the facts of Western history. They were familiar with Jay's statement to Gardoqui, the Spanish envoy, that "the Americans, almost to a man, believed that God Almighty had made that river [the Mississippi] a highway for the people of the upper country to go to sea by." [1] They knew of the efforts made by the frontiersmen to secure the free navigation of the river, which had resulted in the purchase of Louisiana. They fully realized the importance of the majestic, fast-flying steamboats which brought to New Orleans the varied products of the Northwest. There was a fallacy in their conclusion, however, for they had failed to take into account the economic changes that had occurred in the decade before 1860. They had forgotten the railroads which linked the West with New York, Philadelphia and Baltimore—or if they had considered them, they had utterly failed to estimate their true importance. They can scarcely be blamed, since the people of the Borderland did not themselves fully realize the significance of the new connection with the East. If the secessionist movement could have been delayed for another decade, the economic changes in the Borderland would have been completed so as to have been patent to the most ardent subject of King Cotton. In that case the Southern people must have realized the futility of expecting help from the Borderland, and would have weighed more carefully than they did the possibility of the failure of the secessionist movement.

Considering the Southern estimate of the economic strength of their section, it is not difficult to understand why the leaders of the secessionist movement did not take the border slave States into their confidence and attempt to secure their coöperation from the beginning. In the South the movement had a solid basis in the widespread

[1] F. Wharton, editor, *The Revolutionary Diplomatic Correspondence of the United States*, vol. iv, p. 135.

popular indignation at the election of a sectional President. If the leaders had delayed the proceedings for the period necessary to win over the border States, it is possible that the ardor of their own followers might have cooled. On the other hand, there seemed to be nothing that could be lost by independent action, for the Southerners believed that when secession had actually occurred, and when the border States had to face the alternative of going with the South or remaining with the North, they could not fail to join with them. They therefore lost no time in asserting their independence, confidently expecting that the other slave States would follow them.

The cool reception which the northern tier of slave States at first gave to the secessionist movement led some of the more determined Southerners to attempt to bring economic pressure to bear. The "sovereignty" convention of Alabama proposed that the Mississippi River should be closed to the people of the upper valley.[2] Two or three of the governors of States that had seceded recommended that their legislatures pass laws prohibiting the importation of slaves from the border States. Governor Magoffin, referring to this threatened measure in his reply to the commissioners from Alabama, declared that it was not calculated to prove conciliatory to the people of his State.[3] The policy of coercion had everywhere the same effect, irritating many sincere friends of the South. Consequently, the more sagacious secessionist leaders, realizing the evil results of attempting to coerce the border States, afterward procured the abandonment of the policy. If the Republicans had been a little more conciliatory on their part, the border slave States might at

[2] Cincinnati *Enquirer*, Feb. 22, 1861.
[3] Magoffin to S. F. Hale, *Official Records*, Series IV, vol. i, p. 15.

this time have been alienated from the South. Unfortunately for the cause of the Union, their newspapers throughout the country just then abandoned their impossible position of favoring the secession of the South and plunged to the opposite extreme of advocating the coercion of the seceded States to return to the Union. The result was that numerous States' Rights men on the border who had worked for compromises were driven to the advocacy of secession.

In January, 1861, the secessionist party in all the border States brought tremendous pressure to bear on the state officials to take measures which would finally bring about secession. These measures were, first, the calling of the legislatures in special session where regular sessions were not shortly to meet; secondly, the provision by the legislatures for the calling of constitutional conventions; and, thirdly, the passing of ordinances of secession by the conventions. Governor Hicks of Maryland, alone among the state executives, resisted the pressure and refused to call a special session. One or two of the other governors were favorable to secession, and did their utmost to bring it about. The others held to the theory of state sovereignty, under which every State had the right to remain in the Union or to leave it at pleasure. When they called special sessions of the legislatures, they therefore acted on the assumption that there was sufficient public demand to justify the full discussion of state and national relations.

Among the advocates of state sovereignty, as opposed to secession, was Governor Magoffin of Kentucky, who had finally despaired of settling the differences between the sections by compromises. To his mind, the efforts of the border States to secure adjustments had precipitated, rather than retarded secession on account of the opposition of the Republicans to every reasonable compromise. Their triumph, appearing to rest upon "sectional animosity," presented a real danger to the interests of the people of Kentucky. He was therefore of the opinion that the State could not longer remain in the Union without guarantees from the new Republican administration. Early in January he called the legislature into special session for the purposes of providing for military defense and of calling a constitutional convention.[4]

The call for the special session aroused the Union party of the State to take active measures. Robert J. Breckinridge wrote an open letter to his nephew, the Vice-President, declaring that it was the deliberate opinion of Kentucky that secession was no remedy for anything, and was itself the direst of calamities. Garrett Davis, John M. Harlan, Joshua F. Speed and others organized the Union party in preparation for the struggle in the legislature. The center of unionist sentiment was the city of Louisville, which had become prosperous largely through its trade with the South, but which had Northern connections sufficient to more than offset the Southern influences. The two leading newspapers were unconditionally in favor of the preservation of the Union, and the majority of the people agreed with them. On January 8th, a great Union demonstration was arranged in the city, which showed definitely the sentiment of the people. This was nothing less than the simultaneous meeting of conventions representing the Douglas Democrats and the Constitutional Union party, which together had cast nearly two-thirds of the vote of the State two months

[4] Message of Governor Magoffin, House *Journal*, called session, January, 1861, pp. 4 *et seq*.

before.   Strong addresses in favor of the preservation
of the Union were made in both conventions, and identi-
cal resolutions were adopted which, though not so unequivocal as some sanguine persons in the North had
anticipated, showed unmistakably that the delegates
were devoted to the Union, and desired its preservation
by any means short of coercion.[5]   The most important
act of the conventions was the appointment of an executive committee of ten who were to organize the Union
men of the State in opposition to any attempt to secure
secession.   The action of the conventions produced a profound impression.   In all parts of the State mass meetings approved the sentiments expressed in the resolutions.
Members of the legislature which was about to assemble
were greatly influenced; and the secessionist movement
was effectually halted before the first skirmish began.

During the legislative session the pro-Southern party
made every effort to secure the calling of a "sovereignty"
convention. The Union party, on the other hand, devoted
their efforts toward defeating the measure by delay.   By
a vote of fifty-four to thirty-five, the House refused to
consider it,[6] and the danger of secession was postponed.
There was naturally much discussion of means to restore
the Union.   By an almost unanimous vote the House
expressed its approval of the Crittenden compromise as
a basis of settlement.[7]   A resolution was passed by both
houses requesting the Congress to call a convention of
the States to propose amendments to the Federal Constitution.[8]   In all these measures the legislature made it

---

[5] Lewis Collins, *History of Kentucky* (revised by Richard H. Collins,
who contributed the section quoted), vol. i, pp. 85-86.

[6] House *Journal*, called session, January, 1861, p. 64.

[7] *Idem*, pp. 85-87.

[8] Collins, *op. cit.*, vol. i, p. 86.

plain that Kentucky should continue to be one of the United States. The victory of the Union party was, however, not as complete as might have been desired; for in two other resolutions the legislature tacitly recognized the principle of secession, and expressly declared the right of the State to take independent action if the need should arise. In the first of these, it declared that it had heard with profound regret of the action of New York, Ohio, Maine and Massachusetts, which had tendered men and money to the President for the purpose of coercing certain "sovereign States" of the South into obedience to the national government. In the second, it declared that whenever those States should send men and money for that purpose, "the people of Kentucky, uniting with their brethren of the South, will as one man resist such invasion of the soil of the South at all hazards and to the last extremity."[9] Another ominous note was struck when the legislature refused to adjourn *sine die*, voting instead, early in February, to take a recess until March 20th. The object was partly to await the result of the Peace Conference, partly to ascertain definitely what the policy of the incoming national administration would be.[10] If it should attempt coercion, Kentucky would be ready to combat it. The terms could hardly have been made plainer.

Leaving the later events in Kentucky to be considered in other chapters, let us turn our attention to Virginia where the pro-Southern party was much more active and aggressive. Their strength was mainly confined to the eastern part of the State, though the professional politicians in all sections were almost solidly in favor of seces-

[9] Collins, vol. i, p. 86.
[10] Cincinnati *Enquirer* Feb. 9, 1861.

sion. They could count on the active aid of the Richmond *Enquirer*, then edited by O. Jennings Wise, the eldest son of ex-Governor Henry A. Wise.[11] They had the support of the organizations of both the Southern Democratic and the Constitutional Union parties. More important still for their purposes, they had induced Governor Letcher to renounce his former unionist sentiments and to act as their obedient agent. He made the first move toward secession at nearly the same time as the governors of the Gulf States, issuing a proclamation on November 15th calling the legislature into special session. As the principal purpose, he named the consideration of a financial arrangement which had been made for the sale of state property, but he included also the discussion of calling a convention to determine what should be the future relation of Virginia to the government of the United States. [12] Apparently being certain that the State would secede, he devoted considerable attention to securing arms from the national government in order that he might be ready in case of war. In this matter he was more active than the other chief executives of Southern States, purchasing all the munitions the War Department would sell him. Early in January he was in conference with other leaders of the State over the question of seizing Fortress Monroe as soon as secession should be accomplished.[13]

The people of northwestern Virginia also appear to have believed that the secessionist party in the State

[11] An editorial, Dec. 24, 1860, suggested that Virginia and Maryland should take over the national capital to prevent the inauguration of Lincoln.

[12] House *Journal*, extra session, 1861, pp. 3-4.

[13] G. D. Hall, *The Rending of Virginia*, p. 196. See also Letcher's message to the legislature, December, 1861.

would be successful. Without waiting for the issue to be forced upon them, they quickly came to a decision, aligning themselves with practical unanimity on the side of the Union. The desire for a separate State west of the mountains, which had been in the minds of the people from the time of the Revolution, suddenly crowded itself upon their attention. Recounting afresh the disabilities which had been placed upon them by the ruling class in eastern Virginia, they began a strong movement for the division of the State on the line of the Blue Ridge. "We are for secession at once," said the Tyler County *Plaindealer* on January 4th. "No ties bind us to Eastern Virginia but the unjust laws they have made." At about the same time, the Morgantown *Star* declared: "We have been hewers of wood and drawers of water for Eastern Virginia long enough, and it is time that section understood it." [14] The Clarksburg *Guardian* expressed the opinion that "Western Virginia has suffered more from the oppressive doctrines of her eastern brethren than ever the Cotton states all put together have suffered from the Northern Personal Liberty Bills." A correspondent from Marion County to the Alexandria *Gazette* declared that, if a convention should be called, the western part of the State would accept nothing but the white basis of representation and the abolishment of the exemption of slave property from taxation. "If our eastern brethren," he said, "withhold these rights from the West at this juncture, it will take a hundred thousand bayonets from a southern confederacy to force western Virginia into a union with the cotton states." [15]

If the advocates of secession had carefully considered

[14] Quoted by Hall, *op. cit.*, p. 126.
[15] Quoted by the Cincinnati *Gazette*, Jan. 4 and 5, 1861.

the situation they would have realized that the division of public opinion on sectional lines in Virginia was as dangerous as the sectional division of the nation. The dissatisfaction of the people of western Virginia with the state government, combined with their great love for the Union, set a problem which should have made Wise and others of his party pause in their efforts to hurry Virginia out of the Union. The secessionist leaders in Virginia suffered, however, from the same infirmity as their associates in the cotton States. They had an overweening confidence in their strength, and they apparently believed that devotion to the Union could be overcome by the specious arguments of the leaders who had for a long time carried the Trans-Alleghany section with them in political campaigns. They therefore prepared carefully for the calling of a convention when the legislature should meet on January 7th.

The circumstances under which the legislature assembled, unlike those in Kentucky at about the same time, were decidedly unfavorable to the cause of the Union. There was no great commercial center like Louisville to serve as a nucleus for the gathering of nationalist sentiment. Richmond was almost wholly secessionist in its sympathies. The means by which opinion could be expressed were under the control of the secessionists. The Union party was badly led, and it had no definite program. Its opponents were organized and active. Influential men declared themselves in favor of half-way measures. Thus ex-Governor Wise published a letter on January 8th recommending that Virginia should resume the powers which had been delegated to the national government. He did not favor secession, he said, but only the suspension of relations between Virginia and the

United States until the latter should comply with the ultimatum of the State.[16]   The message which Governor Letcher sent to the legislature was a mixture of sentiments expressing devotion to the Union, criticism of the Republicans, and sorrow for what he termed the hasty and ill-advised act of South Carolina.[17]   Though upholding the legal right of secession, he counseled against hasty action, recommending that no convention be called at that time, and suggesting instead the appointment of commissioners to the States north and south of the Mason and Dixon line for mediation and the compromise of all differences.   Taken at its face value, the message seems to express unionist sentiments of a sort; but when read in connection with other statements of the Governor it appears as an attempt to lull the Union party into a sense of security.

Notwithstanding the unfavorable situation in which the unionist members of the legislature found themselves, the special session accomplished something in halting the secessionist movement.   It called the Peace Conference which met in Washington on February 4th, and it sent commissioners to Washington and to the state capitals of the South to ask that hostilities be postponed.[18]   In case it should be impossible to preserve peace, the legislature declared that every consideration of honor and interest demanded that Virginia should unite with the South.   In order that the State might be in a position to take immediate action if future circumstances required it, provision was made for the election of delegates to a constitutional convention on the day the Peace Confer-

[16] Letters to the Richmond *Enquirer,* Jan. 8, and Feb. 12, 1861.
[17] Beverley B. Munford, *Virginia's Attitude Toward Slavery and Secession,* p. 249.
[18] *Idem,* p. 250.

ence met. The call was somewhat precipitate, only three weeks being allowed for the discussion of the questions at issue. But it can hardly be said to have been a purely secessionist measure, despite the fact that the seceded States had left the Union through the ordinances of conventions. Many persons in western Virginia, whose devotion to the Union could not be questioned, wanted a convention in order to secure important constitutional changes relating to representation and taxation.

The first real struggle between the unionist and secessionist parties in Virginia came in the election of delegates to the constitutional convention. Every shade of opinion was to be recognized among the candidates who offered themselves. There were outright secessionists and unconditional Union men; opponents of coercion and conditional Union men of varying degrees of loyalty. Some among them disguised their true sentiments in order to appeal successfully to the predominant feeling of the constituencies. During the brief canvass it was well-nigh impossible for the people to determine accurately whether or not the candidates would truly represent their opinions. In most of the Trans-Alleghany counties the temper of the people was such that no one suspected of favoring secession had much chance of being elected. Extreme care was taken to make sure of the genuineness of the loyal expressions of candidates. It was felt that no mistakes could be made in this critical election—that no States' Rights politicians avowing a conditional allegiance to the Union should be elected. The candidates were required to stand on a platform of principles that excluded all but the most thoroughgoing Union men. The resolutions adopted by the nominating convention in Harrison County are representative of the sentiments of the people throughout most of northwestern Virginia. It was resolved "that we will support no man as a delegate . . . who is not unequivocally opposed to secession and will not so pledge himself. . . . We will not support any man who believes that the convention . . . or any other State authority can absolve the citizens of this State from their allegiance to the General Government; and that we will support no man who does not believe that the Federal Government has the right of self-preservation."[19] In order that the people might have an opportunity to watch the proceedings of the convention and hold their delegates responsible, it was further declared that there should be no deliberations in secret session. The voters in some other sections, particularly in the Shenandoah Valley, also declared themselves in favor of remaining in the Union.

The results of the election were extremely favorable to the nationalist cause. Of the one hundred fifty-two delegates only thirty were classified as outright secessionists. Most of these came from the "black belt" between the James River and the North Carolina border. About one-fourth of the total number were unconditional Union men, most of whom were from the Valley and the Trans-Alleghany sections. The remainder, more than half of the membership, were conditional Union men, opposing coercion, but strongly supporting measures of compromise and concession. In politics, twenty were classified as Douglas Democrats, one hundred two as Whigs, and the remainder as secessionists.[20] A popular referendum was obtained on the question whether or not the action

[19] Henry Haymond, *History of Harrison County, West Virginia*, pp. 333-334.

[20] *The South in the Building of the Nation*, vol. i, p. 111.

of the convention should be submitted to the people for
ratification or rejection. The voters determined, 100,536
to 45,161, that they should have the final decision.[21]

The victory of the Union men had political consequences of the greatest importance. If a majority of the
people, at such a critical time, had voted to leave the
Union, it is more than probable that Kentucky and the
other 'border slave States would have followed their
example. The election therefore checked the secessionist movement and confined it, for the time being, to the
Lower South. It stopped short the discussion of plans
to seize the national capital. It allowed time for the
popular excitement to cool. And most important of all,
it afforded an opportunity for the new Republican administration to go into office quietly and to formulate its
policies for the preservation of the Union. Everywhere
in the North the people hailed the result joyfully. Seward
declared that it was a rift in the clouds that presaged the
clearing away of the storm.[22]

The convention began its sessions on February 13th,
less than three weeks before the date of the inauguration.
It was composed of many of the ablest men in the State,
including an ex-President of the United States, several
high officials of the national government, and many
notable leaders of state politics. As everyone had
expected, the Union men had complete control of the
organization, forcing the election of John Janney of Lou-
doun County as president, with a full list of unionist officers. The committees appointed were representative of
all parties.

No sooner was the organization completed than the

[21] Munford, *op. cit.*, p. 256.
[22] Munford, p. 257.

convention earnestly attempted to solve the problem of preserving the Union, which had proved impossible of solution in the halls of Congress. The members were actuated to pursue this policy, not by an exaggerated estimate of their own abilities, but rather by a feeling of the importance of their State. Virginia was the "Mother of States" and the "Mother of Presidents," and it had always occupied a leading place in the nation. At this time, too, it stood between the extreme sections. Surely if a solution were possible the convention might achieve it. In the first few days of the session, many resolutions were presented proposing adjustments of the difficulties, which varied greatly. On one point only there was general agreement: there should be no coercion by the national government, only compromise and concilia- tion. True to its conception of its duty as a mediator, the convention took a position of strict neutrality be- tween the seceded States and the national government. One of the first resolutions which it passed declared that if either section began hostilities, Virginia would feel obliged to join with the other in repelling the assault. Desiring to give the South full opportunity to be heard, it received the official representatives of Georgia, South Carolina and Mississippi, and gave them permission to make addresses before it. They declared the intention of their States to remain outside the Union "unless the economy of God were changed." Proclaiming the causes which had induced them to secede, they advised that Virginia should take similar action at once.[23] The con- vention, in making no protest against their attacks on the national government, showed loyalty of a dubious sort.

In reading the proceedings, one cannot help being

[23] Virgil A. Lewis, *History of West Virginia*, p. 333.

impressed by the lack of cohesion among the unionist majority. If they had been united and determined, they could have taken complete control of the convention, passed resolutions favoring the preservation of the Union, and then adjourned. As it was, their great numbers were a source of weakness instead of strength, since the delegates, believing that secession was impossible, were lulled into a sense of false security. The important question upon which their attention should constantly have been fixed was soon complicated by the reopening of the old struggle between the East and the West. The western members demanded the passage of amendments to the constitution guaranteeing reforms in representation. Moreover, they announced boldly their intention to remain in the Union even if the new administration should enter upon a policy of coercion. Their extreme stand in both these matters brought upon them the bitter opposition of the city of Richmond and alienated many moderate Union men. Apparently there was no one among them who sensed what seems now to have been the fairly evident drift of affairs toward secession. The sectional quarrels could easily have been averted if there had been even one unionist leader with sufficient ability to recognize the needs of the situation and sufficient personality to direct his party. Unfortunately there was no such man. President Janney took the position that he should be only the moderator of a deliberative body, refusing to assume the familiar duties of the speaker of an American legislature. Alexander H. H. Stuart and Jubal A. Early were either lacking in ability or were not sufficiently devoted to the Union. John S. Carlile, of northwestern Virginia, could not obtain a following in any other section because of his extreme views. Though all of these men had some support, there was no one capable of planning a course of action which all would follow. Recommendations for compromises and weak resolutions declaring devotion to the Union were the only measures upon which the whole group could agree.

In contrast to the inactivity and disorganization of the unionist party, the secessionists presented a solid front. There were no differences in policy among the leaders. All were working to achieve the same end. They had the tremendous advantage always possessed by a minority with a definite purpose when the majority is tolerant, badly led, and lacking a definite program. Through their noisy demands for a hearing they secured choice seats and important committee assignments. On the all-important committee on Federal relations, they had seven members out of twenty-one. They were marshaled as a solid phalanx by their leaders, who included such men as ex-President Tyler, Robert L. Montague, and John Goode. They were indefatigable in developing secessionist sentiment both in the convention and in the city. And they had the coöperation of leading officers of the State. The commissioners who had come from the seceded States remained in Richmond and abused their privileges as diplomatic representatives to a "sovereign" State by engaging in propaganda to overthrow the government of which it was a part.[24] Sentiment opposed to the Union was overwhelming in the streets, in the hotels and everywhere else throughout the state capital. Secessionists packed the galleries of the convention, applauding the expression of sentiments friendly toward the South.

[24] Carter G. Woodson, *The Disruption of Virginia* (unpublished thesis in Harvard University), p. 222.

The leaders of the party evidently believed that it might be possible to secure a majority for their cause by taking advantage of favorable circumstances and bringing pressure to bear on members whose devotion to the Union was lukewarm. They opposed adjournment at all times, knowing that it was for their interest to keep the convention in session as long as possible. The moderate Union members did not wish to adjourn until after March 4th, in order that they might ascertain the policy of the Republican administration—an attitude that suited admirably the plans of the secessionists. Even the members from the Trans-Alleghany section played into the hands of their opponents by demanding reforms in taxation and the suffrage before the convention adjourned. Thus the State of Virginia, on March 4th, presented a menacing attitude toward the new administration.

It will be remembered that Kentucky also was in a position to threaten the future stability of the Union by reason of the fact that the legislature had fixed a date beyond March 4th for reassembling. But the unionist leaders in that State were in a much better position than in Virginia. By constitutional provisions they were guarded against the hasty and excited action of a small group;—there was plenty of time for excitement and passion to cool. The legislature would not meet until March 20th, after the policy of the new administration had been announced. Some time would be required for it to pass a resolution calling a "sovereignty" convention to meet at a future date. In the interval there must necessarily be a popular election for members of the convention. Finally, the convention would require several days for organization and deliberation. All the influence of a secessionist governor and a secessionist majority in both houses of the legislature could not have passed an ordinance of secession until after momentary passions had subsided. But in Virginia, in case of a sudden unfavorable turn of events, the secessionists might gain control of the convention and take the State out of the Union within forty-eight hours. The necessity for a referendum to the people provided no adequate remedy against hasty action, since it would come after the secession of the State was an accomplished fact. For this reason, an early adjournment was the foremost need of the hour. If it had occurred in February or March, the history of the United States would probably have been materially changed. The new administration would at least have had an opportunity to formulate a policy depending on the country as a whole and not on one State.

The Union men of Missouri were more fortunately placed for their first defense against secession than their fellow-partisans in either Kentucky or Virginia. The position of the State so far north, the close connection between its people and the inhabitants of free territory, and the commercial interests of its great metropolis all tended to increase the strength of the unionists and to diminish the prospects of the secessionists. In nearly all sections of the State there was a predominant unionist sentiment devoted, as in Kentucky and eastern Virginia, to the promotion of compromises and mediation. As in Virginia, there was something of a sectional distribution of sentiment, since a large party in St. Louis threatened to secede from Missouri if Missouri seceded from the Union. The unconditional unionist party in St. Louis was so strong, indeed, that most writers on the period have left the incorrect impression that the

city was the only center of nationalist feeling in the
State. From the beginning they preferred to act alone
without much consideration either for the people of the
rural districts or for the state government. In some respects their intentions bordered on the illegal and the
revolutionary. The advocates of secession were equally
determined that their cause should prevail. In all their
activities they were not ineptly directed by the governor
of the State, who was an active and outspoken secessionist, quite unlike the honest Magoffin or the devious and
cautious Letcher. The two contending factions had a
prize well worth fighting for—the United States arsenal
at St. Louis, which was by far the largest in the South.
Added to other complications was the stationing in the
city of an insubordinate, ultra-abolitionist captain of the
United States army. All in all, the bitter struggles
between the two factions afford one of the most fascinat-
ing chapters in American history.

The positions of the moderate Union men—the great
majority of the people—and of the extreme secessionists
were well set forth respectively in the farewell message
of Governor Stewart and in the inaugural address of
Governor Jackson, soon after the beginning of the year
1861. The former document was probably the ablest
state paper written in the Borderland, containing, as it
did, a forceful presentation of the dominant opinion of
the people toward other sections. Governor Stewart
arraigned the abolitionists for having brought the country to the verge of ruin through their absorption in the
single question of securing freedom for the slaves. At
the same time, he considered the people of the Lower
South equally blameworthy, on account of their precipi-
tancy in leaving the Union without having first made an

effort to secure a reasonable redress of their grievances. In the existing crisis, which had resulted from the intolerance of one section and the selfishness of the other, he recognized that the people of Missouri were in a trying position. He recommended, for the immediate future, that they should devote their efforts to promoting harmony and understanding, remaining in the Union as long as it was possible to secure justice. A general secession of the slave States, he was confident, would mean violence and bloodshed; but Missouri should not be frightened from her position by the past unfriendly legislation of the North or dragooned into secession by the extreme South. If war should come, he recommended that the State should take the position of armed neutrality.[25]

Governor Jackson's inaugural address was in complete contrast to the statesmanlike message of the retiring governor. He appealed to sectional and partisan prejudices and based his arguments upon misrepresentations. The Republicans, he said, formed a sectional party whose only principle was hostility to slavery and whose only aim was to strike down its existence everywhere. Their success in the election constituted a threat at the great property interest of the South, amounting in all to $3,500,000,000. He therefore justified the secession of the Gulf States as a measure of self-protection, indeed, as the natural result of the national election. Apparently taking it for granted that the policy of Lincoln's admin-

[25] The message is reprinted in full in the *Journal* of the Senate, 1860-61, pp. 20 *et seq.* Governor Stewart was a native of New York. His long residence in Missouri had made him conversant with conditions in a border slave State. He was therefore in an excellent position to speak dispassionately on the question of secession. In the campaign of 1860, he had sided with the Northern Democrats. See further in John McElroy, *The Struggle for Missouri,* p. 24.

istration would be the coercion of the seceded States, he recommended that Missouri should take her stand with the Lower South, because "her honor, her interests and her sympathies alike point in the one direction." He made much of the importance of the Southern market for the products of Missouri, all of which, he said, must go down the river either to be consumed on the plantations or to find a foreign market by way of the Gulf of Mexico. In his endeavors to second the policy of some Southern leaders in bringing pressure to bear on the Borderland, he completely ignored the railroad connection with the East and the important commercial relations which the people of the State had with adjacent territory to the north, east and west. In closing his address he threw out the same concession to the Union men that the secessionists had done, stating that the division of the country was not likely to be permanent, owing to the probability that a suitable basis for reunion would soon be found.[26]

It was a typical secessionist message, and might as well have been written in South Carolina, so little did it contain of the prevailing compromise sentiment of the Borderland, and so little emphasis on the true interests of Missouri. Coming from Claiborne F. Jackson, it could hardly have been otherwise. He was a native of Kentucky and had come to Missouri in 1822, when he was fifteen years of age. After practicing law for a time, he engaged in politics, opposing the hard-money and anti-slavery policies of Benton and the people of St. Louis. While in the State Senate, he had proposed the resolution instructing the United States senators to support pro-slavery measures, from which Benton took his disastrous

[26] Senate *Journal*, 1860-61, pp. 46 *et seq.*

appeal to the people of the State.[27] During the troubles
in Kansas he and Atchison were the directing spirits of
the armed invasions from Missouri which attempted to
secure the admission of the territory as a slave State in
defiance of the spirit of the law. Nominated through the
machinations of the pro-Southern group in the Democratic party, he supported Douglas in order to be elected,
and then, as his first act, betrayed the party to which he
owed his office.

Lieutenant-Governor Reynolds, South Carolinian by
birth, had much the same political history as Governor
Jackson.[28] Many of the members of the legislature were
ardent secessionists. Indeed it is hardly an exaggeration
to say that the party advocating immediate secession
was composed of a part of those who voted the Southern
Democratic ticket and of those who had been candidates
on the Northern ticket. There were, of course, a number of Constitutional Unionists and Douglas Democrats
who were secessionists; but the great majority were the
former political leaders among the Democrats. They
comprised a plurality in both houses of the legislature.
In the Senate there were fifteen Breckinridge Democrats,
ten Douglas Democrats, seven Constitutional Unionists
and one Republican. In the House there were forty-
seven Breckinridge Democrats, thirty-six Douglas Democrats, thirty-seven Constitutional Unionists and twelve
Republicans.[29] The organization of the Senate was
made as strongly secessionist as possible through the
committee appointments of the lieutenant-governor. His

[27] Charles M. Harvey, "Missouri from 1849 to 1861," in the *Missouri
Historical Review*, vol. ii, p. 23.
[28] Thomas L. Snead, *The Fight for Missouri from the Election of
Lincoln to the Death of Lyon*, pp. 30-32.
[29] Eugene M. Violette, *History of Missouri*, p. 324.

opening address was a defiance of the national government and an appeal to prejudice against the North.[30]

The legislature had not been in session long before it was apparent that the majority were in favor of carrying out the governor's policies. A bill providing for the calling of a convention was reported from committee within the first few days. Another bill to reorganize the militia of the State was presented in the Senate on January 5th. It was designed to place the military forces entirely under the control of the secessionists, since it would curb the free expression of opinion concerning the policies of the state administration and relieve all members of the force from their superior allegiance to the United States.[31] A third proposed law would have taken the control of the police of St. Louis out of the hands of the Republican mayor and have vested it in a board appointed by the governor.

The secessionist policies of the governor and the legislature were watched by people in all parts of the State with varied feelings. The pro-Southern party, who had always been an outspoken element, hailed the secession of the State as practically an accomplished fact. At isolated places in the rural districts they formed bands of self-constituted defenders of Missouri, and began to punish the expression of sentiments opposed to secessionism. It was reported that several Union men had been obliged to take refuge in Iowa or Kansas.[32] On the other hand, the partisans of the Union were similarly active in other sections. There was a great deal of excitement through-

[30] John McElroy, *The Struggle for Missouri*, p. 32.
[31] James Peckham, *General Nathaniel Lyon and Missouri in 1861*, pp. 24-25.
[32] Peckham, *op. cit.*, p. 29.

out the State, with no very definite means of determining the true state of opinion. In St. Louis the secessionists talked of organizing a military force to be ready when Missouri should pass an ordinance of secession. A much more numerous and influential group, comprising the great majority of the native population of the city, were conservative supporters of the Union, who favored the settlement of the differences between the sections by compromise, and deprecated the haste both of the state administration and of the unofficial partisans of the two groups. On January 8th a meeting of the Douglas Democrats was held in Washington Hall, at which resolutions opposing coercion and endorsing proposed compromises were adopted, and a beginning was made toward the organization of a moderate Union party through the appointment of a committee of twenty to act with a similar committee to be chosen by the Constitutional Union party. The action of the meeting was of tremendous importance, since it provided a means for the organization of the better class of citizens on the side of the Union. At this point occurred an instance of the stubborn intolerance that was all too characteristic of the period. The Republicans, who were the most active opponents of secessionism, were unwilling to coöperate with the newly formed committee. Believing that the struggle would be settled by force rather than by winning the opinions of the people, they took measures to forestall the secessionists by making secret preparations to seize the control of the city. The "Wide-Awakes," a semi-military association which had paraded in the interest of Lincoln's candidacy, were encouraged to retain their organization, and the German *Turnvereins,* which had been drilling secretly since the election, added bayonet practice to their other exercises.[33]

The control of St. Louis was extremely important from the military standpoint because of the location there of one of the subtreasuries and of the arsenal. The latter contained sixty thousand muskets, a million and a half ball cartridges, ninety thousand pounds of powder, several field pieces and siege guns, and machinery for the manufacture of arms. None of the other slave States had secured so rich a prize when they seized the property of the national government within their borders. Its capture would not be a difficult matter in case of an attack in force, because of its location on low ground near the Mississippi River. Besides, it was not then garrisoned, there being only a few staff officers, orderlies and unarmed workmen about the enclosure.[34] At the proper time Governor Jackson and the secessionists hoped to seize it and equip the whole army of Missouri from its stores. The Republicans were equally determined to prevent its falling into their hands. Considering its great importance, it was inevitable that it would become the principal object of the struggle between the two extreme factions.

More active measures for the possession of St. Louis than had yet taken place were precipitated by Isaac H. Sturgeon, the assistant treasurer of the United States in charge of the subtreasury. Fearing that the state authorities would seize the funds in his possession, amounting to $400,000, he telegraphed the President on January 5th, asking that troops be sent to the city. President Buchanan advised with General Scott, who

[33] Robert J. Rombauer, *The Union Cause in St. Louis, 1861*, p. 129.
[34] Peckham, *op. cit.*, pp. 42-43.

ordered a lieutenant and forty men from Newport Barracks to proceed to St. Louis and guard the customs house and the subtreasury. Their arrival on January 11th provoked tremendous popular opposition, for it was looked upon as the beginning of a policy of coercion, which all groups except the Republicans strongly deprecated. The secessionists were furious. A mob quickly formed in the vicinity of the government building, which the mayor found it impossible to disperse with the ordinary means at his disposal. He therefore appealed to the council to devise means to restore the authority of the city government, probably with the expectation of securing their consent to call upon the Wide-Awakes for help. There might have been bloodshed within a short time if General Harney, the commander of the Department of the West, had not interfered by ordering the troops to the arsenal.[35] The mob thereupon dispersed. But the incident was not yet closed. It led to more determined measures by the groups within the city and by the state authorities.

The secessionists were the first to act. Fearing that the city authorities in some future emergency would summon the German military organizations to their assistance, they immediately completed the organization of "Minute Men" who were to be ready at a minute's notice to combat force with force. All told, they numbered about four hundred young men, most of whom had paraded with the Douglas Democrats in the campaign of 1860. They began drilling openly, and made no secret of their intention to capture the arsenal when they considered the time favorable. Their movement was delayed chiefly because the leaders of the pro-Southern

[35] Snead, *op. cit.*, pp. 102-103.

party insisted that the State should secede before any revolutionary action was taken by an armed force. Difficulty in procuring arms further handicapped them, making it impossible for the organization to accomplish anything for the time being.[36]

The action forced the unconditional Union men to a realization of their danger. On the day of the arrival of the Federal detachment, about twelve hundred of them met in Washington Hall to devise more active measures to counteract those of the secessionists. For the first time they abandoned the test of allegiance to the Republican party, and entered into coöperation with Union men of all parties, refusing only to accept proposals for compromise. They disbanded the Wide-Awakes and organized in their place a Central Union Club, with branches in all parts of the city and county of St. Louis, to which any thoroughgoing Union man might belong.[37] A small group of leaders, with Francis P. Blair, Jr., as their guiding spirit, met secretly to take sterner measures. Blair declared his belief that the attitude of the secessionists meant fierce and relentless war, which could be counteracted only by the most thorough preparations on the part of the Union men. Following his advice, the leaders put into effect a measure which indicated that their disbanding of the Wide-Awakes was only a ruse. They formed a real military organization of a secret character which was soon able to dominate the situation in the city. There was no difficulty in securing volunteers—the Germans offered their services in large numbers—but the problem of arming them exercised the ingenuity of the leaders to the fullest extent. A private

[36] General Basil W. Duke, *Reminiscences*, pp. 37-38.
[37] See page 31 of Harvey's article, cited *supra*.

subscription in St. Louis was sufficient to purchase seventy muskets. An appeal to Governor Yates resulted in obtaining two hundred more from the stores of the militia of Illinois.[38] In New York and Boston the citizens contributed several thousand dollars which was used for the purchase of additional arms and equipment. The whole body was placed under the direction of a Committee of Safety, composed of Blair, Oliver D. Filley, James O. Broadhead, Samuel Glover, John How, and Julius J. Witzig,[39] who assumed the task of guarding the cause of the Union from all the elements that menaced it.

Meanwhile the conditional Union men had found an opportunity to express their sentiments. Through inadvertence, the newspapers, in advertising a Republican meeting for January 12th, stated that it would endorse the Crittenden compromise. The leaders who had called the meeting, not wishing their party to be committed to any but a thoroughgoing stand for the Union, took especial pains to advise their followers not to attend it. But other citizens did to the number of fifteen thousand.[40] Under the leadership of Hamilton R. Gamble and Lewis V. Bogy, they passed resolutions endorsing the Crittenden compromise and pledging their loyalty to the United States. In refusing to coöperate with them, Blair and the Committee of Safety cut themselves off from the moral support of the great body of native citizens of St. Louis, thereby creating in the public mind a serious distrust of their own motives.

At the state capital, news of the arrival of Federal troops in St. Louis resulted in a tremendous outbreak of

[38] Peckham, pp. 36-37.
[39] See page 31 of Harvey's article, cited *supra*.
[40] Peckham, p. 52.

feeling. A resolution was immediately presented in the Senate that the sending of troops was "insulting to the dignity and patriotism of the State, and calculated to arouse suspicion and distrust on the part of the people toward the Federal Government." [41] Without delay, the bill to take the police of St. Louis out of the mayor's control and place them under a commission appointed by the governor was taken up and passed. A special sub-committee on St. Louis affairs was appointed for the purpose, it was said, of "purging St. Louis of Black Republicanism." On January 21st the bill providing for a state convention and calling a special election for delegates became a law. [42] On January 29th resolutions were passed declaring that when the national government should undertake to coerce the South, Missouri would aid in resisting the invaders. Only two members of the lower house besides the Republicans voted in the negative. [43] In successfully urging these measures the secessionists took full advantage of the temporary condition of excitement throughout the State. They were enabled to take the first step toward secession through a mere suggestion of coercion.

The calling of the convention led to a spirited campaign. Men of all parties seem to have believed that a secessionist majority would be elected. Even in St. Louis the prospects of victory for the Union party seemed dark, though the Republicans had had a majority in the city for some time. The more extreme leaders advised a straight party ticket; but Blair, realizing that the prejudice against Republicans and Germans would

[41] Senate *Journal*, 1860-61, p. 71.
[42] Laws of Missouri, 1860-61, pp. 20-21.
[43] Snead, *op. cit.*, p. 51.

result in the nomination of another unionist ticket and
thus make the triumph of the secessionists probable,
agreed to coöperate with the conservatives and to advise
his followers to support their ticket."

Governor Jackson was so confident that a secessionist
majority would be elected that he made arrangements in
advance to take possession of the arsenal. On January
24th he sent General D. M. Frost, the commander of the
state militia, to interview Major Bell, the senior officer
in the arsenal. The result was favorable for the secessionists. Major Bell, carrying the doctrine of state sovereignty to its logical conclusion, told Frost that he considered that Missouri had the right to claim the arsenal
because it was on her soil. He assured him that he
would not defend it when the state authorities, at the
proper time, determined to take possession of it. And
he promised not to allow any arms to be removed without notice to the officials of the State." His proffered
aid was of not the slightest value to the secessionists,
since Blair, already suspicious of his loyalty to the Union,
had procured, through his personal influence with the
War Department, an order transferring him to New
York."

Fearing that the secessionists would attack the arsenal
to obtain arms for their followers and carry the election
by force, the Union men employed detectives and maintained a strict guard in the vicinity of the enclosure.
More than once, their volunteers are said to have assembled to assist the garrison. The War Department, recognizing that forty men would be an insufficient force

" Peckham, p. 84; Snead, pp. 57-58.
" Frost to Jackson, Jan. 24, 1861. Senate *Journal*, extra session,
October, 1861, p. 30.
" Peckham, p. 46.

against a sudden onslaught by the Minute Men, greatly strengthened the garrison. The number of recruits in Jefferson Barracks was also increased. Eighty regulars, transferred from posts on the Kansas frontier, arrived in the city on February 6th. A little later Captain Totten came with a detachment which had been driven out of the arsenal at Little Rock when the state authorities of Arkansas captured it. By the middle of February the national government had nearly five hundred men stationed in St. Louis.

Commanding the detachment which arrived on February 6th was Captain Nathaniel Lyon, who subsequently played a dominant part in the councils of the Union men as well as in his own particular field of military operations. He was a native of Connecticut, a graduate of West Point, and a veteran of the Mexican War and of some Indian campaigns, in which his usefulness to the service was somewhat marred by insubordination. In 1856 he was ordered to Kansas to assist in the enforcement of the laws in that distracted territory. At first he is said to have meditated resigning his commission rather than be a party to the extension of slavery; but after some consideration he decided that he could be of use to the free-soil settlers there. During the presidential campaign of 1860 he wrote a series of articles for anonymous publication in the Manhattan, Kansas, *Express,* which, after the manner of most abolitionist writings, were dull, heavy and prosaic, treating mainly of the advantages of free labor and free soil and of the wickedness of the slaveholders.[47]   His attitude toward

[47] These articles have been collected and published under the title, *The Last Political Writings of General Nathaniel Lyon, U. S. A.*

slavery is said to have attracted the attention of Blair at the time, and his transfer to St. Louis is supposed to have been made at the latter's request.[48]

Lyon was at this time forty-three years old. A contemporary has described his personal appearance as being in decided contrast to his character as a determined leader. He was short and rather slender. His face was long and narrow, with a high forehead and mild, deepset blue eyes. As he stood in his favorite attitude of picking or stroking his coarse sandy beard, one would have thought of him as anything but a soldier. Yet at the head of his troops, "his form straightened up two inches taller; his eye dilated and blazed with excitement, and his commands were given in trumpet tones that were heard and *obeyed,* through all the deafening din of battle." [49] His character may perhaps best be described as that of a militant Puritan born two centuries after his time. His New England upbringing, his habit of withdrawing to the company of his own thoughts, and his experiences in Kansas had produced a man whose counterpart can be found only in one of Cromwell's Ironsides. He lacked respect for authority. He was impatient of restraint of any kind. He was absolutely sure of the righteousness of his own motives. And he was supremely confident that he was an instrument in Divine hands for the eradication of evil. The only other leader of the Civil War who can be compared to him was "Stonewall" Jackson; but Jackson lacked the qualities inspired by a long conflict with an abhorred principle which made Lyon's fanaticism so terrible. On January 6th he wrote:

[48] Rombauer, *op. cit.*, p. 150.
[49] *Last Political Writings,* p. 234.

"It is no longer useful to appeal to reason but to the sword, and trifle no longer in senseless wrangling. I shall not hesitate to rejoice at the triumph of my principles, though this triumph may involve an issue in which I certainly expect to expose and very likely lose my life. I would a thousand times rather incur this, than recall the result of our presidential election." [50]

One of Lyon's first acts after arriving in St. Louis was to call upon Blair to learn the condition of affairs. An intimacy at once grew up between the political leader and the militant abolitionist, which resulted in their coöperating closely throughout the crisis. Lyon visited the secret drilling grounds of the German volunteers, and often acted as drillmaster. He advised Blair as to the measures necessary for the defense of the arsenal, and Blair used his influence with the authorities at Washington to have them put into effect. Less than three weeks after Lyon arrived, he criticized his superior. Major Hagner, characterizing his failure to utilize the defense afforded by the stone wall of the arsenal as "either imbecility or d—d villainy." [51] Hagner's assignment appeared to him to be due to General Scott's "usual sordid spirit of partisanship, and favoritism to pets." He urged that Blair secure an order appointing him to the command of the arsenal, promising that he would arm a regiment of Germans—an act that would have been as illegal as the intentions of the secessionists. Before the plan could be carried out General Harney, who kept in close touch with conditions in St. Louis, again interfered, declaring that there was no danger of an attack. He properly

[50] Ashbel Woodward, *Life of General Nathaniel Lyon*, p. 236.
[51] Peckham, pp. 66-67.

refused to take any measures for defense which, on the eve of the election, might have inflamed the popular mind.[52]

The use of "coercion" by the national government in concentrating troops at the arsenal failed wholly to arouse opposition among the people, as it might easily have done if the thoroughgoing plans formulated by Lyon and Blair had just then been carried into execution. Contrary to the expectations of both the extreme factions, the election resulted in a unionist victory so overwhelming that even the secessionist legislature was induced to drop all measures for organizing the militia and arming the State. Every delegate elected to the convention had previously expressed himself as in favor of the preservation of the Union.[53] The popular majority against secession exceeded eighty thousand. Several of the largest slaveholding counties in the State gave the unionist candidates more than twice as many votes as their opponents. Though some of the members-elect were not, perhaps, very strongly Union men, being opposed to coercion, the referendum to the people was a staggering blow to the secessionist movement which was all the more effective in that it followed the unfavorable votes in Virginia and Tennessee.

Greatly surprised though the Union men were at the result, they were not content to rest, but sought to protect the convention from the sinister influences of the state capital. Jefferson City was supposed to be seething with secessionist sentiment. It was said that nothing

[52] Harney to Thomas, Feb. 19th. *Official Records,* Series I, vol. i, p. 654.

[53] Eugene M. Violette, *History of Missouri,* p. 329.

but the *"Marsellaise"* and "Dixie" were to be heard on the streets.[54] The governor, far from accepting the verdict of the people, had become only the more radical in his advocacy of secession. On March 1st he appeared with the commissioner from Georgia when the latter was serenaded, and declared that the honor of Missouri compelled her to stand by the South. On account of these things, the unconditional Union men were convinced that the state capital was not a suitable place to hold the sessions of a Union convention, especially since the complete loyalty of some of the members was doubtful. They therefore obtained from the citizens of St. Louis an invitation for the convention to hold its sessions in their city, holding out as an inducement the free use of a large hall, which was unobtainable at Jefferson City, and the payment of the railroad fares of the members. The invitation was gladly accepted, partly because the state capital could not furnish sufficient accommodations for both the legislature and the convention, partly because the strongly unionist members of the convention wished to remove their weaker brethren from temptation.[55] The date set for the first meeting was March 4th. Since the work of the convention was influenced by the policy of President Lincoln, further discussion of the subject is reserved for the following chapter.

In the other slave States which were closely connected with the Borderland, the course of events resembled that in the three States already studied. Governor Hicks of Maryland flatly refused, on December 28th, to call the legislature into special session, on the ground that it

[54] Galusha Anderson, *The Story of a Border City During the Civil War*, pp. 43-44.
[55] Anderson, p. 44.

was unnecessary. His action was warmly endorsed by the people of the State.[56] Thus the Union men in Maryland were in a much better position at the beginning of 1861 than in any other slave State. In Tennessee, Governor Harris called an extra session of the legislature in December, which in due time provided for the election of delegates to a convention. The people voted overwhelmingly against secession, the unionist majority being nearly 65,000. East Tennessee was almost solidly for the Union, and the remainder of the State returned a majority of nearly 39,000.[57] In Arkansas, as in nearly all the other Southern States, the governor and the legislature were avowed secessionists. Shortly after the beginning of the year they made provision for a constitutional convention. Pending the result of the election, a mob in Little Rock attacked the arsenal, whereupon the governor demanded and received its surrender to the state militia. The Federal garrison was withdrawn from the city, and orders were issued also for the evacuation of Fort Smith. But the citizens of northwestern Arkansas, who were almost unanimously opposed to secession, requested the continued protection of the national government. The orders were then countermanded, leaving a United States force in a position to command southwestern Missouri and to threaten the secessionists at Little Rock.[58]

The account of the early secessionist movement on the border would be incomplete without some consideration of the political developments in the northern part of the Ohio Valley. In a sense, the people of that section held the balance of power between the slave States and the

[56] Rhodes, vol. iii, p. 301.
[57] Gus W. Dyer, *School History of Tennessee*, pp. 106-107.
[58] *O. R.*, Series I, vol. i, pp. 655-656.

North of the abolitionists. If they, through their social
and commercial relations with the South, should take a
friendly, or even a neutral stand on the question of secession, there could be little doubt that the success of the
movement was assured. The people of the North would
be compelled helplessly to accept the division of the
Union as an accomplished fact. If, on the other hand,
the Ohio Valley opposed secession, the balance of power
would be shifted to the North, and the secessionist movement would sooner or later fail.

As we have seen, the first policy proposed by the
extreme secessionists was that of bringing economic pressure to bear. To the proposal to close the Mississippi
River, the people of the whole Northwest united in angry
protest. Nothing that was done in the South before the
firing on Fort Sumter caused so much resentment to be
stirred up. Though the secessionists did not press the
matter further at that time, there remained the danger
that in the future ruinous restrictions might be placed
on the trade of the upper valley. The dictates of self-
interest, therefore,—not to mention sentimental attachments—made the people look to the restoration of the
Union as the most important political end that could be
attained. For its accomplishment, they continued to
urge conciliation and compromises. When the secessionist movement threatened to engulf the border slave
States, they redoubled their efforts, lending their support
to the Union men of Kentucky and Missouri, and working shoulder to shoulder with them to prevent a permanent disruption of the nation. In the first three months
of the year, the Union party, as distinguished from the
Republican party, included in its membership nearly all
the people of the Borderland. No great difference can

be discerned between the national policies advocated by it in Ohio, Indiana and Illinois and those sponsored by the people of the neighboring slave States.

The Republicans were by this time in favor of preserving the Union, though they differed from the conservatives concerning the methods to be used. Most leaders of the party looked upon the secessionist movement as a means of depriving them of the fruits of their victory in the election of 1860. They therefore naturally refused to yield an inch of ground, and proposed to use Jacksonian methods. Governor Yates of Illinois constantly urged Lincoln to intervene by announcing a strong position in opposition to secession. Governor Morton of Indiana declared that if the Union was worth a bloody struggle to establish, it was worth an equally bloody struggle to maintain. He declared that there were now but two groups, "the party of the Union and the base faction of its foes." [59] The legislature of Ohio, at its session in January, passed resolutions declaring the secessionist movement revolutionary, and pledging the support of the State to the national government in maintaining the authority of the Constitution and laws of the United States.[60] These strong expressions of opinion, though representing fairly well the attitude of the extreme Republicans, hardly expressed the dominant popular feeling. Most of the people favored measures that were calculated to reëstablish the Union. Even among those who had voted for Lincoln a reaction had set in. There is evidence to show that south of the National Road many Republicans gravitated toward the support of compromises. The declarations of leaders and

[59] William D. Foulke, *The Life of Oliver P. Morton*, vol. i, p. 104.
[60] Senate *Journal*, 1861, p. 19.

the resolutions of conventions of the Democratic party can therefore be taken to represent fairly well the sentiments of the section.

In Ohio the state convention passed resolutions approving the Crittenden compromise. The presiding officer declared that if the policies of the Republicans should bring on war, they should be allowed to fight their own battles. And David Tod, later the Union war governor, went to an even greater length when he stated that if the Republicans should attempt to coerce the South they would find the two hundred thousand Democrats of the State in front of them.[61] In Indiana the Democratic state convention, which met on January 8th, pledged the party to devote its efforts toward preserving the Union, or reconstructing it if it should be dissolved. It was resolved that, in the event of a civil war, Indiana should act with other conservative States as a mediator between the contending sections; and if all attempts at settlement proved futile, that the legislature should then summon a convention "to declare authoritatively the position of Indiana at the present crisis." The retiring governor, Hammond, in his final message to the legislature, asserted that the cause of the difficulties that existed was the "fanatical agitation on the question of slavery," promoted by a "dangerous class of political teachers who belonged to the ministry." He appealed to the people to stop the discussion of moral issues and regard slavery "only as a political question." [62] In the legislature several proposals were made to secure a settlement of the controversy by some sort of compromise; but that body, being under the control of Republicans

[61] George H. Porter, *Ohio Politics in the Civil War Period,* p. 55.
[62] Foulke, *op. cit.,* vol. i, pp. 99-100.

led by a determined chief executive, failed to make any great concession to the South. Public opinion, as expressed in the resolutions of mass meetings held in various parts of the State during the first two months of the year, seemed to favor almost any sort of compromise that would leave the Union intact. An extreme position was assumed by citizens of Cannelton, Perry County, who declared that if the division of the Union between free and slave States should prove permanent, they would never consent that the Ohio River should be the boundary: it must be a line drawn north of the town.

In Illinois opposition to coercion and sympathy for the secessionist movement were even more strongly expressed. The Democratic state convention, in resolutions passed January 16th, absolved the Southern States from blame, and placed the responsibility for the disruption of the Union upon the anti-slavery agitation and the election of a sectional President. As a means of settlement it was proposed that a convention of all the States should be called, as provided in the Constitution of the United States, for the purpose of proposing amendments. Members of Congress from the State were asked to make concessions and to accept any propositions that would restore harmony.[63] During the session of the legislature, the Democratic members, by maintaining a solid front against the rather timid Republican majority, were able to secure the passage of measures looking toward conciliation, and to prevent the enactment of laws desired by Governor Yates for the maintenance of the authority of the United States. One of the first acts was to ask the Congress to call a convention of the States. Another

[63] Alexander Davidson and Bernard Stuvé, *A Complete History of Illinois from 1673 to 1884*, p. 867.

act provided for the calling of a constitutional convention. No attention was paid to a recommendation of the governor for the reorganization of the militia, because it was felt that such an action would indicate to the South that the State was in favor of coercive measures to preserve the Union.[64]

Various expressions of opinion among the people showed, not merely opposition to coercion, but a great deal of sympathy with the secessionists. The people of southern Illinois regarded themselves as practically a part of the South, on account of their kinship with its people, their dependence on the river trade, and their close relations with Kentucky and Missouri. As the secessionist movement spread northward, it found a ready response among them. The sentiment in favor of secessionism was so strong that Republican state officials advised against holding sessions of the district court at Cairo because they thought it would be impossible to secure the conviction of the most outspoken opponent of the government of the United States. In all of Illinois south of Springfield there was scarcely a prominent leader who from the beginning took an unequivocal stand for the Union. The attitude of John A. Logan, who represented the southern district of the State in the Congress, was regarded by his constituents as being strongly sympathetic toward the South. They circulated widely a speech of his in which he is said to have compared the secessionists to the patriots of the American Revolution. Ex-Governor John Reynolds did not hesitate to declare his pro-Southern sympathies. It was generally understood that W. H. Green, A. J. Kuykendall and other leading Democrats were advocating that southern Illi-

[64] Cole, *op cit.*, p. 273.

nois secede from the remainder of the State and join the Confederacy. Secret meetings with this object in view were held at various points.[65] Fortunately the action of Kentucky and Missouri prevented, for the time being, any open attempt to take drastic measures. But the situation pointed to conciliation and compromise as the only safe policy for the incoming national administration to pursue.

Taken as a whole, the Borderland stood, on March 4th, in an attitude of hopeful expectancy that measures would yet be devised to preserve the Union. Though it can scarcely be said that there was much confidence in the new administration, yet the circumstances were such as to give it full opportunity to put into force its policies. In Kentucky the legislature had refused to call a convention. In Virginia there was a convention in session in which the Union men outnumbered the secessionists by nearly four to one. In Missouri there were no avowed advocates of secession in a convention which was soon to begin its sessions. And in all the States north and south of the Ohio River the people were devoted to a policy of conciliation. It was hoped that the seceded States would return to the Union if the Republican party refrained from interfering with their domestic affairs and gave guarantees for the future. On the other hand, there was only slight sentiment in favor of a policy of using force as a means of preserving the Union. At the first sign of coercion it seemed evident that all the border slave States, with the possible exception of Delaware, would leave the Union. There was danger also that southern Illinois would attempt to join them. In both Ohio and Indiana it was doubtful whether the people would sup-

[65] Cole, pp. 260-261.

port the national government in making war on the seceded States. The Republican administration seemed therefore to have only the choice of continuing the policy of Buchanan or of submitting to a permanent division of the Union.

CHAPTER V

LINCOLN AND THE BORDER STATES

It was fortunate for the United States in the critical year 1861 that Abraham Lincoln understood perfectly the people of the Borderland. Lincoln was superlatively great as a statesman, standing higher than any of his contemporaries and ranking with the great popular leaders of all time. Better than most men, he possessed the power to frame wise policies of government; and he had the ability, infinitely more uncommon, of compelling public opinion to support his policies. He did this, not by establishing his light on a mountain top and calling the masses to come to him, but by estimating almost intuitively their position and then marching three feet in advance of the throng, leading them along the course which he had planned. His long residence in southern Indiana and Illinois and his wide acquaintance in Kentucky and Missouri gave him a knowledge of the people of the Borderland which enabled him to frame surely the policies upon which the fate of the country depended; for without their support the Union could not have been preserved. That he made mistakes in carrying out some of the details of his policies may be granted; but his failures were due, not to defects in the policies themselves, but to his reliance upon the advice of leaders who were not as far-sighted as himself.

Little mention has been made of Lincoln thus far

because he was not the leader of the Republican party, and it was not expected that he would formulate the policies of the administration. That task was regarded as too great for an inexperienced prairie politician. Instead, the position of leadership was, by common consent of the people, assigned to Seward, who had been schooled through years of training in state and national affairs. Shortly after the election the report gained circulation that he would be offered the post of Secretary of State in the new administration—a position which offered tremendous possibilities of wielding power. During the session of Congress from December, 1860, to March, 1861, he stood head and shoulders above every other man in the Republican party. Loyal members of Buchanan's cabinet communicated to him information concerning the activities of other members whom they suspected of disloyalty. General Scott conferred with him on matters relating to the disposition of the military forces. Even a communication from Lincoln to a special committee of the Senate was referred to him before action was taken upon it. In all these matters, Seward accepted his responsibilities as if the future of the country depended upon him alone. He took the office of Secretary of State in Lincoln's cabinet, as he said, to "try to save freedom and my country." Afterward he declared that he had "assumed a sort of dictatorship for defense." [1]

With all his political wisdom and experience, Seward failed to bring forward any constructive program for the Republican party to follow in settling the distracted affairs of the country. All through the winter he steadfastly refused to agree to compromises which might

[1] Alonzo Rothschild, *Lincoln, Master of Men*, pp. 128-134.

reconcile the people of the South, even when other leaders
of the party seemed willing to support them. He devoted
his efforts to the single purpose of gaining time by the
exercise of "forbearance, conciliation and magnanimity,"
hoping that the people of the South would repent of the
extreme step they had just taken and return voluntarily
to the Union when they had had an opportunity for
deliberation. Such a policy differed little, if at all, from
the helpless waiting of Buchanan. It was not until Lincoln had definitely embarked upon a policy for the
preservation of the public property of the United States
in the seceded States that Seward had anything of a
constructive nature to offer. Then the proposal of a war
with France and Spain, which he put forth in the hope
that the common danger to all of North America would
cause the South to return to the Union,[2] was so chimeri-
cal that no attention could have been given to it.

The only other positive policy that was proposed by
Republican leaders in the winter of 1860-61 was that of
using force to compel the seceded States to return to the
Union. It had the support of influential newspapers and
public men, and was strongly championed by the Blairs,
who continued to have great influence in the councils
of the party. The arguments in its favor were drawn
from the analogy of Jackson's experience in crushing the
nullification movement and from the fact that some of
the Southern leaders had declared that the people of the
North, being a nation of money-changers, would not fight
for the preservation of the Union. It was believed that
if the national government took a strong stand against
secession, the people of the South would abandon their

[2] "Some Thoughts for the President's Consideration," printed in
Nicolay and Hay, *Abraham Lincoln, A History*, vol. iii, pp. 445-447.

position and accept such concessions as a united North
felt free to offer. In the facts of the situation, however,
there was no basis for the expectation that the use of
force would prove successful. The almost unanimous
protests of the border States should have caused its
advocates to abandon it. Lincoln understood the temper of the people sufficiently to know that it would only
bind the secessionists more firmly to their purpose and
add populous States to the number that had already
seceded. He therefore rejected this proposal, together
with the opportunist plan of Seward and the policy of
settlement by compromise which was proposed by the
Northern Democrats and other conservatives.

Lincoln's own policy apparently developed slowly during the winter. Shortly after the election he determined
to give the former Democratic element of the Republican
party a strong representation in his cabinet, with a view
to uniting the North. Two members, Bates and Montgomery Blair, represented the border slave States. He
desired to have John A. Gilmer of North Carolina in the
cabinet in order that he might obtain the support of the
people farther south.[3] From the beginning, therefore,
he recognized that the prime requisite for the restoration
of the Union was the formation of an administration in
which the people of the North and of the border slave
States could have confidence.

On the question of recognizing the legality of secession, he took a decided stand from the beginning. On
December 13th he wrote: "The very existence of a general and national government implies the legal power,
right, and duty of maintaing its own integrity."[4] He

[3] Nicolay and Hay, vol. iii, p. 362.
[4] *Idem,* p. 248.

rejected proposals for compromise, not so much because of opposition to any particular plan, as from the belief that no compromise would be a final settlement of the question. He had no objection to the passing of a new fugitive slave law or to the admission of New Mexico. He might even have given his assent to an extension of the line of the Missouri Compromise. But he believed that such concessions would only lead the South to renew the agitation for the acquisition of Cuba and to begin "filibustering for all south of us." [5] That he understood clearly the attitude of the Southern people toward the Union is indicated in a confidential letter to John T. Hale, in which he wrote: "They can never have a more shallow pretext for breaking up the government, or extorting a compromise, than now." [6] He was extremely careful to make no statement in advance of his assuming the reins of the government that could be construed by the secessionists to their advantage. To all inquiries concerning the policy he intended to pursue, he directed attention to the platform upon which he had been elected and to the speeches he had previously made.

There is nothing in the published writings of Lincoln which manifests the slightest wavering on the question of maintaining the Union. Everything he wrote indicates that he had a positive policy, even to the extent of going to war as a last resort. In December, when it was stated in press dispatches that the forts in the harbor of Charleston would be surrendered to the state authorities, he asked General Scott to be prepared at the time of the

[5] Lincoln to Thurlow Weed, Dec. 17, 1860, quoted by Nicolay and Hay, vol. iii, p. 253.

[6] Jan. 11, 1861. Nicolay and Hay, vol. iii, p. 288.

inauguration either to hold or to retake them.[7] A little
later he wrote to Senator Trumbull that if the forts were
surrendered he would take counsel with his friends in
Washington and, with their approval, announce publicly
that they were to be retaken after the inauguration.[8] But
he desired peace above all other things, and was determined to adopt forcible measures only if the United
States should be attacked.

It must have been in connection with the incident
just discussed that Lincoln devised the policy of retain-
ing possession of the Southern forts as a way out of the
difficulties. Early in February his program was practically determined upon. He wrote his inaugural address
at Springfield almost exactly as it was afterward delivered. During his journey to Washington he took the
opportunity to prepare the country for the proposals
which he intended to announce. In his address to the
legislature at Indianapolis he expressed doubts concerning the Southern conception of the unqualified sovereignty of States, and defined the terms "invasion" and
"coercion." Admitting that marching an army into the
South would be both, he asked the question: "If the
United States should merely retake and hold its own
forts and other property, and collect the duties on foreign
importations, or even withhold the mails from places
where they were habitually violated, would any or all
these things be 'invasion' or 'coercion'?"[9] This speech
was roundly condemned by the Cincinnati *Enquirer*
because it was regarded as a blow to the patriotic party

[7] Lincoln to E. B. Washburne, Dec. 31, 1860, *Complete Works*, Gettysburg Edition, vol. vi, pp. 84-85.

[8] Dec. 24, 1860. Quoted by Horace White, *The Life of Lyman
Trumbull*, p. 112.

[9] *Complete Works*, vol. vi, pp. 112-114.

which had been endeavoring to save the Union.[10]   The later addresses delivered before he reached Washington were less definite and positive.

Lincoln's first inaugural address combined a masterly discussion of the constitutional principles involved in the secessionist movement with a clear statement of the policies of the government and an appeal for popular support in efforts to preserve the Union.   It deservedly ranks among the greatest American state papers.   Lincoln regarded the Union as resting upon far more than the basis of a mere contract.   But even if the Constitution were only a contract, he pointed out that it could be broken only by the consent of all the parties to it.   He disclaimed any intention to interfere with slavery in the States where it already existed.   He upheld the fugitive slave laws.   And he pointed out the fact that if the South had grievances, these grievances might be redressed by constitutional amendments or by laws.   As to the policy which he intended to pursue as the chief executive of the nation, he reminded his hearers that he was charged with the enforcement of the laws of the country.   But he promised that there would be no invasion, no using of force against or among the people anywhere beyond what might be necessary to hold, occupy and possess the property and places belonging to the government and to collect the duties and imposts.   Obnoxious strangers would not be forced among the people of the South, because he thought the attempt to do so would be irritating and nearly impracticable.   The mails would be furnished in all parts of the country unless repelled.   The people everywhere were "to have that sense of perfect security which is most favorable to calm thought and reflection."

[10] Feb. 13, 1861.

Disavowing any desire to begin a war upon the South, he declared: "In *your* hands, my dissatisfied countrymen, and not in *mine,* is the momentous issue of civil war. The government will not assail *you.* You can have no conflict without being yourselves the aggressors. . . . We are not enemies, but friends. We must not be enemies. Though passion may have strained, it must not break our bonds of affection. The mystic chords of memory, stretching from every battlefield, and patriot grave, to every living heart and hearthstone, all over this broad land, will yet swell the chorus of the Union, when again touched, as surely they will be, by the better angels of our nature." [11]

The address had a political purpose of the greatest significance. A Northern President, elected by a sectional vote, gave up his whole message, without flinching, to a discussion of the policies of the government toward a section that had left the Union. Lincoln could hardly have expected, by constitutional arguments and promises of non-interference, to convince the disunionist party of the error of their ways. For them the address was a denial of the rights they had asserted as an independent government. No such government could brook the possession of forts along its seacoast or the collection of customs at its ports by a foreign power. It was generally believed in the North that there was a large group favorable to the Union in all the seceded States except South Carolina; and it was to this group, in part, that Lincoln appealed. He doubtless wished also to crystallize public sentiment in favor of the Union at the North. But in the main his desire seems to have been to appeal to the judgments and the unionist sentiments of the peo-

[11] Nicolay and Hay, vol. iii, pp. 327-344.

ple of the border States. For that purpose a declaration of principles could hardly have been more skillfully phrased. He definitely proved that the reasons which the secessionists had given for disrupting the Union were without substantial basis in fact. And he placed upon them the burden of taking further extreme measures.

The effects of the address were immediately evident. In the South it was received with indignation and defiance.[12] In the North the people were electrified. It was like Jackson's famous toast to the Union in solidifying public sentiment. In the Borderland it caused some misgivings. The people found little fault with the statement of constitutional principles which it contained, but they feared that the policy of the President would lead to war. The reaction against the Republicans which had begun soon after the election continued to gain in force. In April a Democrat was chosen mayor of Cincinnati by a plurality of four thousand on a platform promising support to the Crittenden compromise,[13] and the Republicans were defeated in the municipal elections of the four other large cities of the State of Ohio. In the municipal elections in St. Louis, How, Republican, was defeated by Taylor, Constitutional Unionist, by twenty-six hundred votes—the first time since 1857 that the Republicans had lost control of the city government.[14] It is doubtful, however, if the Republican reversals were wholly due to the inaugural address. In general, its effect seems to have been salutary.

The secessionists of St. Louis had planned a demonstration on March 4th with the view of influencing the

[12] William R. Garrett and R. A. Halley, *The Civil War from a Southern Standpoint*, p. 40.
[13] G. M. D. Bloss, *Life and Speeches of George H. Pendleton*, p. 27.
[14] Snead, *op. cit.*, p. 95.

convention, which began its adjourned session in the city
on that day, and of securing possession of the arsenal,
if possible. They laid their plans carefully so as to
create a difficult situation and then take advantage of
every false move of their opponents. A Southern flag
was raised above the courthouse in the hope of provoking attempts on the part of the Union men to tear it
down; and sixty Minute Men, armed to the teeth, were
stationed in the Berthold mansion nearby. If the Union
volunteers appeared in force to remove the flag, the Minute Men determined to fire, and thus bring on a street
conflict which the police would be powerless to stop.
It was expected that then Governor Jackson would call
out the militia to restore order. Once the state troops
were in possession of the city, the secessionist leaders
expected that the arsenal would be taken over by them.[16]
Thus the Union volunteers would be without support
from the United States troops, and the secessionists
would be in complete control of the situation. It was a
desperate scheme, with its immediate success dependent
upon drawing the Union men into the trap, and its final
success upon the President's declaring in favor of coercion.

When, in the early morning, the displaying of the
Southern flag was first noticed, an excited crowd of citizens quickly gathered. Having first removed the flag
from the courthouse, they proceeded to the Berthold
mansion where a similar flag was being displayed. Here
they engaged in a verbal conflict with the garrison,
until some secessionist sympathizers came up and began
a series of rough and tumble fights with the Union men
in the streets. Meanwhile, the German volunteers were

[16] General Basil W. Duke, *Reminiscences*, pp. 38-40.

called to arms so as to be ready in case of a secessionist attack on the arsenal, though their leaders had no intention of marching them to assault the headquarters of the pro-Southern party. The first part of the plan of the Minute Men was thus defeated, as it should have been, since the provocation they offered was insufficient to merit notice. The second part was defeated through the refusal of General Frost to order the militia under his command to seize the arsenal. He gave them no encouragement whatever, even refusing to attempt to disperse the crowd as long as it appeared that the police had the situation in hand.[16] Finally some members of the Committee of Safety appeared upon the scene and persuaded their partisans to go to their homes.[17] The rioting was not resumed.

At the state capital the secessionist members of the legislature interpreted the inaugural address as a threat of war against the South. On March 5th they made a tremendous effort to pass the bill for the reorganization of the militia. The Union members ranged themselves in vigorous opposition, arguing that no one proposed to attack Missouri. The moderate group who were in the majority objected to the bill because it would make necessary higher taxes when the wealthy classes were unable to pay them on account of the stoppage of trade. Furthermore, the provisions giving the governor almost unlimited power were considered dangerous.[18] The measure was therefore easily defeated. A little later the House refused to consider resolutions passed almost unanimously by the Senate instructing the senators and

[16] Duke, p. 40.
[17] Peckham, pp. 82-83.
[18] Snead, pp. 74-75.

requesting the representatives in the Congress to oppose
the passage of bills granting supplies to coerce the seceded
States.[19]

On March 4th the convention quietly resumed its sessions in St. Louis under the complete control of conditional Union men, with ex-Governor Sterling Price as the
presiding officer. Resolutions were presented reflecting
every shade of opinion. For the most part they opposed
the beginning of hostilities by either party. Several of
them clearly recognized the common interests of the border States. Mr. Calhoun proposed, on March 8th, that
if both the North and the South should refuse to make
concessions for the preservation of the Union, the States
bordering on the Ohio and Mississippi rivers should meet
in convention and determine upon concerted action. The
same day Mr. Leeper suggested the formation of a central republic of the border States, with the Constitution
of the United States as the supreme law and the Stars
and Stripes as the flag, which should "invite our wander-
ing sister States to resume their original positions in the
family of States." [20]

There was practically no sentiment in the convention
favorable to secession. Only one adverse vote was cast
on the passage of a resolution that no adequate cause
existed to impel Missouri to dissolve her connection with
the Federal Union. Among other resolutions passed were
the following: that grievances should be adjusted by a
fair and amicable settlement, and that the Union should
be restored; that a convention should be called to amend
the national Constitution; that the Crittenden compromise offered a satisfactory settlement of the difficulties

[19] W. F. Switzler's *Illustrated History of Missouri*, p. 311.
[20] *Journal* of the Convention, March, 1861, p. 32.

before the country; that there should be no employment
of force by the national government to coerce the seceded
States, or by these States to assail the national government; and that Federal troops should be withdrawn from
forts within the seceded States where there was danger
of a collision.[21] On the resolution presented by the Committee on Federal Relations that Missouri should secede
if the Union were permanently broken up, there was
much difference of opinion. The majority of the members preferred to await the course of events before taking
any action. On March 22nd the convention adjourned
without having considered the passing of an ordinance
of secession, for which purpose it had been called. It did
not even pass a resolution criticizing the conduct of the
Republican administration. The disappointment among
the secessionists was keen. Governor Jackson referred
to it as "Governor Price's submission convention," and
characterized its position as "miserable, base and cowardly."[22] But the great majority of the people regarded
its action as eminently satisfactory.

The strong love for the Union which had halted the
secessionist movement in the beginning was reinforced,
after a time, by considerations of reason and interest.
The people realized that the climate of Missouri was
better adapted to the white race than to the black. In
the decade from 1850 to 1860 the white population had
doubled in numbers, while the slaves had increased by
only twenty-five per cent. It was recognized that the
immigration of white men, on which the future of the
State seemed to depend, would be greatly diminished if

[21] Switzler, *op. cit.*, p. 327.
[22] Jackson to J. W. Tucker, April 28, 1861; printed in the *Collections*
of the Missouri Historical Society, April, 1903, p. 21.

Missouri joined the Confederacy. Furthermore, in such a case she could never have a transcontinental railroad, to which the business men looked as one of the most brilliant possibilities of future prosperity. In the event of war, also, the exposed position of Missouri would invite attack. The taxable property of the State, which, aside from slaves, amounted to $315,000,000, would all be exposed to destruction in a war waged to protect slave property valued at only $45,000,000. Even if war did not follow the secession of the State, the value of the slave property would be greatly diminished because of free territory on three sides of Missouri into which the slaves could easily escape.[23] This "bringing Canada to the borders of the State" did not appeal to the hard-headed slaveowners of Missouri, who formed a considerable portion of the Union party. The Southern historian of the war in the State laments that "of all wealth, property in slaves was the most timid and the most cowardly." The rich landowners, he said, were "fast learning the duty of submission" when the convention met.[24] Though the statement goes too far in impugning the motives of the slaveholders, it is undoubtedly true that the ownership of slave property exerted a greater influence for the Union than for the Confederacy.

The decisive action of the Missouri convention relieved the national administration of worries concerning the future course of the State. With good management, there should have been little difficulty in combating the militant pro-Southern policy of Governor Jackson and in holding the State in the Union. Blair and Lyon, however, were not satisfied that all danger was removed.

[23] Anderson *op. cit.*, pp. 58-59.
[24] Snead, p. 64.

They still feared that Governor Jackson, with the aid of the Minute Men, would attempt to gain possession of the arsenal. Blair easily procured for Lyon the command of all the troops there, and Lyon made every preparation to repel an attack. He had holes made in the walls through which to point cannon. He placed batteries in position to command the approaches. He established strict guards at all the gates. In order to bring musketry fire to bear upon an attacking party, he provided banquettes. Signals were arranged between him and the Union leaders in the city by which he could gain early information of activities among the secessionists. In addition, he promised the Committee of Safety that the men drilling under their orders should have arms if the necessity arose.[25] In the midst of his preparations he was ordered to report for temporary special duty at Fort Leavenworth; but Blair procured the revocation of the order. At the time of the firing on Fort Sumter the Union position was so strong and the forces were under such capable direction that the secessionists could hardly have captured the arsenal under any circumstances.

The response of Kentucky to Lincoln's announcement of his policy was similar to that of Missouri. The conservative citizens seem to have felt depressed, owing to their belief that it would now be more difficult to devise compromises. The pro-Southern party were jubilant because the inaugural address seemed to foreshadow a policy of interference in the internal affairs of the South which would bring on a conflict and precipitate Kentucky into secession. Early in March they began the circulation of petitions in the rural districts requesting the governor to call a convention without waiting for the action

[25] Peckham, pp. 74-75.

of the legislature; but this unconstitutional scheme proved so unpopular that it was soon abandoned. They then turned their attention to the organization of chapters of a Southern rights association in various localities. With a view to influencing the legislature, they called a convention of the association to meet in Frankfort on the opening day of the legislative session.[26]

All their artificially stimulated public opinion proved to be of no value to them. When the legislature met after its adjournment of six weeks, it was apparent that the opinions of the members were unchanged. Consequently no serious efforts were made toward secession. The only measure passed that could be interpreted as being in favor of the secessionists provided a small appropriation for the construction of an arsenal at Frankfort. On the other hand, the members showed a desire to remain in the Union by ratifying a proposed amendment to the Constitution prohibiting the United States from interfering with slavery in the States, and by calling a convention of the border slave States to meet in Frankfort in May.[27] The leaders of the Union party, fearing a clash between the United States and the South, wisely secured an early adjournment to prevent precipitate action. Another possible source of embarrassment to the national administration was thus removed.

In Virginia, the President's policy was variously received by the three parties into which the people were divided. Those who were unconditionally for the maintenance of the Union accepted his views as logical and necessary for the performance of his duties under the

[26] W. P. Shortridge, "Kentucky Neutrality in 1861," in the *Mississippi Valley Historical Review*, vol. ix, pp. 291-292.
[27] Collins, *op. cit.*, vol. i, p. 87.

Constitution. The secessionists were delighted because they thought this policy foreshadowed coercion, which would compel Virginia to leave the Union. On March 5th they made a strong effort to secure a declaration of independence and a close alliance with the seceded States. A proposed resolution recited that "Whereas, it is now plain that it is the purpose of the Chief Executive of the United States to plunge the country into civil war, . . . the legislature [should prepare to] resist and repel any attempt on the part of the Federal authorities to 'hold, occupy and possess the property and places' of the United States." [28] The third group, composed of conditional Union men, continued to counsel moderation in the hope of eventual adjustments. They were pleased with the pacific spirit of the address, though they found fault with some of the constitutional interpretations. [29]

The Committee on Federal Relations reported its recommendations about the middle of March. The minority report, signed by seven of the twenty-one members, advised the immediate adoption of an ordinance of secession. [30] The majority, declaring that the maintenance of peace was the foremost duty of the hour, proposed a rather involved amendment to the Constitution of the United States which would protect the interests of the slaveholders. The territories were to be divided on the line of the Missouri Compromise, with slavery forever prohibited north of the line. No more territory should be acquired except by a majority vote of the senators from each section. The Congress should never have the right to abolish slavery in the States, or in the

[28] *Journal*, p. 83.
[29] Munford *op. cit.*, p. 265.
[30] Munford, p. 271.

District of Columbia without the consent of Virginia
and Maryland. The slave trade should be forever prohibited within the District of Columbia. Finally, the
Congress should reimburse the owners when fugitive
slaves were rescued in the Northern States.[31] Thus far
Virginia would have been willing to go after the inauguration of Lincoln. On the other hand, the resolutions
demanded no guarantees from the seceded States. Even
if the national government had accepted the proposal,
the Union would still have been divided, with Virginia
on guard to prevent attempts by the government of the
United States to maintain its authority. For the committee had further declared that the use of force by either
side would be deplored by Virginia, and that, unless satisfactory assurances were forthcoming, the State would
feel compelled to resume the powers granted by her under
the Constitution.

The majority report appears to have received the
approval of the conditional Union men in the convention.
If they had been as well led as their fellow partisans in
Missouri and Kentucky, they would probably have
embodied it in resolutions and then adjourned. Apparently such an action was not strongly urged. The unconditional Union men from west of the Alleghanies were
intent upon securing reforms in the taxation of slave
property, and were unwilling that the convention should
cease its sessions until something had been accomplished.[32] The conditional Union men also opposed
adjournment, wishing to delay until the policy of the
new administration was more fully disclosed. The future
therefore depended upon events at Washington.

[31] See the appendix to the *Journal*.
[32] As late as April 5th. See *Journal*, p. 134.

In putting his policies into effect Lincoln was greatly handicapped from the beginning because of the attitude of the border slave States. On going into the War Department on March 5th, he was informed that Major Anderson's provisions in Fort Sumter would last but a few weeks longer, and that the relief of the garrison could be accomplished only by a force of twenty thousand men. The President, appealing to General Scott for professional advice, received the disconcerting reply that "evacuation seems almost inevitable." [33] The situation was extremely difficult, for Lincoln had counted on allowing as much time as was necessary for conditions in the border slave States to adjust themselves. He was anxious to maintain possession of Fort Sumter because it was located in South Carolina, the center of the movement for Southern independence. If he should weakly yield possession of the only foothold of the United States within its borders he would expose himself to the risk of losing the favorable opinion of the people of the North. Yet there was real danger that if he sent a relief expedition, the action might be interpreted by the border slave States as an attempt to coerce the South, and might precipitate them into secession. Lincoln realized that they were temporarily demoralized by a sympathy with the South which made them forget their allegiance to the Federal government. He therefore proposed to conciliate them for a short time longer, realizing that he was conceding more to them than they could reasonably expect. "But in administration," he said, "we must deal with men, facts, and circumstances, not as they ought to be, but as they are."

On March 15th, Lincoln requested the written opinions

[33] Rhodes, vol. iii, pp. 325-326.

of members of his cabinet on the question of sending a force to relieve Fort Sumter. With one exception, the cabinet were opposed to sending an expedition. Seward thought it would bring on war. He proposed that the policy of conciliation should be continued, in order to deny to the disunionists any new provocation and prove their apprehensions of coercion groundless and false. If any expedition were sent, he thought it should be only a naval force, sufficiently small so as not to antagonize the border slave States. It should be announced that its sole purpose was the collection of the revenues, a necessary and legitimate minor object within the province of the President, which would probably be accepted by Union men everywhere.[34] Bates declared that he would evacuate the fort rather than be a party to the beginning of a civil war. He was convinced, besides, that it was of little value, since the real struggle between the North and the South would be for the possession of the lower Mississippi.[35] Smith advised that no force be sent because "if a conflict should be provoked . . . a divided sentiment in the North would paralyze the arm of the government, while treason in the Southern States would be openly encouraged in the North."[36] Cameron and Welles were opposed to sending the expedition, and Chase's conditional reply amounted to the same thing. Only Montgomery Blair, true to his Jacksonian antecedents, advised positive action in order to show the people of the South that the national government had the requisite firmness to deal with the situation.[37]

Seward was so confident of his great influence in the

[34] Lincoln's *Complete Works,* vol. vi, pp. 196-200.
[35] *Idem,* p. 220.
[36] *Idem,* p. 213.
[37] *Idem,* p. 216.

administration that, on his own authority, he gave
assurances to Justices Nelson and Campbell, who were
acting as intermediaries for Confederate commissioners,
that the order for the evacuation of Fort Sumter would
be delivered within three days.[38] He had previously
informed one of the editors of the *National Intelligencer*
that such action was contemplated, with the result that
the report soon gained currency over the country. The
people of the North were dismayed. The South, jubilant
at the news, believed that it foreshadowed the recognition
of their independence. In Virginia the report brought
about a reaction in favor of the Union, and caused the
outside pressure upon the convention to be greatly
diminished. The unionist party felt confident of their
ability to prevent the passing of an ordinance of
secession.[39]

For a time after the middle of March Lincoln seemed
to hesitate. On March 28th, he again requested the
opinions of the cabinet. At this time only Seward and
Smith were opposed to sending relief. The President
thereupon directed the heads of the war and navy departments to prepare an expedition to move by sea by the 6th
of April. This force, however, was to be "used, or not,
according to circumstances." [40] A little later Fort
Pickens, off Pensacola, was ordered reinforced. The situation in Missouri and Kentucky had cleared by this
time, relieving the President of worries on their account.
But the Virginia convention remained an obstacle to the
accomplishment of any positive measure.

Before actually setting the expedition on foot Lincoln

[38] Rhodes, vol. iii, p. 331.
[39] *Idem,* pp. 344-345.
[40] *Complete Works,* vol. vi, p. 302.

determined to use his influence to have the convention adjourn. He wrote to George W. Summers, one of the Union leaders, asking him to come to Washington for a conference. What Lincoln had in mind was to offer to evacuate Fort Sumter on condition that the convention would adjourn without exacting any guarantees as to the use of force in the seceded States.[41] The invitation was not accepted, nor did Summers at once send a substitute. On April 6th, however, John B. Baldwin, a member of the convention, came to Washington and had an interview with the President. He was informed that he had come too late, since the expedition to provision Fort Sumter was already on its way. Lincoln nevertheless told him of the offer he had intended to make, and impressed upon him the necessity for an early adjournment. Baldwin, on returning to Richmond, apparently said nothing to anyone about the interview. If he had done so, the result might have been favorable, since as late as April 4th, the convention had rejected, by a vote of eighty-nine to forty-five, a resolution to submit an ordinance of secession to the people.[42]

In order that his intentions could not be misunderstood, Lincoln took pains to inform the country at large, and especially South Carolina, that an attempt would be made to supply the fort with provisions only. If the expedition were not resisted, Lincoln promised the governor of South Carolina that "no effort to throw in men, arms or ammunition will be made without further notice, or in case of an attack upon the fort." [43] As far as possible, he made it clear that if any conflict took

[41] Munford, p. 270.
[42] Rhodes, vol. iii, p. 345.
[43] *Official Records,* Series I, vol. i, p. 291.

place it would have to be commenced by the seceded States.

The expedition still failed to receive the approval of Seward, who was convinced that it would precipitate war. Consequently, he did everything in his power to prevent it. At the last minute he proposed the alternative of provoking a foreign war, and failing to win over the President with that fantastic notion, he detached the powerful ship *Powhatan* from the expedition, thus rendering the provisioning of the fort impossible if the South resisted.[44]

The notice of Lincoln's intention to provision Fort Sumter was of course transmitted to the Confederate government; and that government unwisely determined to reduce the fort before the garrison could be relieved. It was practically forced to do so by the war spirit of the South.[45] The secessionists in Virginia also advised positive measures in order to hasten the action of their convention. Roger A. Pryor, a member of Congress, went to Charleston, and on April 10th promised the people that if they would strike a blow Virginia would be in the Southern Confederacy within "less than an hour by Shrewsbury clock. The very moment," he declared, "that blood is shed, old Virginia will make common cause with her sisters of the South." [46] Though the decision to attack was made at Montgomery, the Virginian had a part as one of the four aides of General Beauregard who took the responsibility of ordering the bombardment.

The news of the firing on Fort Sumter was the signal for renewed activity on the part of the secessionists in

[44] White, *op. cit.*, p. 157.
[45] Rhodes, vol. iii, p. 348.
[46] McPherson, *op. cit.*, p. 112.

Virginia. They omitted nothing that could bring influence to bear on the convention to accomplish their purpose. The people of Richmond, stirred to the highest pitch of enthusiasm for the Confederacy, paraded gaily through the streets. The galleries of the convention were filled with secessionists who hissed and groaned at every expression of sentiment favorable to the Union. In the streets the unionist members of the convention were spit upon, and threats were made that they would be driven out at the point of the bayonet.[47] Governor Letcher, having received from the governor of South Carolina an account of the bombardment, immediately transmitted it to the convention. He took good care, however, not to send a Northern version of the affair.

The next step in the plans of the secessionist leaders was to have the convention go into secret session—a policy which the unconditional Union members had opposed from the beginning. The secessionists cleverly made use of an interview which a committee of the convention had had with the President on the day after the bombardment. What he had said to the committee only reaffirmed the declarations in his inaugural address and applied them to the present case. If Fort Sumter had fallen, he said, he felt at liberty to repossess it, and would in every case repel force by force.[48] There was therefore no necessity for receiving the report in secret session. But a sufficient number of unionist delegates were won over to secure the passage of the resolution. Once the convention went into secret session, it was found impossible to revert to the former system.

Even more important measures to promote secession

[47] G. D. Hall, *The Rending of Virginia*, p. 181.
[48] *Complete Works*, vol. vi, pp. 244-245.

were taken by Governor Letcher. In reply to the President's call for 75,000 militia to enforce the laws, he wrote on April 16th that no men would be furnished by Virginia. "You have chosen to inaugurate civil war," he said, "and having done so, we will meet it in a spirit as determined as the Administration has exhibited toward the South." [49] The next day he called out the militia, ostensibly to protect the State against an invasion, but really to use them in such a way as practically to force the convention to adopt an ordinance of secession. Orders were issued for the seizure of the arsenal at Harper's Ferry, the navy yard at Gosport, and Fortress Monroe; and the forces were put in motion for the accomplishment of these designs. The stage was finally set for action in the convention.

On the morning of April 17th, Henry A. Wise secured the floor, and, drawing a large horse pistol from his bosom and laying it on the desk before him, delivered a violent address denouncing the government of the United States. At the close he took a watch from his pocket and declared that events were then occurring which caused a hush to come over his soul. At such an hour, he said, Harper's Ferry and its armory were in possession of Virginia soldiers. At another period the Federal navy yard and property at Norfolk had been seized by the troops of the State. [50] A member who asked by what authority the troops had been ordered to move was silenced by the reminder that some of them were his own constituents. The staunchly Union men, disconcerted by the suddenness of the announcement, could only protest feebly to the last. The vote on the question of sub-

---

[49] *O. R.*, Series III, vol. i, p. 76.
[50] Hall, *op. cit.*, p. 183.

mitting an ordinance of secession to the people was carried by eighty-eight to fifty-five. Of the forty-six delegates from what is now West Virginia, twenty-nine voted against the resolution, nine for it, seven were absent, and one was excused.[51] Shortly afterward troops were introduced into the State from the South. In eastern Virginia the war spirit was extremely strong, overcoming all dictates of reason. Secession was an accomplished fact long before the voters registered their approval of the ordinance at the polls. The popular vote was 125,950 to 20,373, not including returns from thirty-four counties in western Virginia.

[51] Virgil A. Lewis, *History of West Virginia*, p. 337.

CHAPTER VI

THE RESPONSE OF THE NORTH

When the question of preventing the reinforcement of
Fort Sumter was being discussed in the Confederate cabinet, Toombs declared that an attack on the fort would
cause the loss of every friend that the South had among
the people of the Northern States. His prediction was
amply justified. The whole North regarded the bombardment, not as an evidence of the resistance of a free-
dom-loving people to external aggression, but as an
unjustified assault upon the nation. There was no
thought of criticizing the President for his act in ordering the provisioning of the fort. His carefully laid plans
were far more successful, indeed, than he had hoped they
would be; for the defense made by Major Anderson's
little band, on short rations and with a scanty supply of
ammunition, appealed powerfully to the imagination of
the people. It diverted from the South all the sympathy
that had formerly been bestowed upon that section. For
the first time in years the North was united upon a single policy. The people rose as one man, irrespective of
classes, political parties or factions. There was no longer
any thought of patching up the differences by compromises or offers of conciliation. With one accord the people determined to meet force with force.

In no section of the country was the response of the
people more unanimous than in Ohio, Indiana and

northern Illinois. The legislatures at once voted to raise
and equip armies. Volunteer companies, formed when
the news came of the surrender of Fort Sumter, vied
with one another for the coveted assignment to one of
the regiments for which the President had called. The
people of large communities gathered in mass meetings
and pledged their full support to the government. Private citizens took measures to prevent the expression of
secessionist sentiments and the shipment of supplies to
the South. In southern Ohio and southern Indiana,
where the people had shown the greatest sympathy for
the institution of slavery, the common danger impelled
them to devote their efforts to the preservation of the
Union. They cheerfully pledged their all in the full
knowledge that the war might be fought at their very
doors.

In Ohio public opinion, forgetful of compromises and
offers of concessions which had been so strongly urged in
the months just preceding the outbreak of the war,
swiftly advanced to the position of the Republican newspapers. For the moment the Democratic party seemed
to lose its identity and merge with the opposition into a
great Union party. On the day of the bombardment,
David Tod, one of the foremost leaders of the party,
wrote to the President pledging the support of the two
hundred thousand Democrats of Ohio.[1] Mass meetings
held in all parts of the State endorsed the President's
policy, especially strong resolutions being adopted in
Democratic centers like Columbus and Cincinnati. In the
last named city the movement of public opinion was
pretty accurately reflected by the *Enquirer,* which, until
the attack on Fort Sumter, had been a bitter critic of

[1] George H. Porter, *Ohio Politics During the Civil War Period,* p. 75.

the administration. On the day afterward it declared that "the Southern army . . . broke the *status quo,* . . . and upon them rests the immediate responsibility for the bloody strife which has been inaugurated. . . . If war and bloodshed rage throughout the land, our sympathies will be with the stars and stripes." The next day it asserted: "If the fort has surrendered, it will be not only a gross political, but a military blunder upon the Administration, which has set out to relieve it with an inadequate force." The success of Lincoln's policy could hardly have been more complete.

The people of the city moved quickly both in expressing favorable sentiments and in giving actual aid to the cause of the Union. An appropriation of $200,000 was made by the city council for the purpose of equipping troops.[2] On April 27th a mass meeting denounced as a traitor anyone who sold an article contraband of war to any person or State that had not declared a firm purpose to support the national government. Even previous to that time the people had enforced an embargo on shipments to the South, including points in Kentucky.[3] The young men of the city were naturally in the forefront of the movement, swarming to the enlistment offices to enroll themselves in regiments. The Germans were first with their fine *turner* regiment, the Ninth Ohio; and the Irish citizens soon afterward completed the organization of the Fifth and Sixth Ohio. Within a week from the fall of Fort Sumter, ten thousand men had enlisted in the city, and Camp Dennison was soon established nearby as a center for training.[4]

[2] Henry Howe, *Historical Collections of Ohio,* vol. ii, p. 43.
[3] D. W. McClung, *History of Cincinnati and Hamilton County,* p. 345.
[4] Howe, vol. ii, pp. 44-45.

The state administration found it difficult to measure up to the standard which the people demanded. Since Ohio had no militia, Governor Dennison was obliged to call for volunteer companies to fill the quota of the State. Within twenty-four hours after the receipt of the President's call, twenty companies had offered their services from all parts of the State—from Cleveland, from Toledo, and from Portsmouth on the Ohio River. In the confusion of the first few days the adjutant-general accepted all offers without keeping records of the numbers. When an accounting was made it was discovered that there were in service several times the six thousand men the President had asked for. It was then necessary to organize several regiments of state troops and even to send many volunteers to their homes.[5] The difficulty in obtaining arms was extremely great, for all the States were organizing armies, and the competition among them sent the prices soaring. Nevertheless, troops from Ohio were soon ready to defend the national capital.

In the legislature party lines were obliterated, and both houses rose to the occasion as few such bodies have done. On the day that President Lincoln called for troops the Senate voted to appropriate a million dollars for defense, one-half to be disbursed by the national government, the other half by the state authorities. A contingent fund was also provided to be used as the governor might direct. Within three days the House passed the bill unanimously.[6] As soon as it became known that more troops had been accepted than the President had called for, the legislature passed an act providing for the organization of six additional regiments to serve as state

[5] Whitelaw Reid, *Ohio in the War*, vol. i, pp. 27-29.
[6] Porter, *op. cit.*, pp. 75-76.

troops until they were needed by the national government. For there were far-sighted leaders who expected more than a "three-months' war."

Before the close of the session there appeared among a small group of Democratic leaders a spirit of opposition to the war. Clement L. Vallandigham, the congressman from the Dayton district, was the most prominent of them. He went to Columbus, and in the lobbies did everything possible to defeat measures for national defense. His influence, however, was of no effect at this time. The only result of his efforts was the presentation of a bill "to define and punish treason against the State of Ohio." [7]

The governor of the State, William Dennison, was a Republican politician of some prominence. Needless to say, he devoted his efforts to the promotion of the military establishment. Though he lacked the capacity for detail and the genius for organization that made Morton and Yates great war governors, his public measures were in the highest degree important. Leaving administrative details to his subordinates, he devoted his own talents to diplomacy and the larger problems of government. He directed much attention from the beginning to securing the defense of the State from a possible invasion by the Confederates. Along the southeastern boundary, Ohio was contiguous to the seceded State of Virginia for more than four hundred miles. The river provided an excellent line of defense against an invasion in force, but it would be difficult to guard against marauding parties. After studying the problem, Dennison came to the conclusion that the line of the Alleghanies was the best possible for the defense of Ohio, since it would remove the

[7] Daniel J. Ryan, *A History of Ohio*, p. 152.

scene of conflict and would require a much smaller army to ward off attack.

A further consideration leading to this conclusion was the attitude of the people of northwestern Virginia who had taken a decided stand for the Union and against secession. If they should be overpowered by the military forces of the South and of Virginia, much would be lost. Dennison determined to take advantage of the opportunity in time to save them. In response to their requests for aid in driving back a Confederate force, he took the responsibility for arranging an invasion of Virginia at a time when the national government still allowed the soldiers of the State to guard the southern end of the Long Bridge leading from Washington to Alexandria. He met with no difficulty in obtaining the approval of President Lincoln for the proposed expedition, but his request for a body of Federal troops to take part in it was refused, since all the available men were needed for the defense of Washington. Fortunately for his plans the six additional regiments which had been formed in Ohio had not yet been ordered out of the State. With them and a similar body of troops which Morton had organized in Indiana, Dennison ordered McClellan to prepare to invade Virginia.*

There was some delay while the unionist leaders in Virginia awaited the result of a popular referendum on the question of secession, which was held on May 23rd. Four days later McClellan ordered his force to cross the river at Parkersburg and Wheeling. Within a short time he had driven the weak, disorganized and badly led Virginia army into the mountains, winning great glory for the arms of Ohio and the command of the Army of the

* Reid, *op. cit.*, vol. i, pp. 45-48.

Potomac for himself. General Rosecrans completed the
work of clearing northwestern Virginia, and later drove
the Confederates from the Kanawha Valley. By the
end of the summer there was no large Southern force
within two hundred miles of the borders of Ohio.

Another source of possible danger to the State of
Ohio was the attitude of Kentucky, which hesitated a
long time before definitely deciding for the Union. Dennison early entered into negotiations with Governor
Magoffin with a view to keeping Kentucky in the Union.
Later, as a matter of policy, he virtually recognized the
neutrality of the State, sending McClellan on June 8th
to hold a conference with General Buckner, who was in
command of the militia of Kentucky. The two leaders
agreed that if Kentucky should be invaded by the Confederates, an army would be sent from Ohio to drive
them out. As long, however, as Kentucky maintained her
neutrality, McClellan agreed to respect it.[9] The arrangement went far toward quieting the fears of the people of
Ohio, as well as toward conciliating the Kentuckians.

The response of Indiana, like that of Ohio, was spontaneous and almost unanimously for the Union. The
news of the attack on Fort Sumter united all classes
against the South. As the bulletins were published telling the progress of the bombardment, crowds began to
gather in Indianapolis and other cities to wreak vengeance on Confederate sympathizers. First visiting the
offices of newspapers whose expressions toward the administration had been unfriendly or lukewarm, they
compelled the proprietors to display the national colors.
Afterward they marched through the streets, stopping at
the homes of citizens whose sympathies were thought to

[9] Reid, vol. i, p. 280.

be with the South and compelling them to take an improvised oath of allegiance.[10]   After the passions of the moment had cooled somewhat the people met in orderly mass meetings and pledged their support to the President.

The state government was poorly prepared for Lincoln's first call for troops. As in Ohio, there was no organized militia. Though volunteers offered their services in numbers several times greater than the six regiments asked for, there was an insufficient supply of arms to place in their hands. At the beginning of the year there were fewer than five hundred stand of small arms in the State, and only eight weather-worn and dismantled cannon. The military reputation of Indiana was at a low ebb on account of official reports of the misconduct of her soldiers under fire at Buena Vista which had been made over the signature of Colonel Jefferson Davis. The financial standing of the State was extremely low.[11] All in all, it was an appalling situation. Under any other than the wisest leadership the result must have been disastrous to the cause of the Union in the State.

Oliver P. Morton was just the type of governor that Indiana needed in the emergency. His passionate conviction of the justice of the cause in which he was engaged was united with a genius for leadership and an ability for organization which have seldom been surpassed in state administration. There was no interest of the State or of its soldiers too unimportant to receive his attention. There was no department that was not infused with new vigor by his tremendous energy. If his subordinates were incompetent, he got rid of them and put men in their places who could accomplish the tasks which he

[10] William D. Foulke, *The Life of Oliver P. Morton*, vol. i, p. 115.
[11] Foulke, vol. i, pp. 110-112.

had set. Through the sheer force of his indomitable will
he transformed the administration of the State, and made
it an efficient agency in carrying on the war. In matters
connected with the disposition of the troops, he gave wise
counsel. General McClellan wrote of him once that he
"was a terrible alarmist and not at all a safe head."
Coming from McClellan, the remark was rather compli-
mentary.

Lincoln's first call had apportioned but six regiments to
Indiana, but so certain was Morton that the war was a
serious undertaking that he secured the consent of the
legislature to enroll six additional regiments as state
troops, to be organized and drilled until they were needed.
The scarcity of arms was an obstacle which Morton overcame at first by purchase and later by manufacture. On
his own responsibility he established an arsenal in Indianapolis which supplied not only the soldiers of Indiana,
but also furnished thousands of muskets to the government of the United States.[12] The regiments furnished
by the State were better armed and better clothed than
those of most of the other States. When Morton's state
troops passed through Cincinnati on their way to take
part in the West Virginia campaign, the excellence of
their uniforms and equipment and their proficiency in
drill excited remark, though he had had but a few weeks
in which to organize them. In financial matters he
showed great ability, relieving the difficulties of the State
to some extent by the practice of economies. In every
way he sought to work in close coöperation with the
authorities at Washington, realizing that the war was a
matter of national concern. He held frequent conferences with Lincoln and Stanton, and more than once

[12] Foulke, vol. i, p. 180.

brought about improvements in the methods of carrying on the war.[13]

Though Morton was primarily concerned with the problem of furnishing men and supplies to the national government, he early directed his attention to conditions along the southern boundary of the State where an immense trade had grown up with points in the South. With his approval, a vigilance committee was organized which stopped shipments from Vincennes, Evansville and New Albany. In order to prevent the incursions of marauding bands into the State and to watch the frontier, he organized the "Indiana Legion" in all the southern counties at the beginning of the war.[14] Though the companies were frequently broken up by enlistments into the army, the Legion rendered efficient service, even taking part in some of the campaigns in Kentucky. Moreover, Morton frequently counseled with the Union men in Kentucky on matters concerning the attitude of that State toward the Union. No small credit for keeping it loyal belongs to him.

The legislature was almost unanimous in its devotion to the Union. Called into special session on April 25th, it gave its approval to most of the measures submitted by Morton, and voted sufficient appropriations to carry them out. A resolution to respect the neutrality of Kentucky because of the connections of that State with the South, was unanimously rejected after the House had refused permission to withdraw it.[15] The attitude of United States Senator Jesse D. Bright, who had had

[13] William B. Weeden, *War Government, Federal and State,* pp. 146, 171, 190.

[14] See the *Report* of Major-General Love of the Indiana Legion, 1863, p. 4.

[15] Foulke, vol. i, pp. 121-122.

some correspondence with the Confederate authorities, was condemned. A ringing resolution was passed demanding his resignation. Near the close of the session the legislature declared that he had forfeited all rights to represent the State, and it requested the Senate to declare his seat vacant. With the exception of Bright and a few other Breckinridge Democrats, there was no opposition in Indiana to the vigorous prosecution of the war in the first few months following the attack on Fort Sumter.

The reaction of northern and central Illinois to the events beginning the war was not different from that of Ohio and Indiana. There was the same unanimity of public opinion vigorously expressed in the press and in mass meetings. There was the same rush of young men to join the colors.[16] As in those States, too, party and factional differences were forgotten. Members of all parties vied with one another in showing devotion to the Union. John A. McClernand, the Democratic representative in Congress from the Springfield district, was one of the first to offer his services to the government. His example was sufficient to secure to the authorities of the State the almost solid support of his constituents. South of his district, however, the people continued to show a friendly disposition toward the Confederate States. There were offers of troops for the Union on the first call in excess of the quota,[17] and there was a considerable Union sentiment in many of the counties of the section. But there were other counties which seemed to be overwhelmingly for the South. The movement for the division of the State and the annexation of

[16] In addition to filling the quota of their own State, it is estimated that 10,000 citizens of Illinois enlisted in Missouri regiments. See the *Report* of the Adjutant-General of Illinois, 1861-66, vol. i, pp. 11, 20.

[17] Cole, *op. cit.*, p. 279.

"Egypt" to the Confederate States, which had been smouldering for some months, threatened to break out into open secession and rebellion. At a mass meeting held at Williamson, Marion County, on the day President Lincoln called for troops, resolutions were adopted openly announcing the determination of the people to secede.[18] These resolutions were widely reported to have received the approval of John A. Logan, who still remained in Washington, apparently uncertain as to the course he should take. In other communities, nearly an equal degree of disaffection was evident.

Recruiting for the Southern armies began almost immediately after the firing on Fort Sumter. Many young men from Williamson and Franklin counties hastened to offer their services, among them a brother-in-law of Logan.[19] In some instances the leaders of the Democratic party in southern Illinois are said to have encouraged these enlistments. One member of the legislature, James D. Pulley, was arrested on the charge of having recruited men for the Confederate army.[20] And as late as June, Logan's name was used to secure volunteers for the same service. The cause of the Union was in such a difficult situation that the efforts of patriotic leaders of the State were largely directed for a time toward changing the course of public opinion in this section.

The task might easily have been an insuperable one had not Stephen A. Douglas without hesitation thrown the weight of his powerful influence on the side of the

[18] Cole, p. 260.

[19] Mrs. John A. Logan, *Reminiscences of a Soldier's Wife*, pp. 89-91. Bluford Wilson, however, declares that only a handful of boys joined the Southern army from all of "Egypt." See the *Transactions* of the Illinois State Historical Society, 1911, p. 98.

[20] Cole, p. 262, note.

Union. At the time Fort Sumter was fired on he was in Washington seeking to bring about an understanding between the sections which would not involve a surrender to the South. Upon receiving the news of the attack, he did not delay for a moment to declare that force must be used for the preservation of the Union. He called upon the President at the White House and pledged his support to him, afterward issuing a public statement that he was "prepared to fully sustain the President in the exercise of all his constitutional functions, to preserve the Union, maintain the government, and defend the Federal capital." [21] For a few days he devoted his efforts to securing united action from the Democratic leaders at Washington, and then, with Lincoln's approval, he hurried to Illinois, whence the most alarming reports had come of opposition to the national government.

At Springfield, April 25th, he delivered before the legislature of Illinois the greatest address of his career. For an immortal hour he held his audience spellbound by the magic of his powerful oratory. He was never more masterful than in this, the last great speech of his life. His "trumpet tones" roused his hearers to the highest pitch of enthusiasm and made them "hysterical with the divine madness of patriotism." No one could have any doubt concerning his position. "When hostile armies," he said, "are marching under new and odious banners against the government of our country, the shortest way to peace is the most stupendous and unanimous preparation for war." [22] He frankly confessed that he had made the mistake of leaning too far toward the South in his

[21] Allen Johnson, op. cit., p. 477.
[22] Johnson, p. 483.

previous career, and he warned his hearers of the dangers that lay in following a similar course. Appealing to their self-interest, he asked whether anyone would be "willing to sanction a line of policy that may isolate us from the markets of the world, and make us dependent provinces upon the powers that thus choose to isolate us. . . . If a war does come, it is a war of self-defense on our part. It is a war in defense of the Government which we have inherited as a priceless legacy from our patriotic fathers, in defense of those great rights of freedom of trade, commerce, transit and intercourse from the center to the circumference of our great continent." Near the close, rising to a great climax, he declared: "I believe in my conscience that it is a duty we owe to ourselves and to our children, and to our God, to protect this Government and that flag from every assailant, be he who he may." [23]

The effects of the address were all that the most sanguine advocate of the Union could have wished. Everywhere throughout the State, the people were inspired to greater service and devotion to the cause for which he had spoken. In southern Illinois, where the people had been in the habit of following his leadership for a generation, there ensued an almost magical change in public opinion. Instead of mutterings of opposition to the Union and agitation for secession, the expression of sentiment indicated a great outpouring of national patriotism. Two days after the address was delivered, Lyman Trumbull wrote to a friend that opposition in southern Illinois had practically died out and that the section was a unit in supporting the administration. [24]

[23] Johnson, pp. 483-485.
[24] The letter is reprinted in the *Journal* of the Illinois State Historical Society, July, 1909, p. 44.

The prompt declaration of Douglas undoubtedly turned the tide and saved the State from an internecine struggle. It had a tremendous influence upon the timid and hesitating Logan, on whom the mantle of his leadership fell.

Logan's attitude is somewhat difficult to understand. In Washington during the session of the Congress, his influence was certainly on the side of the Union; but in his relations with his constituents he failed to declare himself in favor of the Union at a time when a declaration would have done an immense amount of good in checking secessionist activities in his district. At the first outbreak of war he proved a timid follower rather than a leader of public opinion, evidently hesitating to risk his political future until he was sure of his ground. Possibly he overestimated the strength of secessionism in his district. His closest friends were the leaders of the movement, and his family was divided in its allegiance. It was several weeks after Douglas's great address when Logan finally decided to return to his home and make a public announcement of his position. Before a large audience at Marion, in the very heart of the former secessionist activities, he declared his belief that the duty of all patriots lay in supporting the national government. This statement having been well received, he further announced that he purposed raising a regiment for the Union, the first company of which should be recruited from Marion. A few of his friends, who knew of his intentions, constituted themselves enrolling officers on the spot, and before the meeting disbanded the first company had been filled.[25]

Though a few minor instances of dissatisfaction with the government occurred in southern Illinois in the sum-

[25] Logan, *op. cit.*, pp. 96-99.

mer, the great majority of the people gave their whole-hearted support to the Union. Having once made up their minds as to the proper course to pursue, they were better Union men than others of the Borderland who had not undergone early divisions of opinion and conversion. Several counties furnished to the Federal armies almost as many men as the combined vote for Lincoln, Douglas and Bell. Their quotas were always full. The draft was never resorted to among them.[26] In 1863 it was reported that the enlistments were fifty per cent in excess of the quota of the section; and a newspaper in Cairo complained that Illinois was being deprived of her man power through the great number of enlistments.

The public authorities of the State acted promptly to carry out the wishes of the people. Though some members of the legislature showed a disposition to cause hindrances if they saw an opportunity to make their opposition effective, the body as a whole gave its support to measures proposed by the governor. An appropriation of $3,500,000 was made to raise and equip troops in addition to those requested by the national government.[27] In order to discourage secessionist activities, an act was passed imposing severe penalties upon anyone who should be convicted of giving aid to the enemies of the United States. Another law was designed to prevent obstruction of the transportation of troops and supplies. Still another provided for the establishment of magazines and the purchase of arms. All these acts were passed within ten days from bills that had been prepared in the governor's office with the advice of committee chairmen.[28]

[26] Bluford Wilson, in the *Transactions* of the Illinois State Historical Society, 1911, pp. 98-99.
[27] Cole, p. 274.
[28] Gustave Koerner, *Memoirs*, vol. ii, pp. 137-138.

In Richard Yates, Illinois had a governor who was equal to the occasion in every respect. Like Morton, he possessed a remarkable capacity for organization, and he was extremely fortunate in being able to choose capable subordinates. He was an even better leader of men, for he had a knack of easily making friends among all classes. Above all, he was diplomatic in his dealings with others. It was necessary that he should be, since in many respects the situation confronting him was more difficult than that in any other Northern State. To his statesmanship a great part of the credit is due for the magnificent efforts that Illinois put forth during the war.

Yates was quick to see the dangers which menaced Illinois and the Union both from internal dissensions and from the activities of secessionists in Missouri and Kentucky. In common with the other leaders of the Northwest, he was concerned also with the problem of opening the Mississippi River to its mouth. He therefore requested the President not to order the troops from Illinois to the defense of Washington, but to allow them to remain under his command for the time being. An immediate objective that he wished to accomplish was to overawe the latent secessionist element in his own State, and to be prepared to give aid to the defenders of the Union in Missouri. He accordingly established the volunteers of the State in camps along the Mississippi River at East St. Louis and at Camp Defiance at Cairo, where they would be in a position to move against either of the elements that menaced the cause of the Union."

In the beginning he would have been willing to send an army into Missouri to overawe the state authorities, but he was dissuaded by some of the conservative Union men of St. Louis, who protested against the proposed

" Cole, p. 262.

measure on the ground that it would provoke violent antagonism among the people. Yates therefore patiently waited until the actual outbreak of war in Missouri, when regiments from Illinois were placed at the disposal of Lyon and Fremont. Under the capable Grant, whom Governor Yates promoted from an enrollment clerk, the troops from Illinois distinguished themselves at Belmont and Fort Donelson, and later bore the brunt of the campaigns in Tennessee.

Perhaps the best understanding of the tremendous efforts of the three States just north of the Ohio River can be gained from a study of the totals of men furnished to the army by the end of 1861. The quota of Ohio under the calls of the President and the acts of Congress of July 22nd and July 25th was 67,365; the State furnished 84,116 men. Indiana was asked to send 38,832, and actually sent 61,341. The share of Illinois was 47,785, but the state authorities enrolled 81,952— nearly seventy-five per cent more than the quota. At the same time New Jersey had furnished only 11,523 men when her quota was 19,152, Massachusetts had failed by two thousand men to fill her quota, and Pennsylvania had raised only two regiments in excess of the number apportioned to the State.[30] The people of the Borderland were as willing to fight for the preservation of the Union as they had been to make compromises before the actual break occurred. Not many of the soldiers, probably, were actuated by a desire to secure freedom for the slaves. They fought with the object of compelling the Southern States to return to their allegiance.

[30] *Official Records*, Series III, vol. i, p. 384, note.

CHAPTER VII

THE "RESTORATION" OF VIRGINIA

In twenty counties, containing by far the greater portion of the population and wealth of western Virginia, the response of public opinion to the firing on Fort Sumter differed but little from that of the free States of the Borderland. With practical unanimity the people chose the side of the Union. Unfortunately there was no organized government in the beginning through which their opinions could be transformed into actions. Nor were there leaders capable of discerning the fundamental problem and of guiding public opinion aright. In consequence, the question of how best to preserve the Union was complicated by a movement toward the formation of a new State, which was secondary in character, depending for its success upon the popular attitude toward the national government. It soon gained such headway as to obscure the larger question upon which it rested, and to divide the efforts of the people. As a result of its ultimate success nearly every writer on the subject has neglected the national loyalty of the people and their extremely important services in preserving the Union. In point of fact, the people had definitely made their decision before the announcement of the virtual secession of Virginia afforded an opportunity to discuss seriously the formation of a new State.

In widely scattered sections the people rose sponta-

neously and without concert to the support of the
national government. The flag of the United States
was displayed in the principal towns. In Parkersburg,
Wheeling and other places the people met in mass meetings to pledge their efforts toward preserving the Union.
The resolutions adopted at Grafton, April 19th, are
fairly representative. It was declared: (1) that secession cannot exist under the Constitution, and that revolution, under existing circumstances, is uncalled for;
(2) that the interests of civil and religious liberty and
of civilization demand the maintenance of the government of the United States; and (3) that if eastern Virginia should secede from the Union the western part of
the State should secede from Virginia. The citizens of
Brooke County, covetous of the honor of organizing the
first company for the United States, appointed a committee to secure arms from Governor Letcher or, failing
in that quarter, from the War Department. When Governor Letcher's orders to seize the United States customs
house were received in Wheeling, a mob of several hundred citizens collected to prevent their being carried into
execution. The mayor, taking the popular side, promised that the police force, augmented by the swearing
in of a hundred officers on that day, would be used
against anyone who attempted to haul down the flag
of the United States. The orders were never carried
out. At Weston, far in the interior, a Confederate flag
which had been surreptitiously placed over the courthouse was hauled down by a crowd of citizens and publicly burned by the presiding justice of the county
court. Still another fact that might be cited to indicate
the sentiment of the people is that several young men
of the Panhandle, being denied the privilege of fighting

to preserve the Union in Virginia regiments, enlisted under the banners of Ohio or Pennsylvania.[1]

The predominantly unionist feeling of northwestern Virginia had been authoritatively expressed over a period of several months, and the dissatisfaction of the people with the domination of eastern Virginia had been notorious for a half century. Both must have been known to the secessionist leaders, who could hardly have avoided realizing the dangers of seceding without having first secured the united support of all sections. Why they did not at least attempt to mollify the feelings of the northwestern part of the State by granting concessions in taxation and representation is a mystery. Possibly they held the "peasantry of the west" in such low esteem that they did not think it worth while to consider them; or they may have counted upon their well-known sentiment of state patriotism to overlook one more act of flagrant disregard for western opinions and interests. Whatever the correct explanation is, the leaders of the secessionist movement proceeded with singleness of purpose to secure a complete disruption of all bonds that connected Virginia with the national government. Notwithstanding the fact that the ordinance of secession could have no legal validity until after it had been approved by a popular referendum, the governor and the convention made an offensive and defensive alliance with the Confederate States under which Southern troops were introduced into the State; and they began raising an army which threatened the defenses of the national capital. The direct consequence of these measures, following the questionable methods by which the ordinance had been passed, was to estrange the people of north-

[1] Wheeling *Intelligencer*, April 13-26, *passim*.

western Virginia still farther from their state government and to lead them to take drastic action against it much sooner than they would otherwise have done.

The members of the convention from the northwestern counties appreciated the sentiments of their constituents much better than the secessionist leaders. As soon as the ordinance of secession had been passed they realized that their usefulness in the convention was at an end. It was no longer desirable for them to work for reforms in taxation and representation, since they were certain that their constituents would never accept them as part of the constitution of a seceded State. Some of the delegates left Richmond for their homes on the day the ordinance was passed and succeeded in reaching Washington before orders for their arrest could be carried into execution.[2] Others, meeting in caucus the same evening in the rooms of one of their number, resolved to go to their homes as quickly as possible. Before they were allowed to leave Richmond, it was found necessary for them to obtain passes from the governor. They were threatened with violence in some communities through which they traveled; but all reached the northwestern counties in safety.[3]

Their return tended to confirm rumors among the people that the convention had passed an ordinance of secession. The citizens were extremely anxious to be fully informed of the proceedings at Richmond; and for their own part, the delegates were desirous of defending themselves and of explaining how the unionist majority in the convention had been led to change its position so quickly

[2] Virgil A. Lewis, *History of West Virginia*, p. 337.
[3] William P. Willey, *An Inside View of the Formation of the State of West Virginia*, pp. 51-53.

and so radically. On April 20th, the citizens of Wheeling met in American Hall to hear the report of Chester D. Hubbard. Complaining bitterly of the treatment of the western delegates by the people of Richmond, he denounced the course taken by the convention and declared that his constituents need not feel themselves bound by it. He advised independent action within the Union. Recommending that the people prepare to defend their opinions by force, if necessary, he urged that the military organizations which were already in process of formation should be completed at once. As a result of his advice, two full companies were enrolled the next day to defend the city. A week later the officers of ten companies of volunteers met to form a regimental organization.

At almost the same hour the people of Wellsburg, in an adjoining county, listened to the report of Delegate Campbell Tarr, who, like Hubbard, recommended military preparations. The committee which had previously been appointed to obtain arms left immediately for Washington, where, through the assistance of Edwin M. Stanton, a former neighbor, they succeeded in securing from the War Department two thousand stand of small arms and a supply of ammunition. These munitions were distributed among the volunteer organizations of the Panhandle, which were later to become Virginia regiments in the Federal army.[5] In consequence of their effective preparations, the people were secured from interference by the authorities at Richmond, and were enabled to pursue their own course in furthering the causes of the Union and of local autonomy.

[4] Lewis, *History of West Virginia*, pp. 338-339.
[5] *Idem*, pp. 340-341.

Outside the Panhandle the people were nearly as prompt in their resistance. The greatest public gathering in the history of Monongalia County met on April 22nd, and adopted resolutions commending the course of their delegates in voting against the ordinance of secession and in afterwards leaving the convention. Without a dissenting voice they declared that they would never follow the remainder of the State into the Southern Confederacy.⁶ Similar meetings were held in nearly every other county of northwestern Virginia. From Berkeley County on the Potomac to Wood County at the mouth of the Little Kanawha River, practically every public address and resolution expressed a firm determination to stand by the Union and to resist the state authorities. At Grafton a military organization was formed to combat the activities of a minority of the people who favored the policies of the governor and the convention. In Mason County, in the Kanawha Valley, a mass meeting called by the secessionists was so largely attended by Union men that resolutions against secession were adopted almost unanimously. In the central portion of what is now West Virginia the secessionists were stronger —in some counties they included a great majority of the people—yet even here the Union men were active. Where it was found impossible for them to hold public meetings they gathered secretly by night to discuss plans for resistance. Despite the orders of the governor and the convention that no one should act in any way under the authority of the United States, they nominated candidates for the House of Representatives in three districts, in order that they might be represented in the

⁶ Virgil A. Lewis, *How West Virginia Was Made*, p. 32.

special session of Congress called by President Lincoln.[7]
Practically everywhere in northwestern Virginia a revolution against the state government was actively fer-
menting before the close of April, when the news of
the passage of the ordinance of secession was first definitely announced.

The action taken by the Union men had thus far been
local and practically without general concert. There was
no arch-traitor against the State, no junto of political
leaders whose influence caused the people to turn toward
the Federal government. The movement was, as a matter of fact, a spontaneous uprising of the people which
was long in achieving its purpose because there was no
one in the beginning who had the reputation, courage
and wisdom to direct it. It was of no use to look for
leadership in the Democratic party, to which most of
the people belonged, since the office holders and politicians were almost all secessionists. Among the Whigs
were two men of considerable ability, George W. Summers and Waitman T. Willey; but the former took no
active part in the movement until 1863, and the latter's
unionist sentiments were so lukewarm that once when
he was addressing a meeting, someone in the crowd
demanded that he "talk Union." [8] Realizing that they
must seek new leaders for their movement, the people
of the interior counties turned to Wheeling, the largest
town in the section. Ten days after the attack on Fort
Sumter committees of citizens in a half dozen counties,
like the committees of correspondence in the beginning

---

[7] For the resolutions passed by the convention in one district, see
Thomas C. Miller, and Hu Maxwell, *op. cit.*, vol. i, p. 319.
[8] Hall, *op. cit.*, p. 546.

of the American Revolution, wrote to Wheeling asking what the people there intended to do.[9]

The greatest single contribution of the city to the cause of the Union—not even excepting the military organizations—was the Wheeling *Intelligencer,* a Republican newspaper then under the able editorship of Archibald W. Campbell. He constantly championed the principles of nationalism, appealing to every sentiment and interest that could affect public opinion favorably. In case the state authorities should succeed in their attempt to leave the Union, he pointed out the dangers of invasion from the North, of the loss of industrial prosperity, of the cessation of commercial and manufacturing development, and of the continued domination of the eastern and Southern slavocracy; but he never made the mistake of introducing purely party issues or abolitionist arguments. By printing in full reports and letters from the interior counties, he encouraged the Union men there and made the cause one for the whole northwest and not merely for Wheeling. Thus the Republican editor who six months before had been denounced as a mischievous disunionist became one of the most important figures in the movement to save western Virginia for the Union. He did not, however, take an active part in organizing the movement; nor were the other leaders in Wheeling ready with a plan for united resistance.

Meanwhile the initiative had been taken by the people of Clarksburg, in the interior. On April 22nd a mass meeting of twelve hundred citizens of Harrison County issued a call for a convention to meet in Wheeling on May 13th "to consult and determine upon such action

[9] Wheeling *Intelligencer,* April 22, 1861.

as the people of Northwestern Virginia should take in
the present fearful emergency." It was recommended
that each county should choose at least five citizens as
delegates. An address to the people of northwestern
Virginia was prepared by John S. Carlile, in which the
necessity for the proposed convention was set forth. The
resolutions were carried by special messengers mounted
on horseback to points not located on the railroads.
Within twenty-four hours they had reached nearly every
county seat and hamlet in the section.[10]

The call for the convention received an enthusiastic
welcome. Meetings of the people at county seats, at
country schoolhouses and at cross-roads stores and dwell-
ings echoed the sentiments expressed. To a person living
in the twentieth century, it seems almost incredible that
there could have been as many voluntary mass meetings
as are reported to have been held in northwestern Virginia in the month following the secession of the State.
Literally tens of thousands of people must have mounted
their horses and ridden for miles out of their hollows
in order that they might listen for several hours to some
local orator or orators, vote approval of resolutions
expressing a warm loyalty to the Union, and elect delegates. Some of the more active Union leaders, like Carlile and Francis H. Pierpont, busied themselves in the
work of organization, though for the most part the
movement continued to be spontaneous. The widest
variations in the method of election occurred. In some
sections it was by counties, in others by election pre-
cincts, and in three counties the mass meetings appointed
as delegates all citizens of the county who could
attend the convention. No definite mandate for the

[10] Lewis, *How West Virginia Was Made*, p. 34.

members was generally agreed upon. It was expected everywhere that the convention would find a way to organize the resistance of the people to the state authorities.

On May 13th more than four hundred determined men, representing twenty-five counties, gathered in Wheeling. It was by no means a remarkable body, as

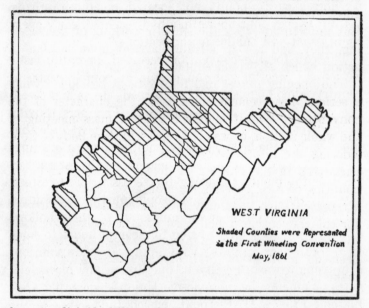

WEST VIRGINIA

Shaded Counties were Represented in the First Wheeling Convention May, 1861

far as political ability was concerned. The former leaders of the people were nearly all absent. One who had been accustomed to attend political meetings in the section saw few faces that he recognized.[11] Most of the delegates were lawyers, merchants, millwrights and farmers whose lives had been spent on lonely farms

[11] Willey, *op. cit.*, p. 58.

among the hills or in the straggling villages of weather-
boarding-over-logs that had been designated as county
seats. Their leaders were chiefly lawyers whose practice
had consisted mainly of litigating land titles, and whose
political experience had been, in most instances, confined to a term or two in the General Assembly. Many
of the former members of the convention were in attendance, and their influence was felt from the beginning.
But unfortunately for the smooth working of the meeting, they had not in advance agreed upon a plan of
action which all would support.

The opening prayer had hardly been concluded when
a serious disagreement arose as to the character of the
convention. Was it merely a general mass meeting of
the whole section, or was it a representative body? Considering the informality of the elections and the wide
variations in the number of delegates among different
counties of nearly equal population, it could be called
a representative body only in a loose sense. In the call
for the convention it had been specified only that there
should be a minimum of five delegates, and there had
been no mention of particular business which would
make necessary an accurate representation of the people.
It therefore partook of the nature of a mass meeting
which could express opinions authoritatively, but could
not transact business that would have a binding effect
upon anybody. Carlile, in opposition to nearly every
other leader, insisted upon calling it, not merely a representative body, but a sovereign convention with powers
similar to those of the state convention which had met
at Richmond. As he explained, the work which it was
intended to do was to separate the northwestern counties

from the remainder of Virginia and set up a new State.[12]

Carlile had greater prestige than any other man in the convention. He had been a poor boy who had educated himself; he had served a term in the Congress; and, though greatly overshadowed by two or three other men in his own county, he had been sent to Richmond because of his outspoken unionist sentiments. There he had fought against secession with such vehemence and unwavering zeal that he had been singled out for special vengeance by the mob.[13] Having returned to his own county, he at once began planning measures of resistance. It was he who had been instrumental in having the convention at Wheeling called, and he was regarded as the proper man to give it direction. A bold and forceful speaker, he was far more eagerly heard than other men who sought by logical persuasion to check the effects of his impetuous haste. On the first day of the session he had little difficulty in having a committee on credentials appointed, which might give the proceedings the color of legality, and in fixing a proportional basis for counting the vote of each county delegation. This done, he proposed an ordinance to dissolve the connection between certain of the northwestern counties and the State of Virginia and set up the "State of New Virginia." A committee was to be appointed by the convention to draft the constitution for the new State, which was to go into operation as soon as the Congress

[12] The account of the proceedings here given is based upon the reports as reprinted in a volume by Virgil A. Lewis entitled, *How West Virginia Was Made*. Other sources of information are in Hall, *The Rending of Virginia;* Willey, *An Inside View of the Formation of West Virginia;* McGregor, *The Disruption of Virginia;* and the files of the Wheeling *Intelligencer*.

[13] Hall, pp. 575-577.

should give its consent. When objections were made that the proposed action was premature and revolutionary, he replied that it was the only legal and constitutional means of redress which the people would have, since, after the special election to be held on May 23rd to ratify the ordinance of secession, they would be in the Southern Confederacy, and no longer under the authority of the United States. "No people," he said, "ever remained free, or ever will, that were not willing to spill their last drop of blood for the maintenance of their liberty. No people who contented themselves with paper resolves while bayonets were bristling all around them and war had been brought to their very doors as rapidly as it could be, ever maintained their freedom in this way. Show yourselves worthy to be free!"

In spite of the wholly inadequate constitutional arguments offered in its behalf, the resolution was enthusiastically received by the great bulk of the delegates. It suited the desires of the radicals—and most of the members were radicals—who wanted to establish a new State at once; and it gave the best possible expression to the vindictive spirit of the hour against the secessionist party in eastern Virginia. Among the abler and more conservative members it met determined opposition. Though favoring eventual separation from Virginia, they believed the time was not ripe for this action. As they knew, there were in most parts of western Virginia conditional Union men who might be driven into the arms of the secessionists if the issue were shifted from merely resisting the state authorities to dismembering the State. The struggle over Carlile's resolution, in their opinion, presented a grave danger to the cause of the Union. General Jackson, who knew something of the feelings of the people in the interior, declared that its adoption would inaugurate internecine war. He urged that all action except concerting plans to defeat the ordinance of secession in the popular referendum be postponed. Another delegate, arguing from the constitutional side, said that a new State could not be created by the method proposed, and that the passage of the resolution would constitute treason against the United States as well as against Virginia and the Confederate States, if their governments should succeed in maintaining their existence. Then Francis H. Pierpont, who had done more than any other man except Carlile to bring the convention to pass, declared that Carlile's attitude amounted to an attempt to drive other members of the convention from the floor. He opposed hasty action based on the plea of necessity because he said there would shortly be any amount of men and money sent to the northwestern counties to protect the people from the state authorities.

The result of the combined assault on Carlile's resolution was successful. At the conclusion of Pierpont's address, an informal poll showed that three-fourths of the delegates were opposed to the measure—a complete about-face for most of them. Carlile then asked leave to withdraw it. A report prepared by the Committee on State and Federal Relations, on which Pierpont was the moving spirit, was then adopted by the convention with but two dissenting votes. In brief, the report declared: (1) that the policy of the state authorities was unwise and "utterly subversive and destructive of our interests," and that efforts should be made to defeat the ordinance of secession in the special referendum; (2) that, in case the people of the State should ratify the ordinance, a special election should be held in the northwestern counties to choose delegates who, with members of the General Assembly, would meet as the second Wheeling convention; and (3) that the people of the northwestern counties might rightfully appeal to the proper authorities of Virginia to permit them peacefully to leave the State. Who the "proper authorities" were to be became evident later. Before it adjourned the convention appointed a central committee of nine members to supervise the conduct of the campaign against the ordinance and to take such other measures as might be necessary in the interval before the assembling of the second convention.

There can be little doubt that the course of the convention was statesmanlike in the highest degree. Its program of action would alienate not a single man. It would, indeed, enlist men of every shade of loyalty—and once enlisted, even the lukewarm could be led to take more positive measures when the occasion demanded. In many parts of the North the results of the convention were disappointing.[14] But the people of that section did not understand the conditions in the border States. What they probably wanted was to humiliate Virginia at once. They apparently could not see that if they did so, they must be content with the support of twenty or twenty-five counties when they might gain fifty by a less extreme course.

After the close of the convention the Central Committee, which included Carlile and Pierpont in its membership, found plenty of work to do. It first devoted its attention to the campaign for the rejection of the ordinance of secession. A pamphlet prepared by Carlile was distributed all over western Virginia, and able speakers were sent into many counties. One of the most telling

[14] James C. McGregor, *The Disruption of Virginia*, pp. 202-203.

methods of arousing resistance was a quotation from a
speech of Howell Cobb of Georgia, which was to the effect
that the people of the South need have no fear of war;—
they could raise cotton while the people of the border
States kept back the enemy.[15] The committee believed
—as did nearly everyone else in the State—that the
ordinance of secession would be ratified by the people.
They therefore looked beyond the election and made
plans for independent action within the Union. They
saw to it that candidates for Congress were voted for
in the tenth, eleventh, and twelfth congressional districts. They urged upon all citizens the duty of electing members of the legislature who were outspoken in
favor of the Union, since these members would have seats
in the second Wheeling convention. Finally, the committee entered into correspondence with President Lincoln and the governors of Ohio and Pennsylvania to
secure their assistance. Governor Dennison willingly
acceded to their request, ordering General McClellan to
concentrate the troops of Ohio on the northern bank of
the river so as to be ready to cross into Virginia when
the ordinance of secession should be ratified.

Meanwhile the secessionists had also been active.
During the weeks following the outbreak of the war their
influential leaders sought to bring the people into line
with the policies of the authorities at Richmond. In the
Panhandle, the Wheeling *Union* espoused their cause
from the beginning with, however, steadily diminishing
support, which obliged the owners to sell their paper
before the middle of May.[16] In Harrison County
ex-Governor Joseph Johnson, for forty years the leading

[15] Lewis, *How West Virginia Was Made*, p. 75.
[16] Wheeling *Intelligencer*, May 13, 1861.

politician in northwestern Virginia, succeeded in holding a fourth of the people of his county to the policies of the state leaders. In Marion County Thomas S. Haymond, who had been appointed a general officer in the state military establishment, succeeded in securing twenty-one recruits, with whom he at first attempted to break up unionist meetings; but upon second thought he abandoned this policy and sought to conciliate the people. In the sparsely settled counties of the interior the secessionist party was much more successful. They had vigilance committees and home guards organized and, in one instance at least, secured an appropriation from the county court for the support of the state forces which had begun to concentrate for the purpose of bearing down opposition to the government at Richmond. Their meetings generally took the position that, since the State had left the Union, it was the duty of the people to follow it and defend its soil against invasion. By the date of the special election, the secessionist party was pretty thoroughly organized.

As to the election, accusations have been made on both sides that many citizens were intimidated, under the *viva voce* system in use, from voting their true sentiments. The Union men claimed that the presence of troops from the South reduced greatly the vote against the ordinance in eastern Virginia; and the secessionists retaliated by declaring that the Union men in the northwestern section prevented many persons from voting by the use of force and threats, and that troops should have been sent there to insure a fair polling.[17] There appears to have been little ground for the accusation

[17] Rhodes, vol. iii, p. 387 note, quoting the Richmond *Examiner*, May 24 and 25, 1861.

as to northwestern Virginia, since votes were cast for the ordinance in every county; but in two counties south of the Kanawha River there are pretty well substantiated reports that men who voted against the ordinance did so at the risk of personal violence.[18] But if there had been no intimidation the general result would not have been changed.

East of the Alleghanies the stir of military preparations, the plans for the establishment of a powerful new confederacy, and the common danger of invasion, all contributed to break down loyalty to the Union. The people voted for the ordinance of secession by more than five to one, and their numbers were easily sufficient to overcome the adverse vote polled west of the mountains. On June 14th Governor Letcher issued a proclamation announcing that the ordinance had been ratified by a popular vote of 125,950 to 20,373, not including returns from many counties (thirty-four of which were in western Virginia) which had not been received owing to the presence of hostile forces. The official returns have been lost, and there is no way of learning positively what the exact results were. But reports gleaned from the files of various newspapers show that in twenty counties in the present State of West Virginia the people voted against the ordinance by 21,789 to 7,114. Complete figures from all the counties would probably show the same proportion. In twelve representative counties of the northwestern section, where loyalty to the Union was strongest, the people voted by nearly ten to one against the ordinance.[19]

[18] Hall, p. 285.

[19] J. M. Callahan, *A History of West Virginia, Old and New*, vol. i, p. 352.

As soon as the results of the election became known the period of peaceful resistance to the state authorities came to an end. The way was open for whatever action the Union men of northwestern Virginia cared to take. Before proceeding with their plans for governmental reorganization, it seemed desirable to the Central Committee to counteract the increasing danger of military subjection by the state government. With their own volunteers, therefore, and with the help of troops from Ohio and Indiana, they began a movement to clear western Virginia of armed secessionists and thus make it possible to restore the authority of the United States. On May 27th Colonel Kelley and the First Provisional Virginia regiment, which had been in training on Wheeling Island, boarded cars for Grafton in the interior. A few hours later the Sixteenth Ohio crossed the river and followed them, and at the same time the Fourteenth and Eighteenth regiments crossed at Parkersburg and proceeded toward Grafton over the Northwestern Virginia Railroad.[20] Political considerations dictated the movement of the Virginia volunteers in advance of the others, since the Central Committee was anxious to make the campaign appear a rebellion against the authorities at Richmond rather than an invasion from the North.

The provisional regiment could probably have defeated the state troops unaided, for they were few in number and badly led. The plan of defense adopted by General Lee had contemplated that each section should defend itself. The volunteers from eastern Virginia and regiments from the more southern States were concentrated within striking distance from Washington. Those from the Shenandoah Valley were stationed near Harper's

[20] *Official Records,* Series I, vol. ii, pp. 45-46.

Ferry. Those from the Kanawha Valley were to guard the mouth of the river. And those from the northwest were to be used to defend the Ohio River line from Wheeling to Parkersburg. Late in April recruiting had been attempted in northwestern Virginia with results that were disappointing in the extreme. Few men joined the colors. On May 4th Colonel George A. Porterfield was ordered to proceed to Grafton and take up a position for the protection of the section. The plan contemplated the use of at least five regiments—one near Wheeling, one near Parkersburg, and three in reserve at Grafton.[21] Porterfield, arriving at Grafton some days later, found neither the officers nor the men who had been directed to report to him there. Instead he was met by a company of Union men who compelled him to leave on the next train.[22] Two days later he reported that he had found three companies in the territory assigned to him, and that he had heard of two or three other companies. He warned the state authorities that there was great disaffection in the district, and requested that troops from east of the Alleghanies be sent to his assistance.[23] It was not until May 23rd, the day of the election, that he was able to concentrate a sufficient force to move upon Grafton. He had then about five hundred fifty men, most of whom were from the Shenandoah Valley. Within a week he felt obliged by the near approach of Kelley to evacuate the town and retire southward to Philippi to await reinforcements. A few companies joined him there, bringing his total to about

[21] R. E. Lee to Porterfield, *O. R.*, Series I, vol. ii, pp. 802-803.
[22] Hall, p. 224.
[23] *O. R.*, Series I, vol. ii, p. 843.

a thousand; but they were undisciplined and lacking in supplies of all kinds.

The advance guard of the Union force reached Grafton on May 30th, having been delayed on the way by the burning of railroad bridges by Confederate sympathizers. Colonel Kelley at once requested permission to follow up Porterfield. His proposal being approved, the Federals moved upon Philippi in two columns on the evening of June 2nd. After marching all night through a heavy downpour they arrived at Porterfield's camp, and at once opened fire. The Confederates were completely surprised. Their pickets had left their posts, seeking shelter from the rain in the town, and the first warning the commander had was the booming of the Federal artillery. After a feeble attempt at resistance his troops fled southward in a disorganized mass. The Federals, worn out by their long march, and having no cavalry, were forced to give over the pursuit after a short distance.[24]

Porterfield halted at Huttonsville, a hundred miles south of Grafton, and began the reorganization of his command. An appeal for reinforcements and supplies brought assurances from General Lee that both would be sent. About the middle of June General Garnett arrived to take command of the Confederate force, which, with reinforcements that continued to come in, soon numbered more than four thousand men. Acting on the advice of General Lee, Garnett determined to make a stand west of the mountains. He accordingly fortified Laurel Hill and Rich Mountain, two long ridges that commanded the road to the upper Monongahela Valley and the cross-

[24] McClellan's and Morris's reports, *O. R.*, Series I, vol. ii, pp. 64-68. Harman's report (Confed.) p. 69.

ings of the Alleghanies. There he awaited the coming of the Federal forces.[25]

Meanwhile, McClellan's army, which had been thoroughly organized at Grafton and Philippi for the campaign in the interior, was ready to move. The march southward was through a country of winding ridges and narrow valleys, most of the land being covered with virgin forest. The people were friendly, willingly furnishing guides for the reconnoitering parties.[26] With his superior service of information, McClellan soon discovered that the Confederate forts were separated by a deep gorge, with the main body on the northern side of the river. Seizing upon the fact, he determined to make his principal attack against the more southern position on Rich Mountain, where success would mean the capture of the Confederate base of supplies and the cutting off of the retreat of Garnett's main force on Laurel Hill. On July 6th he sent a small force under General Morris to make a feint against the main position, while he himself approached the southern position from the flank. A portion of his force, gaining the Confederate rear with only slight resistance, compelled the garrison at Rich Mountain to abandon its position. They retreated in the night, intending to join Garnett; but having lost their way among the laurel thickets, they were surrounded and compelled to surrender. McClellan easily captured the Confederate base, cutting off Garnett, who had begun to retreat toward the south when he heard of the disaster at Rich Mountain. On learning that the road was blocked, he retraced his steps and attempted

[25] O. R., Series I, vol. ii, pp. 236-238.
[26] The reports of both Federal and Confederate leaders show that the people were almost unanimously for the Union.

to reach the Shenandoah Valley over mountain trails to the north of the main road. The Federals, following in hot pursuit, overtook him at Corrick's Ford and completely routed his army. Only a remnant succeeded in crossing the mountains to safety.[27] The practical result of the campaign was to leave northwestern Virginia within the Union lines. Later in the season General Lee led an army across the mountains in person, but he was able to make no headway against the Federal troops. Thereafter the Confederates abandoned the region.

The Federal authorities were not content to stop here. There remained the more serious problem of driving the Confederate forces from the Kanawha Valley. The state recruiting officers had been more successful here than in northwestern Virginia, and ex-Governor Wise, who had been placed in command of the district, had nearly three thousand men. In order to keep this force occupied while the northwestern campaign was being completed, McClellan ordered General J. D. Cox to move with three regiments into the lower valley of the Great Kanawha.[28] Cox accordingly crossed the river, occupying some of the border counties which were infested with guerrilla bands, but was unable to make headway against Wise.[29] Further movements were delayed by McClellan's transfer to Washington. Late in the summer his successor, General Rosecrans, advanced from northwestern Virginia through the forests which separated the Monongahela Valley from the settlements along the tributaries of the Great Kanawha. The strength of the Confederates had meanwhile been greatly increased by the arrival of General

[27] O. R., Series I, vol. ii, pp. 202-248, passim.
[28] O. R., Series I, vol. ii, p. 197.
[29] O. R., Series I, vol. ii, p. 288.

John B. Floyd with his army which had been raised for the protection of the railroad leading into Tennessee. There was, however, a great deal of jealousy between Wise and Floyd. The former, being inferior in rank, was unwilling that the two armies should be combined. The result was that Rosecrans easily defeated Floyd and advanced far up the valley before the arrival of Confederate reinforcements and the approach of winter led to a postponement of further operations.[30]

The results of the campaigns were important from a political standpoint. The Union men in all parts of western Virginia were relieved of the danger of interference by the state authorities, and were enabled freely to carry out their plans for the establishment of a new government within the Union. The States' Rights party were completely silenced. A judge who had previously declared that attempts to divide the State constituted treason, now issued a proclamation that, the Constitution being the supreme law of the land, the people of western Virginia might refuse obedience to the state authorities and set up a new government if they liked. He called upon the secessionists to go east of the mountains and leave the people of northwestern Virginia in peace. For the most part the active leaders of the Southern party left hurriedly on the approach of the troops. The great bulk of the people, on the other hand, greeted effusively the coming of the Union soldiers, regarding them as deliverers. There was little disorder, and there were comparatively few arrests; for the troops, acting under McClellan's reminder that they were "in a country of friends, not of enemies," abstained from retaliatory measures. Only the most outspoken seces-

[30] *O. R.*, Series I, vol. v, pp. 115-119; 122-127; 128-165.

sionists were made prisoners and compelled to give a parole not to fight against the United States.

In the former Whig counties of the Kanawha Valley, where the majority had accepted the results of the state election, the coming of the troops checked active measures to support the Confederacy. Local officials who had been active in securing recruits and in voting supplies for the Southern armies were deprived of their offices, and Union men were appointed to act for the time being under the military authorities. After the first few months of the war, Confederate enlistments practically ceased. For the remainder of the struggle, most of the formerly active secessionists took a position of neutrality.[31] On the other hand, the Union party steadily gained in strength. Having been released from the necessity of giving outward support to the state authorities, they formed local organizations to promote the cause of the Union, and later joined the people of northwestern Virginia in throwing off the yoke of eastern domination.

Meanwhile the political movement in the northwestern counties had proceeded according to the plans of the first Wheeling convention. Twenty-eight members of the House of Delegates who were elected on May 23rd signified their intention to take part in the second convention at Wheeling rather than sit in the General Assembly at Richmond. Five members of the State Senate did likewise. On June 4th a special election was held at which the people chose two delegates for each member which a county was entitled to send to the lower house of the General Assembly. The object in thus constituting the convention was to secure a body which could

[31] Wise to Lee, Aug. 1, 1861. *O. R.*, Series I, vol. ii, pp. 1011-1012; Woodson, *op. cit.*, p. 232.

speak authoritatively concerning the future relations of the people to the government at Richmond and to the government of the United States. From the standpoint of practical politics, it is difficult to see how the convention could have been better constituted to carry out its purpose. The delegates had a direct mandate from the people on the question at issue; so, in a way, had the members of the lower house, who had been elected on May 23rd; and their presence, with the senators, gave the body a conservative character which made it less likely to act hastily. From the standpoint of legality the problem presented great difficulties. Under the constitution and the laws of Virginia the convention was, of course, an illegal and revolutionary body. The people were, however, acting under the Constitution of the United States. Since the adoption of the ordinance of secession had deprived them of the regular means of carrying it into effect, they found it necessary to provide temporarily an agency that could act for them. Under the circumstances, their makeshift expedient was probably the best that could have been devised. Thirty-four counties, containing nearly four-fifths of the population of the Trans-Alleghany section, sent delegates, making the convention large enough and representative enough to command respect.

The convention, assembling on June 11th, at once began the consideration of the future relations of the people to the State of Virginia. As in the first convention at Wheeling, there were propositions advanced looking toward the formation of a new State. But the leaders, having previously agreed upon a course of action, threw the whole weight of their influence against the proposals. One of their number declared that the business of the convention was not "to create a State, but to save one. . . . Let us save Virginia, and then save the Union; for the banner we are lifting up here will be the banner for the salvation of the country." [32]   The sentiment was reiterated by Francis H. Pierpont, who asserted that putting down the rebellion and lending a helping hand to the national government in the maintenance of constitutional liberty were of vastly greater importance to the world than the formation of a new State out of Virginia at this time.   He proposed instead that the state government be reorganized.   In an elaborate constitutional argument he showed that, although there was no legal justification for the creation of a new State, there was complete warrant for the people, acting under the authority of the Constitution of the United States, to set up a new government in place of the one at Richmond which, he said, had vacated its authority.   Upon the President and the Congress was expressly imposed the duty of guaranteeing to each State a republican form of government.   In carrying out this duty, they had discretion to determine what a republican form of government was.   And if the people of western Virginia should organize a state government to act under the authority of the Constitution, he thought there would be no question but that recognition would be given to it.   In a similar situation that had arisen in Rhode Island, the President, by recognizing one government, had compelled the other to cease exercising any authority; and the Supreme Court had affirmed the legality of his action. [33] Pierpont therefore recommended a postponement of the project to create a new State and the concentration of

[32] *Journal,* p. 123.
[33] In the case of Luther *vs.* Borden, 7 Howard 1.

attention upon ways and means to restore the government of Virginia.[34] His speech was effective in securing
the support of practically every member of the convention for reorganization.

In pursuance of the plans of the leaders, Carlile had
already proposed a "Declaration of the People of Virginia," modeled upon the Declaration of Independence.
In it he asserted that the convention at Richmond had
abused its powers and, with the connivance or active aid
of the executive, had usurped other powers to the injury
of the people. By "pretended ordinances" it had required the people to separate from the Union and wage
war against the United States. It had attempted to
transfer the allegiance of the people to an illegal confederacy of rebellious States. It had attempted to place
the whole military force under that confederacy. It
had instituted, with the governor, a reign of terror to
suppress the free expression of the will of the people,
making elections a mockery and a fraud. It had begun
a war by the seizure of the property of the United States.
And it had attempted to bring the allegiance of the people to the United States into direct conflict with their
subordinate allegiance to the State. Because of these
and other acts, the declaration asserted that the government of Virginia should be reorganized; that all the acts
of the convention and the executive tending to separate
the State from the United States, or to carry on war,
were without authority and void; and that the offices of
all who adhered to the convention and the executive were
vacated.[35] The declaration received the unanimous

[34] The entire address may be found in the appendix to the *Journal*,
p. 159.
[35] *Journal*, pp. 86-87.

approval of the convention on June 17th. After the
roll had been called a delegate remarked that the number who had voted was the same as the number of sign-
ers of the Declaration of Independence. Another delegate recalled that the date was the anniversary of the
battle of Bunker Hill.[36]

The next step was to provide for filling the offices
which had just been declared vacated, and to pass ordinances to meet the situation which had arisen as a result
of the illegal action of the convention at Richmond. On
June 19th the convention adopted an ordinance for the
reorganization of the state government. It was provided that the governor and other important officers
should be appointed by the convention to continue in
office for six months, or until their successors should be
elected by the people; that the legislature should consist
of the loyal members of the existing General Assembly,
together with others who should be elected to fill vacancies; and that all officers of the State should take an
oath to support the Constitution and the laws of the
United States. A special session of the legislature was
called to meet on July 1st.[37] The style of the new government was to be "The Restored Government of Virginia," and the seal was to be the seal of the State of
Virginia, with the addition of the words "Liberty and
Union." Other ordinances were passed authorizing the
apprehension of suspicious persons in time of war, recognizing the constitutional duty of the governor to call out
the militia on the requisition of the President of the
United States, and providing for the collection of the

[36] Hall, p. 318.
[37] *Ordinances of the Convention Assembled at Wheeling on June 11,
1861,* pp. 40-41.

revenues, together with other matters of lesser importance. After having elected the officers of the Restored Government, the convention adjourned until August 6th.

The choice of the convention for the office of governor fell upon Francis H. Pierpont [38] by a unanimous vote. He was a native of northwestern Virginia, having been born in Monongalia County in 1814. Largely through his own efforts he had prepared himself for college, and had been graduated from Allegheny College in 1839. Afterward he had taught school for two years, including a year in Mississippi, where he had an opportunity to observe the plantation system at its worst. Returning to western Virginia, he had become a leading attorney and a manufacturer. In politics he had been a Whig until the failure of the party to deal effectively with the question of slavery, when he had gone over to the Republicans. In the campaign of 1860, he was active as a candidate for presidential elector, with, however, extremely disappointing results. The party ticket received but one vote in his own county. During the winter and spring of 1861 he took a leading part in organizing the resistance of the people of northwestern Virginia to the authorities at Richmond. In the conventions his course was marked by shrewd common sense. He impressed himself upon other delegates as a man of extraordinary political ability.[39]

There may have been people in 1861 who believed that the chief reason for the existence of the Restored Government of Virginia was to provide a means for the formation of a new State; but Pierpont was not one of them.

---

[38] The spelling used here is the one adopted by him in his later life. In official documents of the period the name appears as "Peirpoint."

[39] Miller and Maxwell, *op. cit.*, vol. ii, pp. 418-419.

He immediately entered upon his duties with a zeal and determination that no obstacles could overcome. Having established his office in the United States customs house at Wheeling, he sought the recognition of the President for his government by telegraphing that the civil authorities of Virginia were confronted by a conspiracy that could not be put down with the means at their disposal. He therefore requested the aid of the national government, signing his message, "Pierpont, Governor." A few days later, he received a letter from President Lincoln addressed to "Francis H. Pierpont, Governor of Virginia," in which authority was conferred to organize regiments and commission officers for the military service of the United States.[40] This was the first formal recognition of the Restored Government.

Having obtained legal sanction for his government, the next most important problem which the new governor faced was that of obtaining public funds. The treasury was empty. The funds of the State of Virginia were under the control of the treasurer at Richmond. Nothing daunted, Pierpont met the most immediate needs of his government by giving his personal note for $10,000. He then looked about for other sources of revenue. There was then in the vaults of the Exchange Bank at Weston the sum of $27,000 which had been appropriated by the General Assembly for the erection of an insane asylum at that place. Fearing that it would be withdrawn and used for the support of the Confederate armies, he sent an officer, who secured possession of it. The amount was used to meet ordinary expenses until it could be replaced out of taxes. He then turned to the

[40] I am indebted to Governor Pierpont's daughter, Mrs. W. H. Siviter of Pittsburgh, Pa., for this information.

national government, and presented a claim for $40,000, which was due to the State of Virginia as its share of the proceeds from the sale of public lands since 1841. The amount was duly paid.[1] By strict economy he made these funds cover the expenses of the government until the taxes were paid in.

Upon the meeting of the General Assembly, Governor Pierpont transmitted a message in which he recommended the most complete support to the national government. To this end, he asked for the enactment of a law for the apprehension of suspicious persons, and for the election of senators to fill the places of R. M. T. Hunter and John Y. Mason, who had withdrawn from the Congress and were then actively participating in the government of the Confederate States. He also recommended a redistricting of the State to conform to the census of 1860. As to purely state affairs, he urged that the taxes should not be increased at that time in order, probably, that he might gain the support of those who suspected that the establishment of the Restored Government would mean an increase in their private expenses; and he promised to exercise the most rigid economy in the administration of the State.[2]

These recommendations were favorably received by the legislature, which loyally coöperated with their governor. The necessary authority to carry on the government in time of war was provided. To fill the vacancies in the Senate, the legislature chose John S. Carlile and Waitman T. Willey, both of whom were admitted after a brief and unimportant contest. The House of Repre-

[1] Lewis, *History of West Virginia*, pp. 369-372.
[2] Moore's *Rebellion Record*, vol. ii, pp. 161-162.

THE "RESTORATION" OF VIRGINIA

sentatives had already accepted the credentials from Pierpont of the members of Congress and had allowed them to take their seats. The admission of members from Virginia by both houses completed the recognition of the Restored Government.

From the time he had entered upon his duties, Pierpont had been engaged in raising troops for the Union army—a work that was not immediately recognized by the War Department. The response of volunteers from western Virginia in the beginning had been disappointing to the people of the North, who had doubtless expected that many men would leave their homes in an uncertain and troubled time to join the army. Unofficial observers had reported that many of the able-bodied population remained at home while soldiers from other States fought their battles for them;[43] and General McClellan had expressed the opinion that but few of the troops thus far raised in Virginia were really Virginians.[44] Yet less than six weeks after he took the office of governor, Pierpont had ten regiments ready, all but one of which are shown by the muster rolls to have been composed of residents of Virginia. On August 1st, he wrote to Senator Carlile complaining that no definite call for troops had been received by him. He requested him to obtain an order from the War Department for eight regiments of infantry and two of cavalry.[45] By the end of the year 1861 western Virginia was credited with having furnished 12,757 men, when its quota was only 8,497.[46] The record of the people in this respect was better than that of sev-

---

[43] McGregor, p. 245.
[44] O. R., Series I, vol. lii, part i, p. 157.
[45] O. R., Series III, vol. i, p. 378.
[46] O. R., Series III, vol. i, p. 384, note.

eral Northern States, and is the more remarkable because
of the fact that many men of military age had joined the
armies of the South.

In addition, Pierpont secured the formation of a company, or companies, of home guards in many counties,
which, with the help of volunteer troops, succeeded more
than passing well in establishing order and insuring
domestic tranquillity over a great part of western Virginia. He reorganized the civil authorities in several
counties, infusing into the new officers his own spirit of
loyalty and determination. Conducting his administration as far as possible as if the times were normal, he won
the support of many citizens whose sentiments had been
doubtful. From every standpoint he proved himself to
be almost an ideal chief executive. His extraordinary
energy and capacity in establishing a successful government during the stress of civil war and his effective aid
to the national government entitle him to a place second
only to that of Morton, Yates and Andrews among the
great war governors. The Union men of Virginia had at
last found a worthy leader.

The stand taken by the people of western Virginia
had a profound influence upon the result of the war.
Their adherence to the Union diminished the potential
military strength of the Southern Confederacy by not
less than forty thousand men, and reduced the territory
over which the state authorities at Richmond exercised
jurisdiction by about two-fifths. It deprived the Confederate armies of the advantage of defending the line of
the Ohio River, where they would doubtless have had
opportunities to break the communications between the
East and the West by short raids toward Lake Erie. The
Union armies, on the other hand, gained thirty thousand

men, all fighting to defend their homes against invasion. But this, after all, was a relatively slight advantage. Western Virginia formed a mountainous buffer district protecting Ohio and Pennsylvania, and enabling them to concentrate their whole military resources for invasions of the South. Its position, indeed, determined the strategy of the Union armies; for the War Department was enabled to attack both flanks of the Confederacy, and still threaten the center by raids through western Virginia. Through their control of the Baltimore and Ohio Railroad—the only direct line connecting Washington with Cincinnati and St. Louis—they could transfer their troops from one flank to the other much more easily than the Confederates could. Its possession, secured through the loyalty of the people of western Virginia, was easily worth an army. Furthermore, the example of western Virginia had a great influence upon the neighboring border States, particularly Maryland. In the early days of the war there were in that State some secessionists who urged that Maryland should follow Virginia. Replying, John P. Kennedy asked pointedly, "Which Virginia?" For there were then, he said, two Virginias, one rich in mineral wealth, friendly to Maryland capital, and the guardian of Maryland's railroad to the West; the other having only a sentimental tie with Maryland and always jealous of the material prosperity of the State.[47] These considerations were doubtless of great weight in influencing the people of the State to support the Union. In the State of Kentucky also, which for a time was almost equally balanced between the Union and the Confederacy, the effect of the early and decided action of the people of

[47] See his pamphlet "An Appeal to Maryland," reprinted in Moore's *Rebellion Record*, vol. i, pp. 368-373.

western Virginia must have been extremely great. Their attitude may also have been the inspiration for their kinsmen in the mountainous regions of North Carolina, Tennessee, Alabama and Georgia to resist the Confederate authorities.

The secession of Virginia was a terrible blow to the cause of the Union. That it was not decisive was due in large measure to the resistance of the western part of the State.

CHAPTER VIII

ARMED INTERVENTION IN MISSOURI

Though a conflict between the sections had been expected for months, and though men in public life had long calculated the measures to be taken by the border States if hostilities should begin, the actual outbreak of the war came as a crushing blow that stunned and dismayed the people of Missouri. Only a comparatively small proportion of the population had definitely aligned themselves in advance. For the most part the people had clutched at the straws of conciliation and compromise, and had hoped against hope that some arrangement would be made to avert the threatened disaster. Faced with disagreeable alternatives, they had attempted to take a middle course and await developments. The firing on Fort Sumter and the call for troops brought them scarcely nearer to a decision. There was no motive of defense against possible invasion, such as had caused the people of the South and of the border free States to take a determined stand; nor was there a motive of resistance to the aggressions of a sectional group within the State such as had driven the people of western Virginia to act quickly. The people of Missouri felt themselves under no immediate necessity to take sides. Public opinion acquitted President Lincoln of the charge of coercion in sending the expedition to relieve Fort Sumter, placing the blame for the beginning of hostilities on the Confederates. At the same time the people could not believe otherwise than that the remote causes of the war were the intemperate agitation of the abolitionists, their assistance to fugitive slaves, and their denial to slaveholders of the right, upheld by a decision of the Supreme Court, to take their slaves into the territories. Feeling as they did, it is not strange that the people shrank from plunging into a war which would inevitably be more horrible to them than to the people of either North or South, since it would array neighborhood against neighborhood, family against family, and brother against brother.

There were a few sections of the State where, in contrast to the whole, a clarification of opinion seems to have taken place. In the southeastern counties and in the extreme western portion of the State, along the Kansas border, the people for the most part aligned themselves with the pro-Southern party. The former section, like western Kentucky, was dependent on the commerce down the river. The popular mode of thought was that of the South. A declaration by Judge Albert Jackson that no lawyer could practice in his court without renewing his oath of allegiance to the United States provoked an uprising in which the mob took possession of the courthouse and prevented a session from being held.[1] In the other section were the "border ruffians" who had had bloody conflicts with the free soil settlers in Kansas, and who had only recently suffered from the raids of plundering "jayhawkers." [2] They favored the cause of the Confederacy because they hated Northern men, not because they had a quarrel with the United States. But

[1] Peckham, p. 116.
[2] *Vide* the *Missouri Historical Review*, vol. ii, p. 61.

even in this section, wherever the people were gathered in towns rather than scattered on exposed farms, wherever the interests were commercial rather than agricultural, the sentiment was divided. Military organizations were formed in St. Joseph by both Union and Confederate sympathizers, the former being more numerous, the latter being better armed. In the early days of the war a conflict between them would probably have occurred but for the establishment of a truce.[3]

In the rich slaveholding counties along the Missouri River popular sentiment was decidedly opposed to going into the war, especially on the side of the South, because it was feared that the value of all the slave property would be destroyed by an invasion from the North. Jefferson City was reported early in May as being so strongly for the Union that Governor Jackson refused to have the citizens organized into militia companies.[4] Around Lexington, also, nationalist sentiment was in the ascendancy. The same is true of Sedalia, where the most prominent slaveholder declared that he would offer his negroes at "three bits a dozen" to the slaveholders if they had brought on the war.[5] Throughout the southwestern part of the State the unionists were more numerous than their opponents, though there were frequent complaints that they were suffering from the attacks of lawless bands of secessionists which they could not resist because they lacked arms.

In the city of St. Louis the most noteworthy change following the outbreak of the war was in the outward

[3] John R. Atkinson to the Secretary of War, May 2, 1861, *O. R.*, Series I, vol. i, p. 679; Col. E. S. Miles to Townsend, Apr. 30, 1861, *O. R.*, Series I, vol. i, p. 677.
[4] Peckham, p. 170.
[5] Samuel B. Harding, *Life of George R. Smith*, p. 317.

attitude of the pro-Southern party. From being noisy and turbulent in their advocacy of secession, they became, to all appearances, the most quiet and orderly portion of the population.[6] Most of the people continued to support the national government, though leading citizens looked with deep regret at the ruinous prospects for the trade down the Mississippi, and deplored the disruption of the Union, which, they thought, could never be restored by war.[7] In other words, the support which the majority of the people gave to the national government was passive, and their attitude here, as in other parts of Missouri, amounted practically to neutrality.

In the first few weeks of indecision following the outbreak of the war, the policy of armed neutrality found considerable support as a way out of the difficulty. It was put forward almost simultaneously in Maryland, Kentucky and Missouri as a last desperate effort to save the Union without bloodshed. The advocates of the scheme proposed that the border States should arm themselves and refuse permission to all hostile forces to cross their territories. By thus keeping the belligerents separated, they hoped to prevent further conflicts from occurring, and they would be in a position to force the two headstrong sections to mediate their differences and join the mediators in restoring the Union.

It seems hardly worth while to point out the inconsistencies of the proposal or the impossibility of carrying it out. It would have made the South independent by guaranteeing it from attack. It would have been wholly unacceptable to the North, now thoroughly aroused, if

[6] C. Gibson to Bates, Apr. 22, 1861, *O. R.*, Series I, vol. i, p. 672.

[7] *Vide* the Diary of General Ethan Allen Hitchcock, *Fifty Years in Camp and Field*, p. 430.

only for the reason that it would have left the national capital to be protected only by the slender forces of Maryland. It could not have prevented an invasion of the South, since a wide expanse of Virginia abutted upon Ohio and Pennsylvania, and every seaport in the Confederacy was open to attack from the fleet. The objections might be multiplied. The importance of the movement lies in the fact that it was strongly supported by the people of the border States. Among its advocates were such influential leaders as Governor Hicks of Maryland, Governor Magoffin of Kentucky, ex-Governors Stewart and Price of Missouri, and Colonel Alexander Doniphan, the dashing raider of the Mexican War. It was the natural sequel to the earlier proposals of compromise and conciliation, a straw at which the people clutched in their desire to preserve the Union without bloodshed. At the best, it was only a temporary measure, providing a stopping place for public opinion in its natural drift from proposals of compromise to active and whole-hearted support of the Union. If left to themselves, the people would soon have seen its fallacies and abandoned it. Unfortunately they were not allowed time for quiet reflection. The leaders of both the Union and the secessionist parties in Missouri strove to force a decision favorable to their own causes.

Governor Jackson was the first to act. In response to the President's call for four regiments of militia, he wrote: "Your requisition, in my judgment, is illegal, unconstitutional, and revolutionary in its object, inhuman and diabolical, and cannot be complied with. Not one man will the State of Missouri furnish to carry on any such unholy crusade." [8] This bold defiance was no doubt

[8] *O. R.*, Series III, vol. i, p. 83.

intended to serve as a rallying cry for the people of Missouri to join with the governor in bringing about secession and active participation in the war on the side of the South. Probably the same consideration had been in his mind when he called a special session of the legislature to begin on May 5th. Remembering the former tardy disposition of the members, he now sought to place the State in such a position that they would have no other recourse than to aid in bringing on war with the United States. Following the example of Governor Letcher, he determined to seize the property of the United States which lay within the borders of Missouri, and then point to the existence of war as an accomplished fact. On April 20th a company of militia from Clay and Jackson counties seized the little United States arsenal at Liberty and appropriated thirteen hundred stand of small arms to the use of the State.[9] With a view to securing possession of the much greater prize in the arsenal at St. Louis, he ordered an encampment of the militia from the surrounding district just outside the city. Success in this undertaking would have gone far toward the accomplishment of his ulterior purpose.

In the meantime the Union leaders had been at work with a degree of enthusiasm and energy that matched the governor's. They clearly underestimated the strength of the Union party in the rural districts, and they showed a disposition to distrust the expressions of the conservative element within the city. Being unwilling to confide their cause to the final judgment of the people in either State or city, they adopted the policy of meeting the governor's preparations with equally thoroughgoing measures of their own. In other words, they determined to

[9] Moore's *Rebellion Record,* vol. i, p. 36.

fight fire with fire. On the day after Jackson made it clear that he would furnish no troops for the Union army Francis P. Blair, Jr., telegraphed the War Department that if an order to muster the regiments were sent to Captain Lyon, the requisition would be filled within two days.[10] At the same time Lyon wrote to Governor Yates, requesting him to obtain authority to hold in readiness for service in Missouri the six regiments which Illinois was to furnish.[11] Nothing came of the first communication, though the second was attended to. Without considering the effect that the appearance of Northern troops on the soil of Missouri would have upon the people, the War Department directed that two or three regiments be sent to support the garrison in the arsenal.[12] Fortunately, the order was revoked before it could be carried out, owing to the protests of the more moderate Union men that its execution would have a disastrous effect on public opinion.[13] Another move of Lyon, in his extreme solicitude for the safety of the arsenal, brought upon him the displeasure of his department commander, General Harney. Lyon had begun the practice of sending patrols beyond the walls of the arsenal to make sure that the secessionists were not collecting in force to attack it by night. Fearing that this and other measures would unduly prejudice the people, Harney ordered Lyon henceforth to keep his men within the arsenal, and to issue no arms to the volunteers in St. Louis without his express permission.[14]

Harney's course brought him under the severe con-

[10] Blair to Cameron, Apr. 18, 1861, *O. R.*, Series I, vol. i, p. 669.
[11] *O. R.*, Series I, vol. i, p. 667.
[12] *O. R.*, Series I, vol. i, p. 669.
[13] Anderson, *op. cit.*, pp. 82-83.
[14] *O. R.*, Series I, vol. i, p. 668.

demnation of the unconditional unionist leaders, who
accused him of being lukewarm in the cause of his government, if not actually disloyal. It was charged by
some that he was under the influence of his relatives and
associates, most of whom were said to have been either
avowed secessionists or advocates of neutrality. Others,
admitting that his loyalty was above question, declared
that, being old and a slave of routine, he should not have
had such an important command at a critical time.[15] The
charges contained just enough of truth to make them
appear a plausible explanation of his conduct. But a
careful examination of his record and of his administration of affairs in St. Louis shows him in an entirely different light. Born in 1801, he had entered the army at
the age of eighteen, afterward earning distinction
through his dashing bravery in numerous Indian wars.
In the Mexican War, though his record had been marred
by his insubordination to General Scott, the cloud was
entirely removed at the battle of Cerro Gordo, where his
magnificent cavalry charge turned the tide of battle in
favor of the American army. Some time later he had
sought and obtained the command of the Department
of the West because St. Louis was his home. He had
married an heiress to the great Mullanphy estate, thus
gaining *entrée* to the best social circles of the city. His
fortunate connections and his long residence in St. Louis
placed him in an excellent position to form a correct estimate of the opinions of the conservative classes
throughout the State, and to influence a most important
group toward the support of the Union. From the begin-

[15] M. Blair to Ben Farrar, May 17, 1861, quoted by L. U. Reavis,
The Life and Military Services of General William Selby Harney,
p. 377; Nicolay and Hay, *op. cit.*, vol. iv, p. 198.

ning of the war, he was active in opposing the secession of the State. He expressed better than most of his contemporaries the ruinous results to the future prosperity of St. Louis and the State which would follow a connection with the Southern Confederacy. At all times he declared his firm attachment to the Union and his belief that his allegiance to his State was subordinate to that which he owed to the national government.[16] There was little in his record to indicate that he was either a superannuated slave of routine or an indifferent supporter of the cause of the Union.

Harney differed from the other Union men, but after all chiefly as to the best method to be pursued. From his careful study of conditions, he had come to the conclusion that no necessity existed for firing a single gun in Missouri.[17] Only time was needed, he thought, to bring the people to a realization of the position they should take. Shortly after the beginning of the war he received information that Governor Jackson intended to seize the heights above the arsenal and capture it by artillery fire. There appearing to be no immediate danger, he transmitted his information to the War Department and asked for instructions, instead of risking an offense to local pride by occupying the heights.[18] His policy for the time being was to give protection indiscriminately to all citizens, and to curb unnecessary and provocative measures on the part of both the extreme groups.[19] He wished especially to avoid arming the Union volunteers at this time—a measure upon which Blair and Lyon had set their hearts—because, being Ger-

[16] Reavis, pp. 388-392.
[17] *Idem*, p. 367.
[18] Harney to Townsend, Apr. 16, 1861, *O. R.*, Series I, vol. i, p. 666.
[19] Reavis, p. 367.

mans, they were greatly feared by the remainder of the population.

When the Union leaders found it impossible to overcome Harney's opposition, they prepared to accomplish their purposes by devious means. Lyon proposed to circumvent his superior by arming and mustering in the home guards surreptitiously by night; and Blair exerted his influence with Harney's superiors to have him removed or his orders countermanded. To Governor Curtin of Pennsylvania, he wrote, urging him to secure an order from Cameron for the arming of the home guards. "Our friends," he said, "distrust Harney very much. He should be superseded immediately." He wrote also to his brother, the Postmaster-General, asking that General Wool or some other officer whose loyalty was unquestioned be assigned to the Department of the West.[20] The result of his correspondence was an order, on April 21st, relieving Harney and summoning him to Washington to explain his conduct. The command of the department in the interval was given to Lyon against Harney's protest.

The new commander proceeded with alacrity to carry out his orders to "arm loyal citizens, protect property and execute the laws," by seizing the heights west of the arsenal and by mustering into service four regiments of home guards to take the place of the militia that Governor Jackson had refused to furnish. Besides, he organized a regiment of "Missouri Volunteers," and secured permission to form five regiments of "United States Reserves" as an additional protection for the city.[21] Still being dissatisfied with these precautions, he secured

[20] Peckham, pp. 109-110.
[21] John McElroy, *The Struggle for Missouri*, pp. 64-65.

through Blair's influence, an order directing him to declare martial law on the advice of the Union Committee of Safety." His next step was practically to empty the arsenal of arms and transfer them to Illinois for the use of the Federal army. Governor Yates, having obtained an order for ten thousand stand of arms, sent Captain James H. Stokes to sign for them and convey them across the river. His arrival created a great deal of excitement in the city, since the purpose of his visit was well known. In order to disperse a persistent crowd which had gathered about the arsenal gates, Lyon had a few boxes of old flintlock muskets sent up the river bank as if to be loaded on a steamboat at the levee. The crowd at once followed and seized them. At midnight a steamboat dropped anchor before the arsenal, and the work of loading began. The ten thousand muskets for which the requisition was made, together with a large quantity of ammunition, were soon placed on board, when Captain Stokes suggested that it might be wise to empty the arsenal of its surplus stores. Lyon, not being a man to wait for higher authority at any time, thereupon assumed the responsibility for ordering the transfer of eleven thousand additional stand of arms and other equipment. So great was the weight of the stores that the steamboat at first stuck fast in the mud and could not be moved. It was necessary to shift a part of the cargo to the stern in order to release the vessel. It then proceeded without mishap to Alton. Upon its arrival the fire bells were rung, and the citizens turned out to help transfer the precious cargo to a train, which carried it to a place of safety in the interior." The muskets which were left in the arsenal

22 *O. R.*, Series I, vol. i, p. 675.
23 Nicolay and Hay, vol iv, pp. 198-199.

were soon afterward issued to home guards. The course
of Lyon was approved by General Scott, who gave permission to transfer additional arms and stores to Illinois.[24]
Though of doubtful expediency from a political standpoint, these measures placed the Union forces in a
greatly improved position to meet the threatened coup
of the state authorities.

Governor Jackson had meanwhile chafed at his helplessness to seize the arsenal. He wasted some time in
vain regrets that "Governor Price's submission convention" had not taken the State out of the Union in February when arms could easily have been procured by the
seizure of the arsenal.[25] Then, seeking the advice of
General Frost, he found that the reduction of the arsenal
would be impossible without artillery. The state forces
then had no serviceable cannon, but Jackson, undaunted,
sent Captains Greene and Duke of the St. Louis Minute
Men to obtain them from the Confederate government.
Their mission proved successful. President Davis readily
gave them two twelve-pounders and two thirty-two
pounders which had been seized when the militia of
Louisiana captured the arsenal at Baton Rouge. As the
commissioners left for the South, Jackson completed his
arrangements for a week's encampment of the militia in
St. Louis. He had doubtless intended to locate the camp
on the heights west of the arsenal; but Lyon's seizure
of the position compelled General Frost to choose
another site.[26]

On May 3rd seven hundred of the state militia, consisting principally of Minute Men from St. Louis, went

[24] *O. R.*, Series I, vol. i, p. 675.
[25] Jackson to J. W. Tucker, in the *Collections* of the Missouri State
Historical Society, vol. ii, pp. 21-22.
[26] Snead, p. 163.

into camp at Lindell's Grove in the western outskirts of
the city. Though they had already received some military training, having guarded the Kansas border against
the incursions of the "jayhawkers" after the election of
1860, their effectiveness as a fighting force was doubtful.
Certainly they would not have been a match for the
United States regulars then stationed in the city. When
account is further taken of the ten thousand volunteers
then fully armed in St. Louis, and of the presence of
Kansas, Iowa and Illinois volunteers on three of the borders of the State, the notion of their being able to capture the arsenal, even by siege operations, became a gross
absurdity. They could hardly receive help from the Confederate States, since neither Arkansas nor Tennessee
had yet seceded. Nor could they obtain reinforcements
quickly from the interior of the State, since the other
militia districts had not yet been organized.[27] An appeal
for volunteers in Missouri would probably have resulted
in bringing in more men to defend the arsenal than to
capture it. To make the likelihood of an attack appear
even less, it may be pointed out that the commanding
officer and many of the soldiers were not active secessionists at all, but advocates of armed neutrality.[28]

Though Governor Jackson no doubt intended that the
militia should attempt to capture the arsenal, there is
good reason to believe that General Frost did not share
his purpose. It is hardly possible that he, a graduate of
West Point and an experienced soldier, should have considered seriously warlike measures of any kind. The site
he chose for "Camp Jackson" was poorly adapted for
defense. It was surrounded on nearly all sides by hills.

[27] Snead, pp. 160-162.
[28] Lucian Carr, *Missouri, A Bone of Contention,* pp. 300-301.

It was open to cavalry charges in every direction. And it was within short marching distance of a Union force outnumbering his own troops by at least ten to one. Perhaps Frost, in selecting such a site, desired to impress upon the Union leaders his intention to make no hostile demonstration against them. That the selection of the site was not a ruse is fairly certain from the fact that no secret preparations took place, as would indubitably have been the case if hostilities had been contemplated. The encampment was open to the public at all times. It was a place to which the society folk of the city, who disdained to watch the drilling of the Germans, were in the habit of driving every day. No Confederate flag flew over it—only the flags of the United States and of Missouri. Officers and men alike had taken the usual oath to uphold the Constitution and the laws of the United States. As if these things were not sufficient evidences of his lack of belligerent intentions, Frost had previously offered to the Federal commanders his services and, if necessary, all the resources of the State of Missouri to secure the national government in the complete possession of all its property." Though perhaps this offer was not to be taken at its face value, it ought to have been accepted, as a matter of policy, until there were undoubted evidences of hostile intentions.

Despite these considerations, Lyon was convinced that Camp Jackson was neither harmless nor peaceable. According to his biographer he regarded it as "a fearful menace, which by prompt action would amount to no more than bravado, but if suffered to continue and grow, would become very shortly a source of serious trouble, and might result in terrible conflicts in the very streets

²⁹ *O. R.*, Series I, vol. iii, p. 6.

of the city." Probably a truer explanation of his attitude was that he was impatient that no blow had as yet been struck at slavery and secession, and he was anxious to make war upon both. With an intolerant disregard for the opinions of others, he declared that he wanted to make doubtful citizens become active supporters of the government "under the benignant influence of Union bayonets as readily as they would become active rebels under opposite pressure." [30] Because the commander of the camp and his men had not declared themselves unalterably for the Union, Lyon resolved to attack them, and then follow up the blow with movements of troops into the interior of the State, in order effectually to stamp out the secessionist movement.

On May 8th the steamer, *J. C. Swan,* arrived from New Orleans bringing for the state encampment cannon and powder disguised as marble and ale. Lyon wished to seize the shipment at the wharf, but was dissuaded by other leaders who thought it best to allow it to be taken to Camp Jackson, where it could be easily recovered by a United States marshal with a writ of replevin. When Lyon brought his proposal to attack Camp Jackson before the Committee of Safety, Blair and three other members approved it. The other two members, Glover and How, opposed it because they thought it unnecessary. If, they said, the camp was really a source of danger to the cause of the Union, that danger would be removed within two days when the time limit set for it by the laws of Missouri would expire; for there was then little likelihood that the legislature would authorize an extension. They would consent to an attack only in case General Frost declined to honor a writ

[30] Peckham, p. 137.

of replevin to gain possession of the property of the United States which had been taken from the arsenal at Baton Rouge. Lyon, who had previously visited the camp disguised as the aged mother-in-law of Francis P. Blair, Jr., had seen the arms piled up near the enclosure. He had furthermore noticed that two of the principal streets bore the names of "Davis" and "Beauregard." There was no doubt, he said, that the camp was a nest of traitors. After some discussion, he finally silenced the opposition by reminding the committee that General Harney would return on May 12th, after which time it would probably be impossible for the Union men to take any active measures to counteract those of the state government.[81] Though Glover still insisted that a United States marshal should be at the head of the attacking party, Lyon refused to adopt the suggestion because it might appear to be a ruse hardly consistent with the laws of war.[82] He was, moreover, not so much interested in the recovery of the military stores as in the capture of the state forces.

Information of the proposed attack soon reached Frost, who wrote to the Committee of Safety, assuring them that he knew nothing about the arms stacked outside his camp. They might take them if they wished. He also wrote to Lyon, repeating his former offer to assist him in preserving peace and order in the city, and asserting that he had no designs against the United States.[83] Lyon declined to receive the letter. On Friday, May 10th, the day on which the encampment would have broken up, several thousand Union troops moved upon Camp Jack-

---

[81] Peckham, pp. 140-141.
[82] Carr, p. 304.
[83] O. R., Series I, vol. iii, pp. 7-8.

son and surrounded it. Lyon then sent a note demanding the absolute surrender of the state forces on the grounds that most of them were avowed secessionists, and that they were acting under the orders of Governor Jackson. The commander of the camp could do no more than yield, protesting that he had never for a moment conceived that such an illegal demand would be made by an officer of the United States army.[34] The entire body were made prisoners of war. Instead of being paroled on the field, as might reasonably have been done, they were formed in column to be marched back to the city.

It is probable that the events of the day thus far would have had sufficiently unfortunate effects on the attitude of the native population of the city toward the Union; but the worst was still to come. The marching of the Federal troops toward Camp Jackson had attracted an immense amount of attention, and hundreds of people of all classes, men, women and children, had streamed out toward the camp to witness the proceedings. As the troops returned with their prisoners, the crowds lined both sides of the streets, hurling gibes at the volunteer forces. A little way out from the camp, the column was halted to allow the forming of the rear. The epithets grew in numbers and violence, especially around *"Die Schwarze Garde,"* who were dubbed "Dutch black-guards." As the volunteers remained silent at attention, the crowd was encouraged to begin throwing stones, and, according to the report authorized by Lyon, someone discharged a pistol at the troops. One volley was then sent into the crowd here, and the firing was taken up by other organizations without waiting for the

[34] Reavis, p. 359.

authorization of the commander. By the time that Lyon's order to cease firing had been transmitted, twenty-eight persons had been killed or mortally wounded. Among them were two women and three of the prisoners. Only one of the Union soldiers was killed outright, though the commander of the company that began the firing died the next day from his wounds. Many other persons were injured.[35]

There are residents of St. Louis who, in showing visitors over the city, point to the site of Camp Jackson as the place where Missouri was saved for the Union. It is impossible, of course, to state positively that their view is incorrect. No one can know what would have happened if the camp had been allowed to continue until the close of the day, or if the men had been allowed to go to their homes to spread secessionist propaganda and later to enlist with the armies of the South. But from the events which immediately followed the affair, one is forced to the conclusion that it was a political blunder of the first magnitude, which occasioned inestimably more damage to the cause of the Union than could have resulted from allowing it to continue. The capture of the seven hundred secessionists was dearly bought.

The occurrences of the day caused the most intense excitement the city had ever known. Everywhere the news was spread broadcast with many exaggerations. In every section of the city groups congregated, excitedly discussing the situation. A crowd which gathered at the Berthold mansion was dispersed by the police. But other crowds, swearing vengeance against the German population, raided gun stores and practically took possession

[35] Peckham, pp. 154-155; Violette, p. 344; Lyon to Thomas, May 11, 1861, *O. R.*, Series I, vol, iii, p. 4; Frost to Harney, pp. 7-8.

of the oldest and most important part of the city. Within the area bounded by Cass Avenue and Twelfth and Walnut streets, it was extremely dangerous for a Union man to appear in public. Several Germans were brutally murdered on the following night, and their bodies were left in prominent places as a warning to others.[36] To meet the situation, the civil authorities could do little or nothing. The mayor issued a proclamation closing the saloons and ordering all minors to stay indoors for three days, and all other citizens after nightfall; but the police were unable to maintain order or to check the panic in the minds of the people. General Lyon and the Committee of Safety, who had full power to declare martial law, and sufficient men to patrol the streets effectively, showed a strange helplessness. While the Fifth regiment of United States Reserves was marching through the streets, it was fired upon by citizens. The fire was returned, the conflict resulting in the deaths of two of the volunteers and four citizens; but this sort of activity on the part of the military was calculated rather to increase the disorder than otherwise. The German population, fully aroused by the excesses of the mob, threatened to retaliate.[37]

Intelligence that General Harney had returned from Washington on Saturday caused an increase in confidence among the better element of the population. On Sunday morning, however, the rumor gained circulation that Harney was powerless to maintain discipline among the German soldiers, who were reported to be preparing to plunder the city. A dreadful panic seized upon all classes. Gathering together a few valuables, they hastened to

[36] Peckham, p. 158.
[37] Peckham, pp. 162-163; Violette, p. 347.

leave by any means which they found at hand. Most of them fled into the country districts by train, in buggies and on horseback. Many others embarked on steamboats at the wharfs without caring whither they were bound, thinking only to escape from the doomed city.[38]

The panic was quickly stopped through the energetic measures which General Harney took shortly after his return to St. Louis. His first act was to order all the German troops out of the city, and to station United States regulars at various points whence they could be moved swiftly to all sections upon the appearance of disorder. The arrangement proved to be highly effective. The turbulent element who had armed themselves to avenge the massacre had no quarrel with the soldiers of the regular army; furthermore, they respected their ability to maintain order. Shortly afterward, they disappeared from the streets. Under Harney's supervision all gatherings were broken up, crime was rigidly suppressed, and a careful search for arms was made among the citizens, which resulted in the confiscation of twelve hundred rifled muskets and two small cannon. Small detachments of soldiers were sent to Potosi and De Soto, just outside the city, to break up parties of secessionists and seize the arms they had collected.[39] So great was the confidence in the justice of General Harney that most of the citizens who had fled during the panic returned and resumed their accustomed occupations.

In the interior of the State the people expressed their feelings of horror and resentment at the occurrences following the capture of Camp Jackson to as great a degree as the people of the city. The most exaggerated reports

[38] Peckham, pp. 182-183.
[39] Peckham, pp. 186-189.

of the murder of defenseless men, women and children in
the streets of St. Louis by an infuriated soldiery were
spread broadcast, with the result that in many sections
the people rose *en masse* with whatever arms they could
obtain, determined to march to the city and avenge the
slaughter.[40] Later reports caused a subsidence of popular passion. After Harney had restored order the blame
for the massacre was transferred by most persons from
the leaders of the unionist party to the Germans; but
the sentiment in favor of the Union was not again as
strong as it had been. Many who had been ardent supporters of the national government now refused to take
any active part; and hundreds, if not thousands, who
would soon have left the temporary shelter of armed
neutrality for the complete support of the cause of the
Union were precipitated into the camp of the secessionists.[41] Much of the later bitterness with which guerrilla
warfare was carried on in Missouri was probably due to
the feelings engendered by the occurrences at Camp
Jackson.

At the state capital, the first news of the capture of
the militia and the massacre which followed roused the
hitherto circumspect legislature to vengeful action. For
more than a week it had been engaged in debates on the
governor's military bill, which had led to nothing. The
unionist members who had procured the defeat of the
bill at the regular session were still active and watchful.
It seemed quite unlikely that it would become law. But
the report of the massacre changed everything. A scene
of the wildest excitement ensued. Within fifteen min-
utes after a semblance of order had been restored, both

[40] Switzler, *op. cit.*, pp. 356-357.
[41] Duke, p. 53; Violette, p. 350.

houses, rejecting every proposed amendment, had passed the bill and sent it to the governor for his signature.[41] A resolution that the executive should cultivate friendly relations with the Indians was passed without any reading at all.[42] At midnight, after the sitting had adjourned, a telegram was received stating that Lyon and two thousand men were on their way to Jefferson City to capture the governor and the legislature. After what had happened at St. Louis, the state authorities could hardly be blamed for giving the report credence. The bells were at once rung calling the legislature to meet in secret session, and many of the members came heavily armed in anticipation of an attack. Further measures were passed to increase the strength of the state administration for resistance. Within the next five days, the legislature authorized the expenditure of more than $2,000,000. All the money in the treasury was diverted to the military fund, and in addition, the governor was authorized to borrow $1,000,000 to arm and equip men. Further authorizations were to lease a foundry at Booneville for the manufacture of arms; to take over the railroads and telegraphs; to organize the military forces; and, as if these were not enough, "to take such measures as in his judgment he might deem necessary or proper to repel . . . invasion."[43] A resolution protesting against the affair at Camp Jackson was passed by a unanimous vote. Though some of the Union members objected to these measures, they were now in so great a minority that their opposition counted for nothing.

Governor Jackson entered upon his duties of organiz-

[41] Violette, pp. 348-350.
[42] Peckham, p. 167.
[43] Switzler, p. 315.

ing the military forces of the State with alacrity. For the position of major-general which had just been created he chose Sterling Price, a colonel in the Mexican War, a popular politician, a former governor, the president of the state convention, and one of Lyon's recent converts to secessionism. He had been regarded as the principal leader of the conservative faction of the Union party, and his withdrawal left a gap that was extremely difficult to fill. It is true that he had not before coöperated with Blair and the other Union leaders, partly because considerable enmity had existed between them during and after the struggle in which Benton had been ousted from the leadership of the Democratic party in the State;[45] and it is doubtful if they could ever have agreed upon a common policy. Nevertheless, the problems confronting the Union party were varied and difficult enough to have occupied the energies of both Blair and Price, working in different fields. Other prominent members of the conservative group who became members of the state military organization were ex-Governor Marmaduke, Richard T. Morrison and Thomas L. Snead.

In the first few weeks following the affair at Camp Jackson, General Harney seems to have assumed the leadership of the conservative party—at least, most of the measures to restore confidence in the unionist groups were taken by him. The situation was discouraging in the extreme. All the great work that had been done by the moderate unionists in combating the activities of the secessionists and in building up national loyalty seemed irretrievably lost. But Harney was not discouraged. Realizing that strong aversion to the Germans was the

[45] See the *Journal* of the Missouri House of Representatives, 1855, p. 11.

principal basis for the opposition to the cause of the Union, he proposed, in a conference with Blair, that the home guards should be disbanded, evidently not understanding that they had been legally mustered into the service of the United States.[46] When shown the orders from the War Department, he gave way. A little later he sought authority to form a regiment of Irishmen in St. Louis to "do away with the prejudice against the Government troops, which consist almost exclusively of Germans." [47]

Though Harney's course was far more liberal toward doubtful citizens than that of Blair and Lyon, it yet lacked a great deal of giving comfort to the secessionists. In a proclamation on May 14th, he upheld the act of his predecessor in breaking up Camp Jackson, and published all the information in his possession that would establish a suspicion of disloyalty on the part of the state troops. Referring to the recent acts of the legislature—"the result, no doubt of the temporary excitement that now pervades the public mind"—he declared that they could be regarded only as "an indirect secession ordinance," which could not be accepted by him. He served notice that he intended to maintain the authority of the Constitution of the United States within the scope of his command. "Missouri," he said, "must share the destiny of the Union. Her geographical position, her soil, productions, and in short, all her material interests, point to this result." [48] In order to counteract the activities of the secessionists who were arming in most sections outside the city of St. Louis, he asked the War Depart-

[46] Peckham, p. 184.
[47] Harney to Cameron, May 15, 1861, O. R., Series I, vol. iii, p. 373.
[48] Reavis, pp. 363-364.

ment to furnish guns to arm the loyal citizens, and requested that nine thousand volunteers from Iowa and Minnesota be placed under his command.[49]

The political problem of how best to deal with the state military establishment was one of extreme difficulty—much greater than the military problem involved. Harney would have had only to move the home guards and other volunteers under his command into the interior, and the organized state forces would easily have been routed. The advantage gained would, however, have been dearly bought; for the people would have resented the invasion of the Germans, and would have risen against them. The cause of the Union would thus probably have lost thousands of adherents among the conservatives, who now seemed once more to be turning toward it. If, on the other hand, Harney adopted the policy of inaction, the state forces would have time for organization, and the Union men in the interior would suffer for their loyalty from the depredations of irregular local bands. As a way out of the dilemma, Harney chose a middle course calculated to protect the Union men, and at the same time undermine the spirit which had caused some of the people to support the state government against the United States. He opened negotiations with General Price, informing him that the recent military bill was apparently opposed to the President's proclamation for the dispersal of armed bands hostile to the United States, and asking that he suspend its operation until its constitutionality could be determined by a competent tribunal.[50] In an interview between the two commanders which followed, Price agreed to preserve

[49] Harney to Townsend, *O. R.*, Series I, vol. iii, p. 374.
[50] Woodward, *op. cit.*, p. 274.

order throughout the State, directing his whole force to this end. Harney, on his part, declared that "this object being thus assured, he can have no occasion, as he has no wish, to make military movements which might otherwise create excitements and jealousies." [51]

On the whole, the agreement seemed to favor the cause of the Union. There can be little doubt of Price's good faith in making it. He discouraged the enlistment of troops under the military bill by sending to their homes the volunteers who reported at Jefferson City from other military districts; [52] and he did his best, under the watchful surveillance of Harney, to afford protection to all citizens of whatever partisan affiliation. His task was an extremely difficult one, owing to the unsettled conditions in the State. If he failed to curb the unlawful activities of secessionist sympathizers and give full protection to Union men, Harney had only to set in motion the Federal troops, who, under the circumstances, would hardly have been opposed by the great majority of the people. The effect of the agreement was to change Missouri from a position of hostility to the national government to one of armed neutrality—the same position that the State of Kentucky was allowed to occupy throughout the summer of 1861.

Though Harney's policy after the capture of Camp Jackson seems now to have been proper—even statesmanlike—it met with warm opposition at every point from the leaders of the radical Union party. On the day after the affair, Lyon wrote to the adjutant-general that "the authority of General Harney . . . embarrasses, in the most painful manner, the execution of the plans I had

[51] *O. R.*, Series I, vol. iii, p. 375.
[52] Carr, p. 310.

contemplated, and upon which the safety and welfare of
the Government, as I conceive, so much depend." [53] To
another correspondent, he declared: "The villainy of secessionism . . . seems to be taking comfort and consolation
now under the shelter of his authority." [54] Blair con-
curred, in general, with Lyon's opinion. "The agreement between Harney and General Price," he said, "gives
me great disgust and dissatisfaction to the Union men;
but I am in hopes we can get along with it, and think that
Harney will insist on its execution to the fullest extent,
in which case it will be satisfactory." [55] One other
Union leader opposed Harney from motives that are
rather questionable. Ben G. Farrar complained that
much of the government patronage went for the benefit
of the secessionists. "The government purchases," he
wrote, "must always be to the advantage of somebody,
and friends rather than enemies should be preferred. . . .
Can't you have General Harney sent away from here?" [56]

Among the conservative Union men, however, Harney's course was heartily approved. One of them, General ɛthan Allen Hitchcock, a native of Vermont, claims
to have written the Harney-Price agreement. [57] In order
that they might counteract the influence of Blair and
other radicals with the administration, they sent delegations of prominent men to Washington to present their
view of the situation and to ask that matters be left as
they were.

The controversy reached such proportions as to divide
the President's cabinet, Bates representing the conserva-

[53] *O. R.*, Series I, vol. iii, p. 9.
[54] Woodward, p. 260.
[55] *O. R.*, Series I, vol. iii, p. 376.
[56] Quoted by Reavis, p. 374.
[57] Hitchcock, *op. cit.*, p. 431.

tives and Blair acting as the spokesman of those who sought Harney's dismissal and his supersession in favor of Lyon. Cameron objected to the latter part of the plan because he considered Lyon too rash a man to be given such a responsible command.[58] The President, upon whom the final decision rested, hesitated to take any immediate action. He was apparently not satisfied that Harney's policy had been improper. It was, indeed, the same patient, conciliatory course that he himself had used in dealing with the South, and that he was then using in his relations with Maryland and Kentucky. He had, however, formed the habit of trusting the judgment of the Blairs in matters relating to Missouri, and rather reluctantly, he signed an order relieving Harney from his command. He apparently did not intend that the order should go into effect at once. It was transmitted to Francis P. Blair, Jr., to be delivered to Harney if an emergency should arise which, in his opinion, justified such an extreme action.[59] A day or two after the order had been issued, Lincoln wrote to Blair that he had become doubtful of its propriety, and that he was to deliver it only if he considered it "indispensable."[60]

The order did not reach Blair until after the Harney-Price agreement had been concluded, else, as he said, he would have delivered it then. With the order in his pocket, he felt free to point out the measures which Harney should take, even to the extent of practically trying to supervise his conduct. The Committee of Safety circularized the Union men in the interior, asking them to give information of the sentiment in their communities

[58] F. A. Dick to Ben Farrar, May 16, 1861, quoted by Reavis, pp. 374-375.

[59] Reavis, pp. 374-377.

[60] May 18, 1861; quoted by Nicolay and Hay, vol. iv, p. 217.

and to report any outrages that occurred against them. In reply, letters poured in from all sides giving the details of outrages and describing the terrible fear in which the Union men were living. Apparently most of the reports were not worthy of credence, being made up of rumors that were afterward proved to be false, or of inferences drawn from rumors and stated as facts.[61] Blair however brought the reports to Harney's attention and demanded that more aggressive measures be taken.

Harney was not inclined to give the reports much credence. He asked how it was possible for one man to persecute two, since the secessionists were in such a great minority almost everywhere.[62] But he promised to have Price carry out the terms of the agreement. The opportunity both to embarrass the state commander and to prepare the people for gradual intervention by the national government must have seemed to Harney too good to be passed over. He wrote to Price calling his attention to the reported persecutions and suggesting that it might be well to organize Union home guards in the interior. Referring also to reports that a force from Arkansas was about to cross the southern border of Missouri, he proposed to send a regiment of Federal troops to assist in driving them back.[63] The reply of Price was prompt. He stated that the reports had been greatly exaggerated; he thought he could preserve order; he advised against the formation of Union home guards because the arming of one portion of the population might lead to civil conflicts; and he promised to cause the troops from Arkansas to return at once.[64] His tacit

[61] Carr, pp. 310-311.
[62] Reavis, p. 373.
[63] *O. R.*, Series I, vol. iii, p. 378.
[64] *O. R.*, Series I, vol. iii, pp. 380-381.

admission of the right of the United States to send troops into the State and to organize home guards under the agreement opened the way for the gradual intervention which Harney must have begun soon.

Meanwhile the reports from the interior had been forwarded to Washington, where they inspired action altogether out of proportion to their value. The adju-- tant-general wrote to Harney curtly reminding him of his duty to stop outrages "summarily with the force under your command," and apprising him of the fact that the state authorities were not to be trusted."⁵ In reply, Harney gave an excellent justification of the conservative policy he had followed. He pointed out the fact that Missouri was becoming rapidly tranquilized. Though admitting that an aggressive policy might be more brilliant from a military standpoint, he declared that "it could not secure the results the Government seeks, viz: The maintenance of the loyalty now fully aroused in the State, and her firm security in the Union. I entertain the conviction that the agreement between myself and General Price will be carried out in good faith, but while entertaining this belief I shall watch carefully the movements of the State authorities. Any attempt at rebellion will be promptly met and put down."⁶⁶

On May 30th, before Harney's letter could have reached Washington, Blair handed him the order relieving him of his command. The act hardly seems now to have been "indispensable," but Blair, in justifying it, wrote President Lincoln that he had "conclusive evidence that extensive preparations within this State are on foot

⁶⁵ May 27, 1861, *O. R.*, Series I, vol. iii, p. 376.
⁶⁶ Harney to Townsend, May 29, 1861, *O. R.*, Series I, vol. iii, p. 377.

to raise and arm large forces to make war on the United States government. From every neighborhood in the central and southwest portion of the State men are drilling and arming, and both arms and men will speedily be brought to the State from Arkansas." He said he had brought these matters to the attention of Harney, but his answer had been: "I will tell Price about it; I will get Price to correct it." . . . "At times he has promised me that he would interpose, but afterward would say that there was no occasion for doing anything. I ascribe the conduct of General Harney to the influences by which he is constantly surrounded." [67]

With the removal of Harney and the practical accession of Lyon to the command, it became evident that a different policy would be adopted. The new commander immediately made preparations for an extensive campaign into the interior, which the state troops would have been powerless to resist. Their leader did not at once think of resistance. He believed—and rightly—that his agreement with Harney was still in force; and he thought Harney's successor in honor bound to respect it. He even went so far as to issue a proclamation reassuring his brigadier-generals that the widely circulated rumors of approaching Federal interference in the State were unfounded. [68] But among the conservative Union men there was a great deal of alarm. Appreciating the lawless qualities of Lyon's crusading zeal, they feared that a general civil conflict would result from his preparations. With hopes of preserving peace they arranged an interview between Blair and Lyon on the one hand and Jackson and Price on the other.

[67] May 30, 1861; quoted by Peckham, p. 223.
[68] *Last Political Writings of General Nathaniel Lyon*, pp. 45-46.

The meeting took place in St. Louis on June 11th. The state authorities were willing to make far greater concessions than were embodied in their agreement with Harney, even going so far as to propose disbanding their military organization if they were guaranteed freedom from Federal interference. They offered to send home the members of the State Guard; to cease organizing the militia under the military bill; to prevent the importation of arms into the State; to prevent Confederate troops from entering the State; and to guarantee general and impartial protection to all citizens. In return they asked that the national government disband the home guards and agree not to occupy any localities in the State which were not already in their possession. The conditions were wholly unsatisfactory to Lyon, who assumed charge of the negotiations for the other side. He asserted the right of the national government to send its troops wherever it desired, and he refused point blank to disband the home guards.°° A more tactful negotiator would probably have gained even greater concessions than those offered; but Lyon wanted, not concessions, but surrender. After four hours of discussion in which neither side showed a disposition to give way, Lyon dramatically closed the interview with a short speech in which he declared war against the State. "Rather," he said, "than concede to the State of Missouri the right to demand that my Government shall not enlist troops within her limits, or bring troops into the State whenever it pleases, or move its troops at its own will into, out of, or through the State; rather than concede to the State of Missouri for one single instant the right to dictate to my Government in any matter however unimpor-

°° Peckham, p. 247.

tant, I would see you, and you, and you, and you, and
you, and every man, woman and child in the State, dead
and buried. This means war. In an hour one of my
officers will call for you and conduct you out of my
lines." [70] When he had finished he strode from the room,
rattling his sword and clanking his spurs.

The state leaders hastened to leave St. Louis, Jackson
going to Jefferson City, where he issued a proclamation
calling for fifty thousand of the state militia and ordering the brigadier-generals to assemble their commands,
and Price going to Lexington where he took command of
the principal body of the state militia that were under
arms. Their task was of considerable difficulty, since
their forces had been scattered under the Harney-Price
agreement, and they soon discovered that it was nearly
impossible to obtain recruits. Harney's work, after the
affair at Camp Jackson, had been highly effective. Popular passion against the Federal authorities had had
plenty of time to cool. There were now many people in
the interior who were willing, without going to the trouble to ascertain carefully the facts in the case, to justify
Lyon's action in breaking off the agreement. It therefore happened that, instead of the fifty thousand men
that Jackson had called out, only a scant five thousand
joined the state forces within the following six months.[71]

---

[70] The quotation is from Snead, pp. 199-200, who was present as an
aide to General Price. Major Conant, Lyon's aide, quotes him as
saying: "Heretofore Missouri has only felt the fostering care of the
Federal Government. . . . Now, however, from the failure on the part
of the Chief Executive to comply with constitutional requirements, I
fear she will be made to feel its power. Better, sir, far better, that
the blood of every man, woman and child of the State should flow
than that she should successfully defy the Federal Government." *Vide*
Peckham, p. 248.

[71] *O. R.*, Series I, vol. viii, p. 695.

Jackson quickly apprehended the dangers of his situation, and resolved not to defend the state capital. Instead he joined a small force at Booneville, where he decided to make a stand in order to protect the crossing of expected reinforcements from the northern counties.[72]

Lyon gave the state troops little time in which to prepare for defense. Though he made mistakes in dealing with the people of the city and with the state authorities, there can be no criticism of his energy and bravery in the field. Four days after his interview with Jackson and Price, he was in Jefferson City with a considerable force, having come up the river by boat. Delaying only a short time for the arrival of reinforcements, he struck the undisciplined state forces at Booneville and routed them with slight loss on either side. The victory, trifling though it was, had important consequences. It opened the Missouri River. It forced Price to retreat from Lexington to the Arkansas border. It cut off his reinforcements from the northern part of the State. And it still further discouraged enlistments for the state forces. Only Lyon's lack of supplies and facilities of transportation prevented his pursuing Jackson and making his victory complete.

While the Federal commander was forced to wait impatiently on the Missouri, Jackson, retreating southward, crossed the Osage River and joined Price, who had been pursued from Lexington by a superior force of regulars and Kansas volunteers. North of Carthage the state army found the way blocked by Colonel Sigel, who had been sent into the southwestern part of the State to take command of the Union volunteers that had been raised there. After an hour's conflict at long range,

[72] Carr, p. 313.

Sigel withdrew to Sarcoxie and allowed Jackson and Price to pass. They continued their march until they reached Cowskin Prairie in the extreme southwestern part of the State. Here they were safe for the time being, for they had allies in Arkansas, and they had left the Federals far behind, with swollen creeks and muddy roads to impede their progress.

The respite was used by Price in drilling and organizing his men and in procuring supplies. His army had neither uniforms nor ammunition, and there appeared to be slight opportunity to improvise either on Cowskin Prairie. The ordnance officer did not know the difference between a howitzer and a siege gun, but one of his men succeeded in making cartridges for the artillery from a variety of sources, including the iron bars found in a neighboring blacksmith shop, bolts of flannel from the dry goods store, and the reserve supply of a tinsmith. The models were shells captured from Sigel's men. For the small arms, the mines in the vicinity furnished plenty of lead, but there were no facilities for molding it into bullets. One of the officers who was used to service on the frontier made molds from freshly cut trees which served the purpose. The commissary department was often unable to furnish rations for the men, and the paymaster could not pay them; but the soldiers did not greatly object.[73] They were fighting to secure the rights of their State from illegal and arbitrary interference, and their cause was many times more just than that of South Carolina when she seceded. Many of them are reported to have been opposed to secession.[74]

The organization of the state forces was cut short by

[73] Carr, pp. 316-318.
[74] *Proceedings* of the Missouri State Convention, July, 1861, p. 15.

the arrival of Lyon at Springfield on July 13th. After uniting all the Federal forces in southwestern Missouri he had only about seven thousand men with whom to face Price's troops and the Confederate army in Arkansas, which together, according to his reports, numbered thirty thousand. He therefore telegraphed for assistance, promising to hold the superior forces of the enemy in check as long as he could.

Unfortunately Lyon was not in command of the troops in reserve at St. Louis or elsewhere in the western department. It had been the intention of the Blairs that he should be; but Bates and General Scott had demanded, as a price for agreeing to Harney's dismissal, that McClellan's department should be extended so as to include Missouri.[75] For a time he exercised a nominal control over affairs, though it was not an efficient supervision. His interests in western Virginia and elsewhere prevented him from giving much attention to Lyon's campaigns. The arrangement was so unsatisfactory to the Blairs that they looked about for someone else. John C. Fremont was suggested by them as a true Union man, possibly also as a man who would take their advice. Complying with their request, the President issued an order for his appointment on July 3rd. But Fremont was not ready to begin his service at once. He delayed in New York and elsewhere until late in the month before assuming command of the department. During all this period Lyon's urgent telegrams for reinforcements were not attended to. When Fremont finally arrived in St. Louis, he seems to have been overwhelmed with the immensity of the task before him, and with his own importance. His subordinate, campaigning

[75] Peckham, p. 265.

against an active and important enemy on the frontier, was neglected, while he devoted his attention to a small Confederate force operating in southeastern Missouri.[76]

Lyon was loath to give up southwestern Missouri without a struggle. At the beginning of August he moved out from Springfield, intending, if possible, to defeat his enemies in detail before they had an opportunity to unite. Within a day or two he met the advance guard of Price's army and easily defeated it—so easily, in fact, that McCulloch, who was in command of the Confederate army, lost faith in the fighting qualities of the Missourians. The next day Lyon advanced to within six miles of McCulloch's camp, hesitated, then turned back to Springfield to wait for reinforcements. There Price proposed to attack him. But McCulloch hesitated, partly because he had no authority to enter Missouri at all except as far as necessary to protect the Indian Territory, partly because he was afraid to risk a battle with a divided command and such allies as he thought the Missourians were. At length, Price waived his rank and allowed McCulloch to have absolute command, only reserving the right to take charge of his men again when he saw fit to do so. Another advance brought the Confederate force to Wilson's Creek, eight miles south of Springfield, where McCulloch again hesitated.[77]

The approach of the Confederates made Lyon's position dangerous. He had waited at Springfield, hoping that reinforcements would be sent to him from some of the posts along the Missouri River or from St. Louis, until retreat had become perilous, encumbered as he was with a long baggage train for which there was no cavalry

[76] Peckham, pp. 315-320.
[77] Carr, pp. 327-329.

protection. A council of war advised almost unanimously
against risking an engagement; but Lyon overruled it
and determined to fight a battle, hoping at least to cripple the enemy and destroy his baggage, so that an effective pursuit would be impossible. His plan of battle,
formed after a conference with Sigel, was hazardous in
the extreme. Dividing his small force in the face of
superior numbers, he sent Sigel with twelve hundred
German troops to attack the rear, and, if possible, to
destroy the baggage train of the Confederates. With the
remainder, numbering about four thousand, he moved
out, on August 10th, to attack the left wing. The
maneuvers were executed so successfully that almost the
first intimation the enemy had of the close proximity of
the Federal troops was the booming of Lyon's and Sigel's
guns at dawn from opposite sides of his position. The
Confederate leaders quickly broke up a council of war
in which they were engaged. McCulloch hastened with
his forces to beat off the attack in the rear, while Price
led fresh troops to succor a brigade of Missourians who
were falling back under the onslaughts of Lyon. He
succeeded in rallying them, and then led a counter-attack
to within a few yards of the Federal guns. The battle
raged for hours in the thick underbrush, which permitted
the hostile forces to approach within a few yards of each
other without being seen. At this range the hunting
rifles and shotguns of the Missouri troops were effective,
as was the artillery with their improvised cartridges. On
the whole, however, the Federals had the advantage at
this point, forcing Price back into inferior positions. On
the other side of the field Sigel had been completely successful at first, compelling the Confederates to set fire to
their baggage to prevent its capture. But the German

soldiers, forgetting all discipline in their eagerness to plunder the camp, became an easy conquest for McCulloch. When he counter-attacked, they scattered in all directions. Sigel, giving up the battle as lost, led a remnant back to Springfield. The Confederate commander, with his comparatively fresh troops, was then enabled to go to the assistance of Price. His arrival was the signal for a general assault upon the whole Federal line. To meet it, Lyon ordered all his reserves into the battle, and, by determined fighting, he managed to hold his ground. But at this crisis of the battle he was shot down while leading a desperate charge. His second in command soon afterward ordered a retreat toward Rollo, which was not interrupted owing to the exhaustion of the Confederates and their almost complete lack of ammunition.[78]

In its final results, the battle may be set down as a victory for the Confederates, since the whole of western Missouri was opened to them. Though they had suffered severely, they were able to resume operations before the Federals were. The two armies each lost about twelve hundred men, including the missing among Sigel's Germans. The most serious loss of all for the Federals was the death of Lyon, whose place in the field could not immediately be filled.

As soon as the Confederates had recovered from the effects of the battle, Price proposed that they march to the Missouri River. On McCulloch's refusal to take part in the movement, he set out alone. After first defeating Senator Lane and his motley army of Kansas guerrillas, he pressed forward until he reached Lexington, where he compelled the Federal commander to surrender with

[78] Carr, pp. 329-335; Comte de Paris, *History of the Civil War,* vol. i, pp. 332-337.

about thirty-five hundred men. This success enabled him to remain on the river for a time, receiving recruits from most parts of the State. At last, when Fremont had become thoroughly aroused, he sent twenty thousand men into southwestern Missouri to cut off his retreat, and later joined them in person with as many more. Fremont might have proved less incapable in the field than at headquarters, though he had little opportunity to prove it at this time. He was relieved of his command while completing his preparations to bring on a battle with Price, who was waiting along the Arkansas border. General Curtis, who succeeded him, fell back toward the Missouri River in order that a part of his force might be sent to assist in the invasion of Tennessee. About the middle of February he began a forward movement which forced Price to flee from the State. Though joined by McCulloch near the boundary line, he continued the retreat into the interior of Arkansas. Finally, at Pea Ridge, the Southern armies turned about and fought a three days' battle which resulted in their complete defeat.[79] Almost immediately afterward the Arkansas troops crossed the Mississippi River to meet Halleck and Grant in Tennessee. Price, accepting a Confederate commission, took many of his men and crossed with them. Others returned to Missouri to wage a guerrilla warfare against the Federal garrisons.

The Union forces thus finally obtained possession of Missouri to the exclusion of organized enemies; but it was a State that was seething with internal feuds and demoralized by internecine warfare from Iowa to Arkansas. It contributed to the Federal army a magnificent body of volunteers—more in proportion to its population

[79] Violette, pp. 368-371.

than most of the other States,—a majority of whom belonged to the native population. But other thousands joined the armies of the South or remained in the State attacking isolated posts and spreading terror among the loyal population. The conquest of Missouri by Blair and Lyon was dearly bought.

What the result would have been if Harney and the conservatives had been allowed to pursue their policy is, of course, problematical. There would almost certainly have been guerrilla warfare along the turbulent Kansas border. There might also have been considerable disorder in the southeastern part of the State. But it is hardly probable that other sections would have become active theaters of hostilities of that kind. It is possible that enlistments for the Union army would have been postponed by the active opposition of the state administration, since they must have been made at inconvenient points along the borders of the State. It must be borne in mind, however, that there were comparatively few enlistments on either side until after the close of 1861. The delay, after all, would therefore have made little difference in the military strength of the United States. In other respects, the advantages which would have resulted from a waiting policy heavily outweighed purely military questions. The opposition of Governor Jackson and the secessionists had not been formidable in the beginning. Time after time their proposals had been rejected by the people of the State. It was only when the national government, in the most tyrannical manner, invaded the constitutional rights of the State, took away the means upon which it relied for the enforcement of its laws in critical times, and finally made war upon it in disregard of a solemn agreement, that weapons were placed in their hands. Even after the affair at Camp Jackson, it would still have been possible to undo much of the damage that had been done, and to hasten public opinion to take a stand favorable to the Union by the means by which public opinion is best influenced.

It would hardly do to say that there would have been no war in Missouri as long as a firebrand like Claiborne F. Jackson occupied the governor's chair. His intentions were undoubtedly hostile to the United States. It would, however, have been an infinitely wiser policy for the Union leaders to have waited until he forced the issue by making an attack. Such an act would have definitely placed him in the wrong before the people. The Federal troops could easily have repulsed his attacks at almost any stage, and could then have intervened with the law and public opinion on their side. Under these circumstances Missouri would have become a far more powerful reinforcement for the cause of the Union than it was.

CHAPTER IX

THE NEUTRALITY OF KENTUCKY

The response of Kentucky to the events beginning the war, in complete contrast to the state of public opinion in western Virginia and Missouri, showed that the cause of the Union was in a precarious situation. It was not so because public opinion held the North responsible for the outbreak of hostilities, for President Lincoln's carefully formulated policy in regard to Fort Sumter effectually disarmed his opponents in the State, and the sturdy defense of Major Anderson, a native of Kentucky, aroused the admiration of all classes. The correct explanation seems to lie in the fact that sentimentally the people had always considered themselves as Southerners. Upon the outbreak of the war they therefore, without much consideration of questions of right or wrong, or of national or state politics, felt impelled to join in the defense of their section. Probably only the sentiment of devotion to the Union, which moved them in the opposite direction, prevented them from beginning a course of action that, upon sober second thought, they must have regretted. In the first few months following the outbreak of the war, Kentucky was unsteadily balanced between the Union and the Confederacy.

The unconditional Union party in the State was much weaker than in Missouri, and the active secessionists were much stronger. They were, in fact, so strong and so actively engaged in manufacturing sentiment favorable to their cause that it might have appeared to an outsider that the whole State had turned secessionist. On the day of the surrender of Fort Sumter Blanton Duncan mobilized a regiment which he had enrolled for the Confederate army.[1] When he later paraded it through the streets of Louisville, thousands of citizens lined the sidewalk, waving good-bys and cheering for the soldiers and the cause in which they were engaged.[2] On April 15th Governor Magoffin telegraphed in response to the President's call for troops: "I say emphatically Kentucky will furnish no troops for the wicked purpose of subduing her sister Southern States."[3] The action of the governor was outwardly approved by everyone, though some of the unionists ventured to criticize the wording of the refusal. In Louisville, on April 18th, a mass meeting attended by three thousand persons not only approved the reply, but declared that Kentucky should not allow Federal troops to be marched across her territory for the purpose of attacking the Confederate States. If war should come, it was resolved that Kentucky ought to share the destiny of the South.[4] At Paris, a meeting condemned the conduct of the national government and approved Magoffin's course. From Lexington, John H. Morgan wrote to the Confederate government, tendering twenty thousand men to "defend Southern liberty against Northern conquest."[5] A few days later John C. Breckinridge lent his powerful influence to the secessionists, declaring publicly at Louis-

[1] O. R., Series I, vol. lii, part ii, p. 46.
[2] O. R., Series I, vol. li, part ii, p. 38.
[3] O. R., Series III, vol. i, p. 70.
[4] Cincinnati Enquirer, April 17, 1861.
[5] O. R., Series I, vol. lii, part ii, p. 49.

ville that the President's course was illegal, and recommending that the people of Kentucky make one more effort at mediation in the halls of Congress. If they should fail in this, he thought it their duty to unite with the South.[6] In only two sections of the State—in the counties opposite Cincinnati and in the sparsely settled mountainous region—was there an immediate rallying of the people to support the Union. It is probable that if a convention had been in session when the news from Fort Sumter was received, it, like the convention in Virginia, would have passed an ordinance of secession.

The Union leaders, plainly alarmed by the state of public opinion, took a stand much less advanced than that of their government, in the hope of checking the apparent stampede toward secessionism. The Louisville *Journal,* which had been actively engaged in building up sentiment favorable to the Union, took occasion to express the opinion that the President's call for the militia was a blunder. For the benefit of public opinion, it argued that Lincoln was not the government of the United States, and that the government ought not to be held responsible for what he did. It recommended that the people remain calm and await further developments before espousing the cause of the South.[7] Senator Crittenden, who had given his best efforts in the preceding months to secure a compromise, now declared publicly that since Kentucky had done nothing to bring about the war, she should take neither side, but stand firm in the attitude of a peaceful mediator.[8] Even the unionist State Central Committee, composed of men of the most

[6] Moore's *Rebellion Record,* vol. i, p. 35.
[7] April 16, 1861.
[8] Collins, vol. i, p. 87.

unwavering loyalty, felt compelled to ask the people to remain neutral. In its address to the people it gave approval to Magoffin's response to the call for troops, only recommending in the interest of fair play that measures be taken to prevent the enlistment of Kentuckians for the Southern armies. "If the enterprise announced in the proclamation of the President," said the report, "should at any time hereafter assume the aspect of a war for the overrunning and subjugation of the seceding States, . . . [Kentucky] ought—without counting the cost—to take up arms against the government. Until she does detect this meaning *she ought to hold herself independent of both sides,* and compel both sides to respect the inviolability of her soil." [9] Unionist meetings held at Louisville and elsewhere endorsed these views.

The leader of this group, Garrett Davis, soon afterward went to Washington to obtain, if possible, the coöperation of the national government in his plans for saving Kentucky to the Union. In an interview with President Lincoln he explained the delicate condition of affairs in the State, and received from him a reassuring message to deliver to the people. There was no intention, the President said, for the national government to make war on any State that did not take up arms against the Union; nor were there military operations in prospect which would require that Federal troops march across Kentucky. He expressed the opinion that it was the duty of the State to have furnished troops upon his call; but he said that he had not the power, right or inclination to compel her to do so. [10] In adopting a con-

[9] Cincinnati *Enquirer,* April 19, 1861.
[10] Collins, vol. i, p. 88.

ciliatory attitude, the President showed that he had a keen perception of the difficulties of the situation. There can be little doubt but that his policy was correct. Indeed it seems to have been the only one that could have saved Kentucky for the Union at this time.

In the Confederate capital, on the other hand, the course of events in Kentucky was watched with immense satisfaction. Immediately after Magoffin's refusal to furnish troops to the national government, President Davis requested him to send one regiment of militia to join the Confederate army at Harper's Ferry. Although Magoffin would probably have done any legal thing he could to aid the South, he declined the invitation because he did not want to commit the State to a course of action that might prove embarrassing to the legislature. He, however, read the request to Blanton Duncan, who immediately offered his regiment to take the place of the militia.[11] It was accepted by the Confederate government, and part of the men were sent down the river by steamboat on April 17th. The remainder, according to the plan, were to go south on the Louisville and Nashville Railroad. When application for their transportation was first made, the president of the road refused it because of his unionist sympathies, until prominent leaders of the party pointed out to him the fact that the regiment would be less dangerous to the Union if encamped in the South than if it remained in Louisville. It was therefore allowed to proceed.[12] Later on, a number of individuals left for New Orleans and other points to enlist in the Southern armies.

A similar movement was set on foot by some of the

[11] *O. R.*, Series I, vol. li, part ii, p. 37.
[12] Colonel R. M. Kelly, in *Union Regiments of Kentucky*, p. 19.

Union leaders, who desired to enlist men for the Federal army in order both to increase its numerical strength and to afford concrete evidence of the existence of unionist sentiment. The coöperation of the state authorities was not sought, though it is doubtful if they would have interposed obstacles to the establishment of recruiting stations in Kentucky, since they had abetted the departure of men for the South. The President and other Union leaders, however, did not want recruiting camps established in the State. They feared that the enlistment and drilling of men in blue uniforms would bring about accusations that the national government was resorting to coercion. They therefore ordered that recruiting should take place on the northern bank of the Ohio River. J. V. Guthrie of Covington and W. E. Woodruff of Louisville, having obtained commissions as colonels in the Federal army, established Camp Clay on the outskirts of Cincinnati and invited citizens of Kentucky to join them.[18] Many of them responded. But the rush of residents of Ohio to join the colors soon filled up the regiments. It was estimated that only one-fourth of the soldiers were citizens of Kentucky. After the first days of the war few persons in the State enlisted in either army for a long time. The leaders of both parties, sensing the general feeling of hesitancy in the minds of the people about the future course of Kentucky, desired to keep as many of their adherents as possible within the State in preparation for the struggles which were to come.

The period of calm which succeeded the feverish excitement of the first few days was due in part to the extremely circumspect attitude of the Union leaders, in

[18] Kelly, p. 19.

part to the monopolization of the news by accounts of organization and preparation for war. The fact that there were no skirmishes or battles to report gave the too sanguine people a straw to clutch at. This was the belief that it would still be possible to save the Union by mediation and conciliation if enough States joined in the attempt. An insistent popular demand for the action led Governor Magoffin, on April 25th, to ask the governors of Ohio and Indiana to coöperate with him in securing the establishment of a truce between the sections, which should continue at least until the Congress met in July. He expressed the hope that further hostilities could then be averted by a compromise. Both Dennison and Morton disapproved the program as a matter of course. But sensing an opportunity to serve the cause of the Union in Kentucky, they proposed to meet him in conference at some place that he should designate. The proposal was accepted by Magoffin in the same spirit as that in which it had been made. On the date set for the meeting in Cincinnati, he sent General Thomas L. Crittenden with full credentials, but failed to appear in person. The two governors, desiring only to meet Magoffin, telegraphed him that his presence was absolutely necessary to the accomplishment of any work. No reply having been received after several hours, they returned to their state capitals. In a subsequent correspondence, Dennison offered to join Magoffin in appealing to the Southern States to return to their allegiance, though he declared that he could never agree to the establishment of a truce. Morton, much less diplomatic in his utterances, declared that he could not admit the right of any State to act as a mediator between the national government and a rebellious State. He urged that Kentucky remain in the Union.[14] Magoffin's was the last effort made by the chief executive of any State to avert the war by mediation. Whatever his motives were in beginning the negotiations, the results were favorable to the cause of the Union; for his staying away caused his sincerity to be questioned by the majority of the people of Kentucky, who desired the restoration of the Union without bloodshed.

An examination of Magoffin's general policies at this time reveals that he had advanced far toward the support of secessionism. He did not, presumably, intend to aid the military position of the South by his proposed truce. In that matter he seems to have acted merely as the servant of the people, conducting diplomatic relations with other States because they wished him to do so. In other matters, too, he acted wholly within the law. But where he was legally entitled to exercise discretion, he favored the secessionists in every case. Under his legislative powers he called a special session, for the second time in 1861, to consider the question of a convention and to provide means for the arming and equipment of the state forces. As commander-in-chief of the militia, he enlisted thousands of secessionists and instituted improvements in organization, in order, it was believed, that they might become a more efficient part of the Confederate army later on. In the exercise of his emergency borrowing power, he sought to make loans to pay for the arms purchased by the State. But in this matter he could not alone complete the transaction. Only four banks in the State agreed to supply funds. A fifth—the Bank of Kentucky—imposed the condition that the

[14] The correspondence is printed in the *Journal* of the House of Representatives of Kentucky, May session, 1861, pp. 15-16.

money loaned should be used only for defense and the preservation of neutrality.[15] His efforts to be a constitutional executive satisfied nobody. The secessionists fretted and fumed against his policies, and finally excused him on the ground that the military forces under his command were too few in numbers to enable him to act more boldly.[16] The Union men, on their side, openly denounced him as a secessionist and questioned the motives behind his every act. And gradually they won most of the people to their point of view.

In the two weeks just preceding the session of the legislature, a number of events occurred, partly at the initiative of the unionist State Central Committee, which made it appear that there was a decided drift of public opinion toward the full support of the United States. In Louisville the city council, which was composed of Union men, voted an appropriation of $50,000 to arm and equip citizens and place the city in a state of defense.[17] The act was regarded as a reply to the activity of Magoffin in arming the State Guard. In preparation for the municipal elections on May 6th, the Union men nominated a candidate for mayor who had expressed himself as being in favor of compelling the seceded States to return to their allegiance. The polling resulted in his favor by three votes to one, and all the Union candidates for the council were successful.[18] In the State at large, an election for members of the Border States Convention on May 4th resulted favorably for the nationalist cause. There was no direct contest that would indicate the comparative strength of the parties, owing to the fact that

[15] Collins, vol. i, p. 88.
[16] O. R., Series I, vol. lii, part ii, p. 69.
[17] Collins, vol. i, p. 88.
[18] Kelly, p. 11.

the Southern Rights candidates were withdrawn before the election. Even without opposition, however, the unionist candidates received nearly two-thirds as many votes as were cast in the presidential election of 1860.[19] The number of mass meetings held by adherents of the Union greatly increased, as did the intensity of the expression of opinion by unionist newspapers.

It was fortunate for the cause of the Union that its adherents were able to muster so much apparent strength at this time, for the legislature, which began its special session on May 6th, showed an uncertain disposition. Important changes in the opinions of many of the members had occurred since the adjournment in February. Four Breckinridge Democrats had deserted their party, and acted now with the Union men. On the other hand, many more of the conditional Union members had become outright secessionists.[20] There were but two parties now —the States' Rights men, who favored the calling of a convention, and the Union men, who opposed the measure. The Senate was equally divided between them. The House had the weakest sort of unionist majority; five or six of the group were doubtful, and there were others who, according to a Kentucky chronicler, were not unlikely to be intoxicated during the sittings.[21] Under such circumstances it was necessary for the leaders of the Union party to be extremely circumspect. Even a parliamentary mistake might lose the battle for them. Naturally, then, they did not propose that Kentucky should enter the war on the side of the North, or even give that section economic aid. Their whole efforts

[19] W. C. Goodloe, *Kentucky Unionists of 1861*, p. 12.

[20] Nathaniel S. Shaler, *Kentucky, A Pioneer Commonwealth*, pp. 241-242.

[21] Goodloe, p. 9.

were required to prevent the secessionists from carrying
their proposal to call a convention. As an alternative,
they advocated the doctrine of strict neutrality, hoping
that when a new legislature was elected in August, they
would be able to bring the State to the active support
of the national government.

The secessionists, on the other hand, with a whole
State to gain and nothing of consequence to lose, were
outspoken in favor of the South and unsparing in their
criticism of the national government. Governor Magoffin in his message declared: "It is idle longer to refuse to
recognize the fact that the late American Union is dissolved; that ten slaveholding States are now practically
united in a separate and independent government, and
that war exists. . . . The condition of peace, as avowed
by the President of the United States is the overthrow
of the Confederate States Government, and the reduction of the people of the South to unresisting submission
to the United States government." The Confederate
States, he said, asked only to be let alone. He recommended that the people should be asked to determine
what should be the future course of the State." Acting
in the spirit of these declarations, the secessionist members demanded that a convention be called to determine
authoritatively which of the sections, if either of them,
Kentucky should join.

Naturally the people throughout the State were tre-
mendously interested in the session. Many of them
sought in various ways to bring pressure to bear upon
their representatives. The Union leaders were more
active and more clever in organizing this sort of activity

---

[22] *Journal* of the House of Representatives of Kentucky, May session, 1861, pp. 5-12.

than their opponents. From nearly every county in the State petitions, signed by thousands of women, were presented praying for the preservation of peace through neutrality.[23] It is said that these petitions were circulated by unconditional Union men. Many citizens, of course, thronged to Frankfort to watch the proceedings. No sooner would an influential secessionist group appear than the telegraph would summon equally influential Union leaders from Louisville, Covington and other centers to reinforce the unionist lobby already at the capital.[24] By such means as these the supporters of the national government succeeded, by the narrowest of margins, in dominating the proceedings.

The critical point came near the middle of the session, after a desultory series of divisions in which the Union party had had a majority of one. Someone proposed to lay on the table a substitute for a secessionist resolution. It was a matter of little or no practical consequence, but of the highest parliamentary importance. When the vote was taken, the question was declared rejected by a majority of one. A Union member had gone over to the opposition. The secessionists exulted over their victory, for their success at last seemed assured; but on the very next vote the member returned to his party allegiance.[25] The occurrence seemed to take the spirit out of the secessionists, who shortly afterward abandoned their hope of being able to accomplish their purpose at that session. They accepted instead the principle of neutrality by legislative act.

There still remained a question as to the form of neu-

[23] House *Journal*, pp. 24 *et seq.*
[24] Kelly, p. 16.
[25] House *Journal*, pp. 94-96.

trality which Kentucky should adopt. Should she merely request the belligerents to respect her territory, and depend upon their good faith to do so, or should she arm herself to prevent violations? The legislature decided in favor of armed neutrality, against the opposition of some Union members who were unwilling that the State Guard should be further strengthened. Since the session of the legislature in the winter its enlisted personnel had grown to fifteen thousand men.[26] From the beginning of its organization, complaints had been frequently heard that the state authorities were discriminating against the enlistment of Union men. They were accused of having accepted many secessionist companies which had not complied with the terms of the law, while preventing the enrollment of unionist companies which had done so. It was generally known that nearly all the officers and men were of secessionist leanings. The organization was therefore regarded as a menace to the cause of the Union.[27]

In order to counterbalance its power and secure an armed force that would protect the interests of the Union and of Union men against it, many companies of home guards were organized throughout northern and central Kentucky. Near the beginning of the legislative session, Lieutenant William Nelson had surreptitiously brought into the State five thousand muskets which he had obtained from the War Department at Washington. These so-called "Lincoln rifles" were distributed among the home guards by night.[28] By the middle of the session there were two distinct military organizations in

[26] Shaler, p. 246.
[27] Kelly, p. 18.
[28] Collins, vol. i, p. 91.

the State, of not unequal strength. Both were prepared to defend Kentucky against external aggression, though they watched for enemies in different directions.

When the Union leaders found it impossible to prevent the granting of appropriations for the military, they determined to safeguard the funds from being used wholly for the benefit of the secessionists. General Buckner's estimates for the State Guard were greatly pared down. Instead of the $3,000,000 which he asked for, the legislature appropriated $750,000 for equipment and training, half to be spent for the State Guard, and half for the Union home guards. The disbursement of the funds was taken out of the hands of the governor and vested in a commission of five members, a majority of whom were Union men, named by the legislature. Furthermore, it was provided that the home guards should not be called into the service of the State;—in other words, that the governor, who was the commander-in-chief of the militia, should be debarred from exercising control over half the military establishment supported by the State. Finally, a provision was inserted that none of the arms and equipment supplied by the State should be used against either the United States or the Confederate States except to repel invasion.[29]

After the Union leaders had thus succeeded in tying the hands of the secessionists and in getting so great a degree of control for themselves, they seemed somehow to lose interest in the question of neutrality. The secessionists, on the other hand, now insisted upon it. They succeeded in having each house pass a resolution of strict neutrality; but owing to the opposition of the Union members, they were unable to secure the concur-

[29] Collins, vol. i, p. 91.

rence of both houses on any single measure. The result was that the only official pronouncement of the position of Kentucky was an executive proclamation by Governor Magoffin.[30]

There can be no doubt that the neutrality of Kentucky was advantageous to the Southern Confederacy from both a political and a military standpoint. As Lincoln said in a later message to Congress, its consequences would be "disunion completed." For if one State could repudiate its obligations to the national government while remaining in the Union, it was difficult to show why other States might not secede. It was a most far-reaching application of the doctrine of state sovereignty, since it crippled the national government in its efforts to enforce the laws in the regions where resistance occurred. "At a stroke," said Lincoln, "it would take all the trouble off the hands of secession, except only what proceeds from the external blockade. It would do for the disunionists that which, of all things, they most desire—feed them well, and give them disunion without a struggle of their own." [31] Still, he did not think it wise to interfere in the affairs of the State, contenting himself with measures to encourage the Union party which had a tendency toward only peaceful penetration.

On May 7th Colonel Robert Anderson, Kentucky's and the nation's hero of Fort Sumter, was assigned to the duty of raising volunteers for the Union army from western Virginia and Kentucky.[32] He thoroughly understood the sentiments of the people and was in full sympathy with the plans of Garrett Davis and the other

[30] A. C. Quisenberry, in the *Register* of the Kentucky Historical Society, Jan. 1917, pp. 9-10.

[31] *Complete Works,* vol. vi, p. 307.

[32] *O. R.,* Series I, vol. lii, part i, p. 140.

Union leaders. From his headquarters in Cincinnati he exercised a great deal of influence over the course of public opinion in the State. Another native of Kentucky who rendered a great service for the Union was Lieutenant Nelson of the Navy. At the beginning of the war he had expressed a preference for returning to his State and trying to save it from secession, rather than for treading a quarterdeck. His plan was approved by President Lincoln, who gave him a leave of absence and allowed him to go to Kentucky without instructions.[33] One of his first acts was to obtain arms from the War Department and distribute them among the home guards. During the next two months he traveled throughout the State, holding conferences with unionist leaders and making preparations for more aggressive action when the proper time came. A resident of the State who rendered good service was Lovell H. Rousseau, a member of the State Senate. As soon as the legislature adjourned, he obtained a commission and established Camp Jo. Holt in Indiana, opposite Louisville, for the recruitment of volunteers.[34] The only Federal force within the limits of Kentucky for a long time was the small garrison of regulars at Newport Barracks, which was not increased, in deference to popular sentiment.

All along the northern bank of the Ohio River, Governors Dennison, Morton and Yates had established posts to prevent the shipment of arms and military supplies to States that were not completely supporting the Federal government. Camp Defiance, at Cairo, was particularly effective in enforcing the embargo, cutting off nearly all the trade of western Kentucky and Tennessee.

[33] Nicolay and Hay, vol. iv, p. 235.
[34] Kelly, p. 20.

As a result, serious complaint arose among the people of Kentucky, which threatened to develop into rebellion. Notwithstanding the evident danger of losing the State, the restrictions were kept in effect until President Lincoln took control of the regulation of trade and relaxed the embargo. An immense trade with the South at once grew up on all the routes through Kentucky. The southward-borne shipments of foodstuffs and materials of war taxed the capacity of the Louisville and Nashville Railroad. When an inspection was instituted at Louisville, the shippers simply sent their goods by wagon to small stations south of the city. The Federal government had little or no tangible compensation for this aid to the enemy, since the northward-borne shipments amounted to only a fifth of those sent southward. It stood to lose heavily by the policy, and the South to gain, for it could obtain greatly needed military supplies. Before long, however, the defects of Southern statesmanship made themselves felt. The authorities of Tennessee, failing to sense the advantage of the trade, and intent on the dangers of having the North receive a little cotton, placed an absolute embargo upon it, and upon some other staple products; and one of her generals seized a considerable part of the rolling stock of the railroad on grounds that were in no wise justifiable. The action angered the people of Kentucky and alienated many of them from the Confederacy. At the same time, it enabled Lincoln to tighten the restrictions on the Southern trade.[35]

Lincoln's conciliatory, waiting policy in his relations with Kentucky was strongly opposed in some quarters

[35] E. Merton Coulter, *The Civil War and Readjustment in Kentucky*, pp. 57-80; Appleton's *Annual Cyclopedia*, 1861, p. 397.

of the North, notably by Seward and the governors of the three States north of the Ohio River. They wished to take more forceful measures, such as had been used in Missouri. Morton proposed that batteries be erected against Louisville—a step that was prevented by McClellan's objections. Late in May Governors Dennison, Morton and Yates united in advising the occupation of Louisville, Covington, Newport and Columbus to "save Kentucky for the Union." They proposed to use troops from Kentucky as far as possible, or if they were not available in sufficient numbers, they suggested that regulars be employed. An order seems to have been issued at Seward's request directing that the two regiments at Camp Clay should cross the river to Newport, and that General Anderson should move his headquarters from Cincinnati to Louisville; but its execution was opposed by McClellan and by Union leaders both in Kentucky and in Cincinnati. It was notorious, they said, that most of the enlisted men in the two regiments were not citizens of the State at all, and that only a few of the officers were Kentuckians. If the regiments were sent, they feared that it would be considered by the people a transparent trick to smuggle troops into the State. McClellan declared that if such a movement were made, these regiments should go last of all. Nelson added his plea that all military movements in Kentucky be postponed, at least until after the congressional elections on June 20th. The order was not carried out.[36]

The Federal posts on the northern border of the State had their counterparts along the southern border, where the Confederates had fortified Island No. 10, Fort Henry

[36] *O. R.*, Series I, vol. lii, part i, pp. 146-147; 160-161.

and Fort Donelson, commanding the rivers, and had established Camp Boone, to the eastward, for the enlistment of volunteers from Kentucky. Threatened with invasion from both sides, Governor Magoffin entered into negotiations with the authorities of both the North and the South to secure the neutrality of Kentucky from violation. On June 8th a conference was arranged between Generals Buckner and McClellan in Cincinnati, at which an understanding was reached. Buckner promised that the State of Kentucky would protect the property of the United States, and would, as far as possible, compel the Confederate States to respect her neutrality. In the event of an invasion by Southern troops, he promised to dislodge them, if he could; if not, he agreed to seek the aid of the national government. McClellan, on his part, promised to abstain from operations within the State until his help was requested, and then he agreed to withdraw his troops as soon as the Confederates had been driven out.[37] A similar understanding was reached between Buckner and Governor Harris of Tennessee.

The Buckner-McClellan agreement, which differed but little from the one reached between Harney and Price in Missouri at a little earlier date, was approved by President Lincoln in a kindly note to Buckner. It was his duty, he wrote, to suppress insurrection, and he wished to do it "with the least possible disturbance or annoyance to well-disposed people anywhere." At the time there seemed to him to be no occasion to move troops into Kentucky, and he expressed the hope that none would arise.[38] The tone of the letter was pleasing to

[37] Whitelaw Reid, *Ohio in the War*, vol. i, p. 280.
[38] *Complete Works*, vol. vi, p. 325.

the people of the State, who recalled it later in contrast
with an expression from President Davis on the same
subject.

On the day of the interview between Buckner and
McClellan, the Border States Conference met at Frankfort, with delegates present from the western slave
States that had not seceded. The proceedings failed to
attract a great deal of attention outside of Kentucky,
and the conference has been all but forgotten. But the
results were extremely important in their influence on
public opinion within the State. The resolutions
declared that there was no warrant for secession in the
Constitution and no justification for it in the facts existing when the Southern States seceded; that the obligations of the people to the Constitution and the national
government remained unimpaired; and that no changes
in the fundamental law should be made except only the
addition of a constitutional amendment guaranteeing the
protection of slave property in the four slave States
which still remained in the Union.[39] The delegates from
Kentucky issued a separate address to the people, recommending that their State should again appear in the
Congress of the United States and "insist upon her Constitutional rights in the Union, not out of it." [40]

The purpose of the address was to influence public
opinion in the campaign for members of Congress, who
were to be chosen at a special election on June 20th.
After the adjournment of the legislature this was the
next most important trial of strength between the secessionist and unionist parties. The Union leaders exhausted

[39] Moore's *Rebellion Record,* vol. i, pp. 350-356; quoting the Louisville *Courier* of June 8, 1861.
[40] Goodloe, pp. 12-13.

every resource at their command to secure the election
of loyal candidates. The events of the past two months
had encouraged them a great deal, so that, in contrast
to their former cautious advocacy of neutrality and other
more or less harmless expedients, they now assailed the
doctrines of secessionism, and declared boldly that they
favored thoroughgoing support to the national government. They circulated far and wide a letter of Joseph
Holt, a popular leader of state politics who was then in
Washington, declaring that he would as soon remain neutral in a contest between "an officer of justice and an
incendiary arrested in an attempt to fire the dwelling
over my head," as in the present struggle.[41] They
emphasized the natural economic and social connection
between Kentucky and the other States of the Ohio
Valley. They gave plentiful publicity, with appropriate
comments of their own, to a reported statement of Howell
Cobb of Georgia to the effect that the South could raise
cotton while the border States kept back the enemy.
And they pointed out the great service rendered by the
national fugitive slave laws in protecting the property
of the State. The question of slavery had become largely
a racial one in Kentucky, and the Union leaders played
upon the popular fears that the Confederate States
would reopen the African slave trade. It was not then,
in fact, difficult for them to inspire prejudice against the
South; for some expressions of opinion by Southern
leaders that Kentucky had been kept in the Union by
fear had been extremely offensive to their pride.[42]
Before the date set for the election it had become

[41] To J. F. Speed, May 31, 1861; Moore's *Rebellion Record*, vol. i,
p. 284.
[42] Shaler, *op. cit.*, pp. 249-250.

apparent that public opinion had set in strongly toward the cause of the Union.

The results of the election must have been a surprise even to the most sanguine Union men. Their candidates were successful everywhere except in the first congressional district, which included the western counties of the State along the Mississippi and in the lower valleys of the Cumberland and Tennessee rivers. Even there the Union candidate received forty-one per cent of the

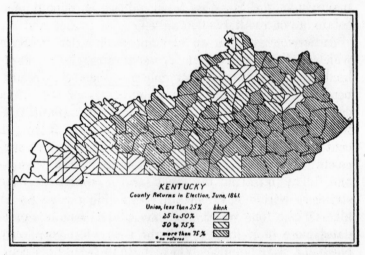

KENTUCKY
County Returns in Election, June, 1861.

Union, less than 25%   blank
25 to 50%
50 to 75%
more than 75%
● no returns

total vote. In the Blue Grass region, where slaves were most numerous, the people gave the majority of their votes to the Union ticket. In the eighth congressional district, embracing the towns of Paris, Lexington and Frankfort, the Union candidate received only fifty-nine per cent of the total; but the party ticket was successful in all the other districts by overwhelming majorities. Only five counties in the eastern part of the State— Owen, Harrison, Scott, Anderson and Morgan—gave majorities for the States' Rights candidates. Daviess and Logan were the only other counties outside the first congressional district in which they had a majority. In the Louisville district, embracing the counties of Jefferson, Henry, Oldham and Shelby, the Union ticket received more than four-fifths of the total vote. In the sixth district, which was composed of mountainous counties in the southeastern part of the State, the States' Rights party cast only 229 votes all told. The Union majority in the State as a whole was 54,700 out of a total vote of about 125,000.

An interesting feature of the result is the relation which it discloses between Union sentiment and slaveholding. Woodford County, where the slaves outnumbered the white population, gave a majority to the Union candidate. In every one of the seven other counties in which the slave population was more than forty per cent of the total the candidates of the party were successful, their votes being in some cases two or three to one. The counties in which the secessionists were strongest were not important slaveholding counties at all. Of the four which gave the States' Rights candidates more than three-fourths of their total vote, only one had a slave population of more than twenty per cent. Generally speaking, it is safe to state that the presence of slaves had little influence on the course of public opinion. What influence it had seems to have been exerted on the side of the Union.

Certain other economic and political factors had a far more potent influence. A close examination of the returns shows that the first congressional district was swung to the secessionists by the vote in the three counties bordering on the Mississippi River. It was quite natural that they should have voted as they did, since their trade was almost wholly with the South, and, as far as they had associations with outside people, these were with Southerners. The people of the lower Tennessee Valley also enjoyed a lucrative trade with the South. Along the Ohio River, on the other hand, all but one of the counties gave majorities for the Union candidates. In some cases the influence of the proximity to free soil and dependence on the trade of the river led the people of inland counties to vote likewise. In the mountainous regions the people voted for the Union candidates because of their love for the national Union, rather than their opposition to slavery. The showing of the secessionists in certain isolated counties is probably best explained as being due to the influence of outstanding political leaders. Humphrey Marshall was the most successful of them, carrying Owen County for their ticket by more than three to one; and George W. Johnson succeeded in carrying Scott County against the opposition of several slaveholders.

The result of the vote seemed to assure the election of a majority of Union candidates to the legislature in August. Some hundreds of Southern sympathizers, losing hope of being able to carry the State out of the Union by peaceful means, left for Confederate camps in Tennessee. The Union leaders continued their patient policy of respecting the neutrality of Kentucky, and of refraining from active measures for the time being. On August 5th the election for members of the legislature resulted in another overwhelming victory for their party. The new House of Representatives contained seventy-six Union, and only twenty-four States' Rights members; and the Senate, including holdover members, contained twenty-seven Union men and eleven secessionists.[43] The distribution of the popular vote in the election was not greatly different from that of the election in June.

August fifth marked a turning point in the policy of the Union leaders. Hitherto, while outwardly respecting the neutrality of Kentucky, they had chafed under the necessity of delaying operations of great importance to their cause; but now that the final determination of the position of Kentucky was no longer subject to a possible wave of popular passion, they felt that they were treading on firmer ground. They therefore began making open preparations for a movement for which they had been making ready over a period of several weeks. This was the arming of the Union men of East Tennessee.

The condition of affairs in this district after the outbreak of the war greatly resembled that in western Virginia. Both were mountainous regions in which the institution of slavery had gained little foothold. Both were conscious of economic interests distinct from those of the more populous sections of their respective States. And in both there had been long-continued political schisms over questions relating to equality and liberty. During the winter of 1860-61 the people had taken a determined stand against secession and in favor of conciliation and the settlement of differences by compromise. When the legislature, in January, submitted to the voters the question of calling a convention, the Union men gained a decisive victory over their opponents, and no convention was held. After the attack on Fort Sumter, Governor Harris called the legislature into special session. That body, without color of constitutional

[43] Quisenberry, in the *Register* of the Kentucky Historical Society, January, 1917, p. 17.

right, entered into a military league with the Confederate States, and passed a resolution of secession, which was to be effective upon popular ratification at a special election to be held on June 8th." Thereupon the Union men, under the able leadership of United States Senator Andrew Johnson and others, began a vigorous campaign to defeat the resolution at the polls and save the State to the Union. They succeeded in rallying the people of East Tennessee to their cause; but finding that the central and western portions of the State were likely to give large majorities for secession, they called a convention of the people of East Tennessee, toward the end of May, to agree upon the measures which should be taken in case the resolution should be ratified. This convention, like the first Wheeling convention, decided to await the result of the special election before taking any definite action. It passed resolutions condemning the attempts that had been made by the opposing party to secure secession by military pressure; advising an adverse vote on the question of secession; and proposing that the State should remain neutral during the course of the war. An adjourned session, to meet after the election, was provided for." The polling resulted in the ratification of the resolution of secession by a vote of 104,913 to 47,238 in the State at large. In East Tennessee, the people indicated their loyalty to the Union by casting only 14,829 votes for it to 34,023 against it.

The inhabitants of the eastern part of the State refused to accept the result of the vote as final. On June 17th —the date of the establishment of the Restored Gov-

---

" William R. Garrett and Albert V. Goodpasture, *History of Tennessee*, p. 203.
" *O. R.*, Series I, vol. lii, part i, pp. 148-155.

ernment of Virginia—the convention began its sessions at Greeneville. On the 20th, it adopted a declaration of grievances against the state authorities and directed the drafting of a petition for the formation of a new State out of East Tennessee. It was decided that if the legislature should grant the petition, another meeting of the convention should be held at Kingston to adopt a constitution and provide for the formation of a provisional government. If, however, the legislature should refuse its consent to the division of the State, the delegates voted to raise volunteers to coöperate with the Federal armies.[46]

The authorities at Washington watched the course of events in East Tennessee with intense interest. There is no doubt that they were anxious, from the beginning of the war, to extend military support to the region. At one time McClellan proposed to march down through southwestern Virginia at the conclusion of his West Virginia campaign, with arms for the people. But the project was not attempted, owing to his transfer to the command of the Army of the Potomac. Further plans were abandoned upon the realization that it would be impossible to conduct a successful campaign on such an attenuated line of communications. Meanwhile Lieutenant Samuel P. Carter of the Navy, a native of Tennessee, had been given an indefinite leave of absence to go to his State and give such encouragement and aid as he could in the development of sentiment favorable to the Union.[47] His activities resembled those of Nelson in Kentucky, except that he was unable to distribute

[46] O. R., Series I, vol. lii, part i, pp. 168-177; Garrett and Goodpasture, op. cit., p. 205.
[47] O. R., Series I, vol. lii, part i, p. 184.

arms. The proposal to transfer guns secretly across Kentucky was rejected for several reasons, the principal one being the belief that the arming of the people would result in civil war within the State, in which they would almost certainly be defeated, severely punished, and perhaps demoralized. In such a case, the arms would fall into the hands of the enemies of the United States. The project of sending arms was therefore delayed until a force could be sent with them large enough to insure for the proposed rising a good prospect of success.

On the first of July orders were issued from the War Department instructing Lieutenant Nelson to prepare an expedition for the relief of East Tennessee from Kentucky. He was to take with him ten thousand muskets, together with field artillery and mountain howitzers. As a support for the expedition, he was directed to raise three regiments of infantry in Kentucky.[48] Upon receipt of the orders he began making preparations for the movement. On July 14th, he held conferences at Lancaster and Crab Orchard with prominent leaders, by whose advice he appointed the colonels of the Kentucky regiments and completed his plans for the wholesale enlistment of volunteers. He dispatched runners in all directions, asking for the organization of companies in various strongly Union communities, with the result that within a short time men were being enlisted secretly for the Federal army in all parts of eastern Kentucky.[49] It was thought best to wait until after the state election in August before ordering the men to mobilize, though

[48] L. Thomas to Nelson, July 1, 1861, *O. R.*, Series I, vol. iv, pp. 251-252.

[49] Nelson to the Adjutant-General, July 16, 1861, *O. R.*, Series I, vol. iv, p. 252.

arrangements for a camp of recruitment and instruction were completed before the election took place.

On the day after the election, and apparently before the result had been determined, Nelson established Camp Dick Robinson in Garrard County, at the southern edge of the Blue Grass section.[50] Though the camp was less than a hundred miles from the Tennessee line, it was safe from the attacks of the Confederates, who would have to approach it through a difficult mountainous region where the people were unfriendly. At the same time, the location afforded unrivaled opportunities to enlist men. Volunteers began pouring in from all sides in accordance with the prearranged plans, and within a few days Nelson had four thousand men in camp, well armed with the now famous "Lincoln rifles."

The Confederate authorities immediately made vigorous protests against the organization of an army in Kentucky for "the avowed purpose of invading Tennessee and transporting arms and munitions to some of her rebellious citizens."[51] Governor Magoffin agreed with them that the establishment of the camp was in violation of the neutrality of the State. He therefore dispatched a commission to Washington to ask the President to order the camp disbanded. Lincoln, now sure of his ground, refused to take any such action, giving as a reason that the camp had been established at the urgent solicitation of many citizens of Kentucky, and in accordance with what he believed to be the wishes of a majority of the Union-loving people of the State. "I do not remember," he said, "that anyone . . . except your Excellency, and the bearers of your Excellency's letter, have

[50] Kelly, p. 22.
[51] Harris to Magoffin, Aug. 4, 1861, *O. R.*, Series IV, vol. i, p. 531.

urged me to remove the military force from Kentucky or to disband it." [52]   A similar mission, dispatched to the Confederate States to obtain further assurances that they would not invade Kentucky, brought the reply from President Davis that "the Government of the Confederate States will continue to respect the neutrality of Kentucky so long as her people will maintain it themselves." [53]   The Confederate troops were not sent in at this time, probably because Davis considered the neutrality of Kentucky an asset from a military point of view.

The secessionists within the State were, of course, bitterly opposed to the presence of Federal troops.   Humphrey Marshall, foreseeing that a conflict was inevitable, duplicated the action of Nelson by establishing a Confederate recruiting camp in Owen County. [54]   General Buckner went to Richmond, where he reached an understanding with the authorities that he should have a Confederate commission if Kentucky declared for the Union. [55]   A number of volunteers crossed the border into Tennessee and enlisted at Camp Boone, expecting to return later and redeem their State by force of arms.

On the other hand, the Union party, which now included most of the people, looked upon President Lincoln's policy in establishing Camp Dick Robinson as a matter of right.   Had not the Confederates used the State as a recruiting ground in April?   It was only fair that the Union military authorities should have the same privilege.   Besides, public opinion had clearly swung around

[52] Quoted by Goodloe, p. 16.
[53] *O. R.*, Series I, vol. iv, p. 397.
[54] Shaler, *op. cit.*, p. 248.
[55] Nicolay and Hay, vol. v, p. 43.   He might also have been a brigadier-general in the Union army if he had chosen the service.   See *O. R.*, Series I, vol. iv, p. 255.

to the point where it was admitted that the national government had the right to raise troops in any State. On August 17th a convention of conservatives in Louisville passed, in addition to the usual declaration favoring the restoration of peace, a resolution deprecating the attempt to destroy the Union by force. It further opposed the continued possession of the mouth of the Mississippi by a foreign power.[56] This was almost exactly the position taken in the winter by the Democrats in the northern part of the Ohio Valley. The action of the convention indicated that Kentucky was nearly ready to take an active part on the side of the Union. All eyes were turned toward the new legislature which was to begin its sessions in the first week in September.

Just at this particularly favorable moment in the affairs of Kentucky, the cause of the Union was placed in serious jeopardy by the stupid and high-handed act of a Federal general in a neighboring State. Fremont, possibly trying to build up his political strength among the extreme anti-slavery group at the North, issued an order, on August 30th, providing that the slaves of citizens of Missouri who had taken up arms against the United States should be liberated upon their application to the military authorities. The report of the action created consternation among the Union men of Kentucky, who had built up their following by stressing the fact that the war was being fought only to reunite a divided country. A whole company of volunteers in a Union regiment threw down their arms when they learned that deeds of manumission had actually been issued under Fremont's authority.[57] The leaders, anticipating further serious

---

[56] Moore's *Rebellion Record*, vol. ii, pp. 532-533.
[57] Lincoln's *Complete Works*, vol. vi, p. 359.

results, appealed to President Lincoln to countermand
the order at once. They declared that the people of
Kentucky would have no part in a war to free the
slaves. "There is," wrote Garrett Davis, "a very general, almost a universal, feeling in this State against this
war being or becoming a war against slavery. The position of the secessionists here has been all the time that
it is, and this proclamation gives them the means of
further and greatly pushing that deception." [58]
President Lincoln thoroughly appreciated the dangers
of the situation and the importance of holding Kentucky
in the Union. "I think to lose Kentucky," he wrote a
little later, "is nearly the same as to lose the whole game.
Kentucky gone we cannot hold Missouri, nor, as I think,
Maryland. These all against us, and the job on our hands
is too large for us. We would as well consent to separation at once, including the surrender of the capital." [59]
On September 2nd, he wrote to Fremont requesting him
to modify his proclamation so as to render it less offensive to the loyal people of the border slave States. Upon
Fremont's refusal to do so, Lincoln himself ordered the
necessary changes. The incident was soon forgotten
among the events that followed. It is nevertheless important in showing the temper of public opinion in Kentucky and the dangers to be anticipated from a single
misstep on the part of even a subordinate.

Fortunately for the national government, it did not
have a monopoly of military commanders who were
incapable of foreseeing the political consequences of their
acts. The Confederates had Leonidas Polk, who, hav-

[58] Sept. 3, 1861; quoted by Rhodes, vol. iii, p. 471.
[59] To O. H. Browning, Sept. 22, 1861, *Missouri Historical Review*,
vol. x, p. 80.

ing been a bishop, ought to have known something of the
peculiarities of public opinion. Evidently the metamor-
phosis which occurred when he threw off his churchman's
gown and exposed his uniform underneath was complete.
It was too complete for the good of the government whose
troops he commanded.

Late in the summer the Confederate authorities sent
him to western Tennessee to oversee the construction of
defenses along the Mississippi River against a threatened
attack from Federal gunboats. His problem was of
more than usual difficulty. Above the bluffs at Memphis both banks of the river in Tennessee, Arkansas and
the southeastern tip of Missouri are extremely low and
flat, rising but little above the level of the water. It was
impossible to find anywhere a position from which guns
could command the river, except some low sandy islands
which had grown up by accretion during past floods. On
one of these, Island No. 10, just below the Kentucky
line, General Pillow had already begun the construction
of fortifications; but this position was objectionable in
that it was subject to inundation.⁶⁰   In case of a flood the
Federal gunboats could sweep past it unopposed and land
troops anywhere in northwestern Tennessee. The only
really good position on the river between Cairo and
Memphis was a line of bluffs at Columbus, Kentucky.
Polk, with the eye of a good soldier, recognized its value,
and resolved to occupy it if the opportunity was pre-
sented.⁶¹   Partly with that end in view, he sent Pillow's
force across the river to New Madrid, Missouri.

There was at this time a small Union force operating
in southeastern Missouri under the command of General

⁶⁰ Pillow to Polk, Aug. 28, 1861; O. R., Series I, vol. iii, p. 685.
⁶¹ William M. Polk, Le ~ idas Polk, Bishop and General, vol. ii, p. 17.

Grant. In his letter assigning him to the district, Fremont had pointed to the occupation of Columbus as one of the movements to be carried out.[92] Grant, however, disobeyed his orders to the extent of refraining from violating the neutrality of Kentucky. Instead, he sent a small force to occupy Belmont on the opposite side of the river. The movement alarmed Polk, who until now had withheld his desire to seize the position. In accordance with his orders, Pillow entered the State, and on September 3rd began fortifying the heights at Columbus.[93] As soon as he learned of Pillow's movement, Grant notified the legislature of Kentucky that Confederate forces had invaded the State in considerable numbers [94]—an act for which he was later reprimanded by Fremont. Directly afterward he took possession of Paducah, Kentucky, at the mouth of the Tennessee River, probably forestalling a Confederate occupation of that point, and making it practically impossible for the authorities at Richmond to rectify at once the error of their commanders by ordering their withdrawal from Columbus. On September 7th the national government further tightened its hold on the situation by removing General Anderson's headquarters from Cincinnati to Louisville.[95]

The significance of Polk's movement was immediately appreciated in some quarters of the South. Governor Harris, whose State had been completely protected from invasion by neutral Kentucky, wrote him at once urging that he give up the position at Columbus; and the Con-

[92] O. R., Series I, vol. iii, p. 142.
[93] Polk, vol. ii, p. 19.
[94] Grant to the Speaker of the House, Sept. 5, 1861, O. R., Series I, vol. iii, p. 166.
[95] O. R., Series I, vol. iv, p. 257.

federate secretary of war ordered his withdrawal.[66] But
Polk justified his action on the ground of military necessity, and stated that it was "entirely acceptable to the
people of Kentucky, or at least this portion of Kentucky." [67] At a time when hesitation was fatal the Confederate government delayed ordering a complete and
unequivocal withdrawal. Instead, President Davis wrote:
"The necessity justifies the action." [68] A little later he
modified this position in deference to the apparent sentiment in the State, writing to Polk that he desired to
treat Kentucky with all possible respect. "Your occupation of Kentucky," he said, "being necessary as a
defensive measure, will of course be limited by the existence of such necessity." [69] At no time did the Confederate government show a disposition to withdraw unconditionally. Nor did they even take the trouble to explain
their position directly to the state officials and attempt
to secure their approval of the invasion.

The delicate question of dealing with Kentucky was
left wholly to Polk, who, although a soldier and a churchman of distinction, was no politician. Six days after the
invasion, he wrote to Magoffin, almost casually informing
him of his recent movement, which he justified by quoting Davis's opinion as to military necessity. He declared
his willingness to withdraw his forces, providing, first,
that the Federal troops be withdrawn simultaneously,
and secondly, "that the Federal troops shall not be
allowed to enter or occupy any part of Kentucky in the
future." [70] Coming from the commander whose move-

[66] Polk, vol. ii, p. 21.
[67] O. R., Series I, vol. iv, p. 180.
[68] Polk, vol. ii, p. 21.
[69] Sept. 13, 1861; O. R., Series I, vol. iv, p. 189.
[70] O. R., Series I, vol. iv, p. 185; vol. lii, part ii, p. 141.

ments were chiefly responsible for the presence of Grant's forces in the State, these were arrogant demands. In dealing with a legislative committee which was later appointed to confer with him, his attitude was even more unfortunate. He committed the unpardonable political sin of attempting to justify his acts before the people of Kentucky by pointing out their own violations of neutrality. Among other things, he charged that the State had allowed the national government to seize at Paducah property belonging to citizens of the Confederacy, and to cut timber from her forests for the building of gunboats. Though both these allegations were true, they were hardly sufficient to justify an invasion before the bar of public opinion in Kentucky. A third charge that the establishment of Camp Dick Robinson constituted a violation of neutrality was easily answered, since it was only necessary to point out the fact that Confederate sympathizers had also established recruiting camps in the State. When Polk further called attention to the fact that representatives of Kentucky in the Congress of the United States had voted supplies of men and money to carry on the war, he exposed, better than had yet been done, the fallacy of the doctrine of neutrality.[71] A State could not be neutral and remain in the Union. In presenting the issue thus clearly, he played directly into the hands of the Union party.

The attitude of the Confederate authorities toward Kentucky brought to completion a realignment of political groupings within the State. After the August election the more advanced Union men looked forward to

[71] Polk's statements to the legislative committee are given in Polk, vol. ii, pp. 24-25.

having Kentucky definitely support the national government. The conservative members of the party and the secessionists were content to continue the policy of neutrality. But after the Confederates entered Kentucky, the pro-Southern minority were left alone, struggling to achieve some arrangement whereby the former policy of the Union men could be continued. Like the Confederate authorities, however, they failed utterly to sense the revolution in public opinion until it was too late to warn their friends in the South. A States' Rights convention at Frankfort on September 10th contented itself with resolutions deploring the unnatural war, advocating neutrality and the dispersal of the Federal camps in the State, and offering to help drive out the Confederates as soon as the Union troops had left.[72]

Upon the assembling of the legislature, one of its first acts was to order the flag of the United States to be raised over the state capitol. After this virtual declaration of policy, it proceeded to pass a series of measures designed to secure the removal of the Confederate troops. On September 11th, a resolution was presented, instructing the governor "to inform those concerned that Kentucky expects the Confederate or Tennessee troops to be withdrawn from her soil unconditionally." It was adopted by the House by a vote of seventy-one to twenty-six, and by the Senate by twenty-five to eight. Governor Magoffin interposed his veto to prevent its passage, but it afterward secured the necessary vote. Thereupon, true to his duty, he issued the proclamation strictly in accordance with the resolution. A substitute proposal that both the Confederate and the Union

[72] Collins, vol. i, p. 93.

armies be withdrawn was defeated in the House by a vote of sixty-eight to twenty-nine.[73]

The States' Rights party, at last alarmed by the seriousness of the situation, resorted to desperate expedients to preserve neutrality. The members in the legislature proposed a compromise, offering to allow the national government the right to keep five thousand men at Camp Dick Robinson and to request the withdrawal of Polk, if the Union members would agree to request that Grant's force should leave afterward.[74] General Buckner, who had assumed the virtual leadership of the party in the State, struck at the heart of the subject by appealing to the Confederate government. On the 13th, he wrote to the adjutant-general at Richmond, informing him that the prompt withdrawal of Polk's army offered the only chance of maintaining the neutrality of the State. "If a withdrawal is authorized," he said, "I can rally thousands of neutrality Union men to expel the Federals." [75]

The plea of Buckner went unheeded, and the decision of the Confederate government was finally made on the advice of their military commanders. Polk expressed the opinion that the Confederate sympathizers in Kentucky overestimated the effect of his invasion on the public mind. It would have been better, he thought, if there had been a respectable pretext for an invasion some months earlier, since the secessionist party had been steadily losing ground. He believed that vigorous action on the part of the Confederates now would cause many of the people of the State again to rally to their sup-

[73] Collins, vol. i, p. 93.

[74] See the message of Governor George W. Johnson of the Kentucky Provisional Government, 1861.

[75] Buckner to Cooper, *O. R.*, Series I, vol. iv, p. 189.

port.[76] General Albert Sidney Johnston, who at this time succeeded to Polk's command, apparently dismissed from consideration the political phase of the situation, and concentrated his attention upon strengthening his military position. He ordered General Zollicoffer to move from East Tennessee into Kentucky and occupy the passes of the Cumberland Mountains. From this position and the one at Columbus, Johnston told President Davis he could not withdraw without exposing the frontiers of Tennessee to an invasion.[77]

The legislature waited a week for the Confederates to leave, and then took measures to compel them to do so. On September 18th a resolution was passed reciting that "Kentucky has been invaded by the forces of the so-called Confederate States, and the commanders . . . have insolently prescribed the conditions upon which they will withdraw, thus insulting the dignity of the State by demanding terms to which Kentucky cannot listen without dishonor; Therefore, Be it resolved . . . That the invaders must be expelled." General Anderson was requested to take command in the State, with full power to call for volunteer forces, and the governor was instructed to order out the militia against the Confederates. The resolution was vetoed by the governor, but was easily passed.[78] Another act required the governor to call out forty thousand men for a period of from one to three years, who were to be mustered into the service of the United States.[79] The Military Board was authorized to borrow $1,000,000 additional for the defense of the State. The arms which had been distributed among the State Guard were ordered recalled. And the

[76] Polk, vol. ii, p. 26.
[77] Polk, p. 28.
[78] Collins, vol. i, pp. 93-94.
[79] Idem, p. 95.

Union commanders in the State were requested to break up camps of secessionists and to protect private property.

To these thoroughgoing measures the legislature added others as time passed, but they were not carried out with the celerity which the impatient Union members demanded. Governor Magoffin's attitude proved a thorn in the flesh for them. He had vetoed every bill designed for the better defense of the State. He had kept in office an adjutant-general and a quartermaster-general who were in sympathy with the Confederates, and who placed obstacles in the way of organizing the armies of Kentucky. Although he had faithfully issued proclamations as required by the legislature, it was recognized that he was not in sympathy with the new policies of the State. From the beginning, the legislature refused to entrust him with any great powers. It virtually deprived him of his position as commander-in-chief of the militia by acts that were probably unconstitutional. It removed him from the Military Board, together with his States' Rights colleague, and filled the vacancies by the election of Union men.[80] Considerable feeling arose for his impeachment, and a resolution requesting his resignation was actually introduced in the Senate. But the sound political thinking which had characterized the Union leaders throughout the struggle now interposed to prevent intemperate action. They recognized that Magoffin had always acted within his constitutional powers. To impeach him at that juncture would probably alienate many citizens of doubtful sentiments; and Magoffin himself might possibly go over to the Confederates and assist in the organization of a provisional

[80] Collins, vol. i, p. 94.

secessionist government. A committee of the Union
leaders, after a conference with him, induced him to
allow the appointment of staff officers from their party
who should have full authority to act without any interference from the commander-in-chief. By these means
they obtained absolute control over all the military
activities of the state government. The next year,
Magoffin, finding his anomalous position distasteful,
resigned his office.[81] Thus passed out of public life in
Kentucky the last prominent figure who had stood consistently for the theory of States' rights. He had, by his
example and influence, performed a service of great value
to the cause of the Union.

Other members of the States' Rights party were
not so consistent. Upon the final decision of the
legislature many leaders left the State to take
their places in the Southern armies. One of the first
to go was General Buckner, who, as early as September 11th, had requested that his commission be made
out.[82] John C. Breckinridge left his seat in the United
States Senate to follow him. At the same time John H.
Morgan summoned his company of State Guards at Lexington, and with them marched to a camp in Tennessee.
Other organizations of these troops from various parts
of the State moved, as if by concert, toward Camp
Boone. Six companies, arriving in a body, were the
nucleus of a regiment of cavalry under Colonel Ben Har-
din Helm. Within a few days enough other citizens of
the State enlisted in the Confederate service to form
the Second Regiment of Kentucky infantry.[83] Over a

[81] Kelly, pp. 24-26.
[82] *O. R.*, Series I, vol. iv, p. 405.
[83] A. C. Quisenberry in the *Register* of the Kentucky Historical
Society, January, 1917, pp. 17-18.

thousand others congregated in the mountains of eastern Kentucky. But not all the State Guards deserted the service of the State. There were many who refused to follow their commanders and who enlisted in the Union army instead; and there were several officers, notably General Thomas L. Crittenden, who preferred the same service.

The Confederate war department assigned General Buckner to the command of the forces at Camp Boone, with the evident purpose of having him begin a military movement to restore the position of the secessionist party in Kentucky. On September 18th, he crossed the boundary line and occupied Bowling Green "as a defensive position," promising to withdraw as soon as the Federal forces had left the State. In a proclamation he asserted that he had come on the invitation of the people of Kentucky to protect them from subjugation by the national government, and to aid the governor in carrying out the policy of strict neutrality which the great majority of the people preferred, but which the legislature, untrue to the trust reposed in it, had overthrown.[84] His conduct toward the inhabitants was designed to prove to them beyond a doubt that the Confederate force had no motives of conquest, but only of deliverance from a foreign yoke. It was against his policy to seize the funds in the banks or to molest private persons. Even the commander of a Union home guard company was to be sought out and given friendly assurances.[85]

Instead of the unbounded enthusiasm which he had expected, he was received by the people with great coolness. He was soon obliged to halt his northward march

[84] *O. R.,* Series I, vol. iv, pp. 413-414.
[85] *O. R.,* Series I, vol. iv, pp. 415-416.

because the popular response did not justify movements beyond his ability to maintain his line of communications. When reinforcements from Tennessee enabled him to move forward into central Kentucky, he found the whole country deserted. The commander of his advance guard failed to find a friend along the road from Jamestown to Thomkinsville. "One old woman," he wrote, "met us with a Bible in her hand, said she was prepared and ready to die." [86] Few recruits joined the Confederate ranks after the first rush of enlistments.

The invasion was rendered of little effect by the activity of the Federal authorities. Until the actual decision of the legislature, General Anderson had been left practically alone in Louisville with only a headquarters guard. Afterward troops which had been massed on the northern border poured across the river in large numbers. Indiana alone sent seventeen regiments, and Ohio nearly as many. Within a month there were about thirty-five thousand Federal troops in the eastern part of the State, besides fifteen thousand Kentucky volunteers who were rapidly being organized. For the "prompt fraternal and effective assistance" rendered by the States of Ohio, Indiana and Illinois, the legislature passed almost unanimously a vote of thanks.[87] The Union forces were collected at Camp Dick Robinson under Thomas, and at the Nolin River, south of Louisville, under Sherman. There was besides a large number of Illinois troops at Paducah under Grant. The necessity of operating on divergent lines which would expose the armies to attack in detail prevented a forward movement until after the end of 1861.

[86] *O. R.*, Series I, vol. iv, p. 545.
[87] Collins, vol. i, p. 95.

In the interval attempts were made, against great obstacles, to consolidate the Federal military strength in the State. Nearly everyone wanted to establish a recruiting camp on his own farm. Instead of coöperation there was competition for men, with the result that the number of enlistments at first was somewhat disappointing. The home guards, in general, did not enlist for regular service—as Nelson said, they were "fireside rangers"—but they did engage in activities which required the constant supervision of the Federal authorities.[88] In spite of all that Anderson and Sherman could do, there were many instances of their persecution of unoffending citizens who were suspected of disloyalty to the Union. General Sherman seems to have been greatly disappointed at the attitude of the people of Kentucky. No one, he complained, had rallied to the cause of the Union, while hundreds were reported to have joined the Confederates at Bowling Green. All the young men appeared to be secessionists. Only the old men and the conservatives, who were content merely to have the Federal armies give them protection, adhered to the Union.[89] On that account every slaveholder was distrusted, and every man who was not a slaveholder was thought to be opposed to fighting his kindred who had enlisted on the other side. Some of the Kentucky regiments that had been raised could not be brought under strict discipline. The commanders in the field reported that the cavalry behaved badly, refusing to drill and spending their time in scouring the country or

[88] Nelson to Greene, Oct. 4, 1861, *O. R.*, Series I, vol. iv, p. 293; to Thomas, p. 304.
[89] Thomas to Cameron, *O. R.*, Series I, vol. iii, p. 548.

in lounging about the villages and drinking establishments.[90] As they received training in the field, however, the soldiers from Kentucky gradually developed
into a magnificent body of fighting men.

With the passing of time it became evident that the
people of Kentucky, as well as her public men, were in
earnest in prosecuting the war. General Buell's reports
indicated that the great mass of the population were
loyal to the Union, irrespective of age. Late in the year
the large number of enlistments showed that the young
men were as loyal as their fathers. The muster rolls
of Kentucky regiments up to December 31, 1861, showed
a total of 26,872 men, not including two regiments then
on service in western Virginia.[91] In the Confederate
service, on the other hand, the report of the secretary
of war in February, 1862, showed but 7,950 soldiers from
Kentucky.[92]

The line of division between Union and Confederate
sentiment ran through all classes of society and through
every section of the State. A careful search failed to
reveal any information indicating that the holding of
slaves and the support of the Confederacy had any rela-
tionship. The question of slavery, indeed, seems almost
completely to have been forgotten. The slaveholders,
instead of selling their slaves, kept them at work in
Kentucky as if there were no powerful abolitionist lobby
at Washington attempting to make the issue of the war
one of slavery or freedom.[93] In the Blue Grass region,
where most of the negroes were congregated, as many

[90] Schoepf to Thomas, Dec. 8, 1861; O. R., Series I, vol. vii, pp. 8-9.
[91] O. R., Series III, vol. i, p. 801.
[92] O. R., Series IV, vol. i, p. 962.
[93] Shaler, p. 255.

men were furnished to the Union armies as went from the whole State into the Confederate service.⁹⁴ In Christian County, the second largest slaveholding county in the State, Congressman James S. Jackson resigned his seat in August, 1861, to raise a regiment for the Federal army. Two more regiments were formed in this county before the end of the war.

It has often been said that the aristocratic families of Kentucky sided with the Confederate States, leaving only the poor and the ignorant and the recent immigrants from the North to fight for the Union. But this statement is not true. There was no monopoly of blue blood on either side. The Clays, the Breckinridges and the Crittendens—to mention only a few—had equally distinguished representatives in the service of both governments.⁹⁵ The lower ranks of the population—the poor farmers and the lumbermen—appear to have enlisted in the opposing armies in about the same proportions as other citizens. It was a peculiarity of sentiment in Kentucky, to a greater degree than in any other State, that hundreds of households were divided against each other.

With such a confused alignment in the different strata of society, it is not surprising to find that there was no clear-cut distinction among different localities. Every county sent men into both the Union and the Confederate armies. Only the proportions varied. In the mountainous counties of southeastern Kentucky the people fought as they had voted, and furnished thousands of men for the armies of Grant and Buell, while only a

⁹⁴ Thomas Speed, *The Union Cause in Kentucky*, p. 161.
⁹⁵ Champ Clark, *My Quarter Century of American Politics*, vol. i, pp. 82-83.

few hundred followed Buckner and Bragg. Along the Ohio River from the Big Sandy to the Green, the Union enlistments were many times those of the Confederates. Louisville and the immediate vicinity sent seven regiments into the Federal army. In the valley of the Green River and along most of the Tennessee border there was the same great majority for the Union. General Ward, establishing his headquarters at Greensburg in 1861, received many recruits who had fought their way with squirrel rifles and shotguns through the Confederate lines. He had losses in killed and wounded before there was an armed company in camp.[96] Muhlenberg County, at the western edge of the Pennyroyal section, sent about 820 men into the Union army as against 150 who joined the Confederates.[97] Union County, opposite the southwestern tip of Indiana, had about an equal number of men in the two armies. To the west of this county the secessionists were in a decided majority, their enlistments being kept down only by the presence, throughout the war, of Federal garrisons.

The mettle of the Union volunteers from Kentucky was first tested in a skirmish at Wildcat Mountain, where Colonel Garrard and the Seventh Kentucky successfully held their positions against Zollicoffer's army until reinforcements came up and drove off the Confederates. Toward the end of the year a few skirmishes of an indecisive nature took place, though there were no important operations. At the beginning of 1862 the Confederates were in possession of the southern one-third of the State, with their principal centers of concentration at Bowling Green, at forts Henry and Donelson, and at Columbus.

[96] Speed, *op. cit.*, pp. 163-178.
[97] Otto H. Rothert, *History of Muhlenberg County*, pp. 252-253.

A considerable force under Humphrey Marshall held the valley of the Big Sandy River. At this time, however, the Union armies all along the line were ready to move. Early in January Colonel James A. Garfield, with a brigade of Ohio troops, defeated Marshall and drove him over the mountains into southwestern Virginia.[98] A little later General Thomas badly defeated G. B. Crittenden and Zollicoffer at Mill Spring, forcing them also out of the State. A simultaneous advance of Foote's gunboats and Grant's army up the Tennessee River resulted in the defeat of General Tilghman, lately an officer in the Kentucky State Guard, at Fort Henry. Without delay Grant marched eleven miles across the country to Fort Donelson, which was then held by a force of fifteen thousand Confederates. After a siege of five days the members of the garrison who were unable to escape were compelled to surrender unconditionally. It is worthy of note that General Buckner was the commander of the Southern army in the final stage of the battle. Four Kentucky regiments, two on each side, bore an honorable part in this campaign.[99]

Grant's successes placed him in a position from which he could threaten the communications of the Confederates at both Bowling Green and Columbus. Before the final result at Fort Donelson, General Johnston began the withdrawal of his troops from the former position, and on February 27th he evacuated without a struggle his strong works at Columbus, for possession of which the Confederates had sacrificed their protection along the whole line from the Alleghanies to the Mississippi. No Confederate force of any size remained in the State,

[98] *O. R.*, Series I, vol. vii, pp. 21 *et seq.*
[99] Shaler, pp. 277-279.

and none appeared there for many months. Though the task of driving them out was completed mostly by the men of Illinois, Indiana and Ohio, the fact that they were able to secure such a poor lodgment was an important contributing factor. And the credit for this belongs to the people of Kentucky themselves, who gave them so little encouragement.

It is hardly too much to say that the decision of Kentucky was the determining factor in the war. It lent aid and encouragement to the Union men of Tennessee and Missouri. It consolidated the cause of the United States in the southern part of what is now West Virginia, making it possible to extend the boundaries of the new State southward with the consent of most of the people. It opened the way into the heart of the Confederacy, making possible the later Union campaigns in Tennessee. South of the Ohio River there was no good line of defense for the Southern armies. From the time that Kentucky finally made her decision for the Union, they fought a losing battle. If the Confederate government in September, 1861, had realized the importance of the neutrality of Kentucky, and had treated the State with the respect to which it was entitled, it is possible that the Union armies would not have been able to use her soil as a base against them. If, on the other hand, the national government had committed one-fifth of the blunders it had in Missouri, Kentucky would almost certainly have sided with the South. A President of the United States who was unfamiliar with conditions in the State would probably have made mistakes. Abraham Lincoln understood the temper of the people better than any other statesman of his time. He realized that he could not force the issue, but must give the people time to make

up their minds and fix their own course.   There are few
better instances of his statesmanship than the manner
in which he dealt with the situation in Kentucky and,
indeed, in the whole of the Ohio Valley in the critical
year of 1861.   Jefferson Davis, in contrast, though a
native of Kentucky like Lincoln, threw away the chances
of his government to survive through his inability to
understand the temper of the people and to deal with
them diplomatically.

CHAPTER X

THE COPPERHEAD MOVEMENT

By the middle of June, 1861, it seemed that the whole populations of Ohio, Indiana and Illinois had rallied to the cause of the Union. In southern Illinois the agitation to form a separate State in the Southern Confederacy had practically ceased, and the whole people had become a unit in supporting the President's policies. Enlistments in all the States had increased. The only important problems of the state administrations seemed to be the supplying of arms and equipment for the soldiers who offered themselves in almost too great numbers. But the unanimity was only apparent. There were many citizens who shouted with the mob, who displayed their flags because it was the fashion to do so, and who outwardly supported every measure of the national government; yet who, in reality, were opposed to the war. In the excited state of public feeling at the outbreak of hostilities, open opposition to the policies of the government would have been everywhere perilous. The danger of mob violence was as real in Ohio, Indiana and Illinois as in Virginia and Missouri. From necessity, therefore, the opponents of the war remained silent until the fever of excitement and passion which had followed the attack on Fort Sumter had to some extent burned itself out. At first timidly, one by one, and then growing bolder as increasing numbers gave them courage, they threw off the mask of professed support of the government and constituted themselves a party in opposition to all the measures of the Union officials, both national and state.

Ohio was the first State in which the friends of the South and the opponents of the party in power found an opportunity to lift up their voices in disapproval. The administration of the military laws left much to be desired. There was no question but that many of the staff officers whom the governor had appointed were inefficient men, whose conduct of affairs caused much complaint among the soldiers.[1] On that account many of those who had volunteered for three months refused to reënlist when their terms of service expired. For a time it was feared that the campaign to clear the Kanawha Valley would have to be abandoned for lack of men. The criticisms of the soldiers were eagerly repeated and magnified by civilians who sought to discredit the party in power.

Neither in Indiana nor in Illinois was there bungling by the state officials in the preparations for war. Most of the staff officers were competent. Those who were not were dismissed without delay, and their places were filled by abler men. All were under the constant supervision of Yates and Morton, whose administrative capacity was above question. In the appointment of field officers, however, Morton brought upon himself a great deal of censure from his political opponents. He believed that the commanders of troops should, above all else, be thoroughly devoted to the Union. He had consequently chosen his trusted friends, a majority of whom were Republicans, for the principal commands. The result was that the Democrats, of every shade of

[1] Whitelaw Reid, *Ohio in the War*, vol. i, pp. 26-29.

opinion, united in denouncing his policy as partisan and
unfair. Their criticisms were echoed by the pacifists,
the pro-Southern party, and the personal enemies that
his bold speech and his vigorous acts had made.[2] Even
Yates did not escape censure for mixing war and politics, though his commissioning of Logan, McClernand,
Grant and others had given full recognition to the minority party in the State. After the death of Douglas the
leaders of the War Democrats expected the appointment
of one of their party as his successor in the Senate. They
had loyally supported the policies of the administration
in the recent session of the legislature, and the disposition of the place presented a most difficult problem.
But Yates felt obliged to deny them their wish because
considerations of national politics seemed to make the
appointment of a Republican necessary. In the ensuing
elections his action was used by the Democrats as an
argument against forgetting the ties of party in time of
war.

The defeats at Bull Run and Wilson's Creek brought
about a new response to the Union, similar to that which
had followed the capture of Fort Sumter. There was
never afterward serious difficulty in obtaining men for
the army in any of the three States. But new criticisms
soon developed, this time directed at the national administration. Confidence in the authorities at Washington
was shaken, and charges of mismanagement became more
and more frequent. The War Department, especially,
fell under the condemnation of public opinion. Secretary Cameron's conduct of his office showed that he was
totally unfitted for his arduous duties either by temperament or training. He displayed none of the qualities

[2] William D. Foulke, *Life of Oliver P. Morton*, vol. i, pp. 171 *et seq.*

necessary to make this most important department efficient; and after a few months he was forced to leave the cabinet under very great suspicion of having been implicated in questionable financial transactions.[3] There was no one who regretted his going.

When, however, President Lincoln, after patiently enduring Fremont's insubordinate and inefficient administration of the Department of Missouri, finally removed him, public opinion took the opposite course. There was no question but that Fremont was incompetent to perform his duties either in the field or at headquarters, and the financial irregularities in his department were too numerous and too great to be disregarded. Even Francis P. Blair, Jr., turned against him, preferring the charges that led to his removal. Fremont had a great political following in the country at large, which had been built up through the legend of his pathfinding exploits, and which had lately been extended by his proclamations for the emancipation of slaves in Missouri. His removal therefore caused great dissatisfaction, especially among the Germans and those of the Republicans who wished to make the issues of the war turn upon the question of freedom or slavery. In Cincinnati the citizens tore down and trampled under foot portraits of the President. In the German section it was unsafe for anyone to express an opinion favorable to him. Subscriptions to the national loan practically ceased. And enlistments were suddenly checked.[4] In Illinois and elsewhere it was charged that Lincoln had removed Fremont because he was jealous of his influence and afraid

[3] Rhodes, vol. iii, pp. 574-577.
[4] Rhodes, vol. iii, pp. 483-484; quoting a letter from Richard Smith to Chase, Nov. 7, 1861.

of his becoming a candidate to succeed him. The Democrats joined in the complaints, not because they loved Fremont, but because they wished to discredit the Republican administration. To them, it seemed only another instance of the policy of the party to conduct the war on a partisan basis. The removal of many Federal officeholders to make places for Republicans had already added to the discontent that had been produced by the appointments of Morton and Yates.[6]

From the time of the dismissal of Fremont, the national government was between two fires in the North. On one side were the abolitionists who demanded the emancipation of the slaves both on humanitarian principles and in order that the people of New England and other strongly anti-slavery sections might be induced to put their whole strength into the struggle. On the other side was the steadily gathering force of partisan opponents of the war who sought to undermine the morale of the people by stressing the great losses in life and property and by proposing a peaceful settlement of the dispute that had rent the nation. Between them, supporting the administration, were those who fought for the restoration of the Union regardless of the question of emancipation. The great majority of the people of the Borderland, both north and south of the Ohio River, belonged to the middle group; though many times in the course of the struggle it seemed that the friends of the administration were outnumbered.

The elections in Ohio and Illinois in the autumn of 1861 indicate very well the trend of public opinion. In Ohio a governor was to be chosen; in Illinois, delegates to a state constitutional convention. The Republican

[6] Davidson and Stuvé, *op. cit.*, p. 871.

leaders in Ohio, alarmed at the condition of affairs, determined to abandon their party name and devote their efforts to the election of a candidate who could be depended on to give his whole-hearted support to the national government. Taking as their slogan the announcement of Douglas that there were now no parties except patriots and traitors, they proposed to the Democratic state committee that a joint convention be held to nominate candidates. That body, anticipating a victory for their party, refused to coöperate. They were in no way responsible, they said, for the condition of the country.[6] Then, having failed to obtain official sanction for their plans, the Republicans and the leading War Democrats appealed to the people. Early in August groups of citizens in about twenty counties issued a call for a convention of the Union party to be held at Columbus on September 5th.[7]

It was obvious that success would be impossible without a strong candidate, able to attract votes from among the Democrats, and a platform that was silent concerning the peculiar principles of the Republicans. The nomination of Governor Dennison for another term was out of the question. Though he was honest and fairly capable, and though he had learned many lessons from experience, the mistakes of his subordinates told heavily against him. There was no other Republican in the line of succession. Besides, it was the prevailing opinion that a War Democrat should be nominated. Among all the men of this group, there was none who had a higher place in his own party or in the confidence of all the people

---

[6] George H. Porter, *Ohio Politics During the Civil War Period*, pp. 81-84.

[7] E. O. Randall and D. J. Ryan, *History of Ohio*, vol. iv, pp. 172-173.

than David Tod. He had presided over the convention at
Baltimore in 1860 which had nominated Douglas. He
had supported vigorously the compromise measures of
the winter before. After the outbreak of the war he had
devoted his efforts to rallying the Democratic party to
the support of the national administration.[8] His nomination was made without opposition. The convention
adopted as its platform a series of resolutions: (1) that
the war had been forced upon the government by disunionists in the South; (2) that it "is not waged upon
our part in any spirit of oppression, nor for any purpose
of conquest or subjugation, . . . but to defend and maintain the supremacy of the Constitution, and to preserve
the Union with all the dignity, equality and rights of the
several States unimpaired; and (3) that as soon as these
objects are accomplished the war ought to cease." [9]

The nomination and the platform of the Union party
practically forced the regular Democrats to take a stand
in opposition to the war. In their platform they criticized the conduct of the war and suggested a national
convention for the settlement of the difficulties of the
country. Their proposal seemed so impractical to the
people that they were not even able to hold their own in
the election. Tod carried the State by a plurality of
fifty-five thousand. The distribution of the vote in different sections of the State was practically the same as
in the election of 1860, the Democrats gaining three
counties and losing six. The result made it evident that
their organization remained unbroken, and that it would
be a source of future danger to the cause of the Union.

In Illinois the issues involved in the election were such

[8] *History of Trumbull and Mahoning Counties*, p. 171.
[9] Porter, p. 83, note.

that a fusion between the Republicans and the War
Democrats was impracticable. The latter group therefore generally supported their party ticket. The results
of the election indicated a decided trend away from the
Republicans. As in 1860, the Democrats were successful in southern Illinois. In addition they carried many
northern counties, including Cook, Will, La Salle and
Peoria, electing in all about three-fifths of the members
of the convention.[10] Their victory created consternation
among the friends of the Union. Governor Yates, fearing that the dissatisfied element in southern Illinois
would be emboldened to attempt to take over the state
administration by violent means, requested that a regiment be stationed at Springfield. "Secession," he wrote,
"is deeper and stronger here than you have any idea." [11]
During the sessions of the convention rumors of disloyalty among some of the Democratic members gained
credence. It was said that one of them held a commission in the Confederate army; that the governor had a
letter proving that another had been engaged in treasonable correspondence; and that almost a majority belonged to a secret organization in full sympathy with
the Southern Confederacy. An investigating committee
appointed by the convention, finding no evidence to sub-
stantiate the charges, exonerated the accused members.[12]

As might have been expected from its partisan com-
position, the convention did not always confine itself to
its proper functions. Resolutions were presented protesting against emancipation and the enlistment of negroes,
and approving the resignation of Cameron "as indicat-

[10] Cole, *op. cit.*, pp. 266-267.
[11] *Idem*, p. 267.
[12] *Journal* of the Illinois Convention, 1862, pp. 942-943.

ing a purpose on the part of the administration of adhering to the conservative principles of the constitution." [13] Shortly after the opening of the session a member asked that the Committee on Federal Relations be instructed to report "whether the odious and treasonable doctrine of secession has not received its vitality and nourishment from the abolition leaders of the north; and whether, in short, the abolitionists of the north and the rebels of the south are not equally and alike traitors." [14] The new constitution, as finally submitted by the convention, was an immense improvement in the existing fundamental law, especially in its provisions relating to taxation and the organization of the government. But these advantages were outweighed by the provision for redistricting the State so as to give the Democratic party a majority in the succeeding legislatures. Equally obnoxious to the Republicans was the clause which decreased the term of the governor from four years to two, thus requiring a new election in 1862 instead of in 1864.[15] Fortunately for the cause of the Union, the draft constitution was rejected by a popular majority of sixteen thousand. Many of the Democrats in southern Illinois voted with the Republicans against it because they feared that its adoption would result in an increase in their taxes.[16]

During the first year of the war the opposition to the policies of the Union officials was almost wholly confined to political agitation. With the exception of Jesse D. Bright of Indiana, who was expelled from the United States Senate for having had correspondence with President Davis, no one of prominence gave direct aid to the

[13] *Journal*, p. 109.
[14] *Journal*, p. 216.
[15] Davidson and Stuvé, p. 877.
[16] Cole, pp. 269-271.

Confederates. The other Democratic leaders limited their activities to criticizing unsparingly the measures of the party in power. In this they performed the proper function of the party in opposition. But the unfortunate position that the Democratic party in Ohio was compelled to take in the election of 1861 soon led to much more dangerous activities than those of mere criticism of the administration. During the following three years their regular organization led a factious opposition, not merely to the Union officials, but to the continued existence of the war itself, failing at all times to give its support to the government.[17]

The Peace Democrats, as they soon came to be called in contradistinction to the patriotic War Democrats, declared that they were in favor of restoring the Union quite as much as the Republicans. They differed from them merely as to the methods that ought to be used. Instead of making war on the States that had seceded, and thus widening the breach between the sections, they declared their belief in the efficacy of negotiations:— and this notwithstanding the practical hopelessness of obtaining anything beyond a weak league of States. Their leaders insisted that the policies of compromise of the preceding winter be resumed, assuring the people that in no other way could the Union be restored.[18] As an argument for the adoption of their policy, they expressed grave doubts concerning the ability of the Federal armies to conquer the South. Furthermore, they tried to build up a narrow sectional feeling by arousing prejudices against other parts of the North, particularly

[17] Randall and Ryan, vol. iv, p. 177; Julia H. Levering, *Historic Indiana*, p. 300; Cole, pp. 298-301.

[18] "The Peace Democrats," Publication No. 99 of the Western Reserve Historical Society, 1918, pp. 17-18.

New England. Thomas A. Hendricks, at the Democratic
state convention in Indiana, January 8, 1862, spoke of
the danger of being enslaved by the capitalists of New
England and Pennsylvania. "To encourage and stimu-
late the people of the South in the production of their
peculiar commodities, that they may be large buyers
from us, has been and . . . will be the true interest of the
Northwest. . . . If the failure and folly and wickedness
of the party in power render a Union impossible then
the mighty Northwest must take care of herself and her
own interests. She must not allow the arts and finesse
of New England to despoil her of her richest commerce
and trade." [19] An address issued later by a disloyal
organization declared that "it was the fanaticism of New
England that caused the war with the Southern States
and brought desolation and sorrow to the hearthstones
of our people. She ransacks the entire country for
negroes to fill her quotas in the Army, and while crying
for a vigorous prosecution of the war fattens on the blood
of Western men." [20]

If the politicians who controlled the party were sincere, their attitude showed that they had not advanced
a step since the attack on Fort Sumter, and that they
were wholly incapable of appreciating the significance of
that event. They apparently could not see, as other leaders did, that the South was in earnest in its desire for
independence. Of their sincerity, however, there is good
reason for doubt. Experienced as most of them were in

[19] Quoted by William C. Cochran, "The Dream of a Northwestern
Confederacy," in the *Proceedings* of the Historical Society of Wiscon-
sin, 1916, p. 238.

[20] Quoted by James A. Woodburn, in "Party Politics in Indiana
During the Civil War," in the *Annual Report* of the American Historical Association, 1902, vol. i, p. 239.

public affairs, they could hardly have escaped realizing that the presence of such a large and active peace party in the North was a source of encouragement to the Confederates, leading them to continue the struggle even when their military success seemed no longer possible, in the hope of the ultimate disintegration of the morale of their opponents. Thus the natural effect of their movement would be permanent disunion.

The rank and file of the Peace Democrats was made up of a number of different groups whose bond of union consisted in their common opposition to the administration. There were many who genuinely believed in the platform of their party—men who actually thought it possible to stop the war at any time and restore the Union. "The Constitution as it is, and the Union as it was" became a rallying cry which brought many otherwise intelligent people into their ranks. Next in order were the advocates of peace at any price, who would have allowed the Union to dissolve into thin air and the States to follow after it if they could only have gone about their business as usual. A third group was composed of bitter partisans who had never voted for any other than the Democratic ticket. They furnished most of the numerical strength of the organization. But they could not have been brought into line with the unpatriotic policies of the leaders if there had not been among them a latent sympathy with the South, which had been carried down from an earlier period in the development of the Borderland. Unmoved by the tremendous social and industrial advances of the preceding decade, they continued to look southward, rather than eastward and northward. To put the matter into plainer words, their attitude seems to have represented a sort of old fogyism.

It is doubtful if there was much economic justification
for the strength of the Peace Democrats. The people,
of course, soon became weary of the waste of life and the
destruction of property in the war. Their commerce
with the South was cut off by the closing of the Mississippi, which, together with the general feeling of uncertainty, caused the prosperity of the commercial centers
to be somewhat diminished. As a reimbursement for
their financial losses, however, there soon developed an
important industry in supplying the army, which took
the place of the Southern trade in provisions to a great
extent. Even in the first year of the war, there was an
inconsiderable number of business failures in Cincinnati.[21] In the succeeding years conditions gradually
improved. The manufacturing and other industries were
stimulated by the war. Just at this time, too, there fortunately arose a tremendous foreign demand for agricultural produce, which brought prosperity to the farmers.
The demand was so great, as a matter of fact, that the
transportation facilities of the section were at first inadequate to meet it. The whole burden of commerce had
been transferred to the railroads by the closing of the
Mississippi, making it difficult for the traffic departments at once to adjust themselves to the new conditions. But after a short time they provided sufficient
rolling stock to carry the surplus wheat and bacon of the
section to the Eastern ports, as well as to care for the
movements of troops and military supplies.[22] In spite
of the adequate provision for transportation the Democratic leaders were not silenced. They continued their

[21] Mayor's *Annual Message*, 1862.
[22] Emerson D. Fite, *Social and Industrial Conditions in the North
During the Civil War*, pp. 15-17.

insistent demands for the opening of the Mississippi, evoking a considerable popular response which apparently grew out of a sentimental preference for the old route rather than dissatisfaction with the new one. But if the railroads had not existed, there can scarcely be any doubt that there would have been many more opponents of the war in the Borderland than there were.

Some of the leading Democrats, in order to make their opposition to the war more effective, assisted in the formation of secret organizations under such names as "The Knights of the Golden Circle," "The Order of the Star," "The Circle of Honor," "The Knights of the Mighty Host," "The Order of American Knights," "The Sons of Liberty," and "The Sons of '76." Such organizations were nothing new in American politics and society. At the time they were a favorite method of advertising a new movement and gaining attention which later resulted in recruiting members. The Know-Nothing party had begun in this way, and as long as it remained secret it had an important influence in politics. Some of the anti-slavery organizations, notably those operating the underground railroad, were secret. In many parts of the South, clubs had been formed under various names to combat the measures of the abolitionists. Some of the organizations established after the Civil War, like the Grange and the Knights of St. Crispin, were secret societies with elaborate rituals. In the establishment of these organizations the opponents of the war in the North merely adopted a well known political expedient of the period.

The most widely known of the societies was the Knights of the Golden Circle. It was originally founded in Alabama, in 1855, for the protection of Southern rights. During the years before the war it made little progress outside a limited section of the South. Upon the outbreak of hostilities, its name, constitution, and ritual were borrowed by Northern opponents of the war, and thereafter its spread was extremely rapid. By the beginning of the year 1862 it had gained so many members in the Northwest that the Union party were thrown into a state bordering on panic. The principal centers of the organization were in Cincinnati, Hamilton and Dayton, Ohio; Indianapolis and Vincennes, Indiana; Springfield and Quincy, Illinois; St. Louis, Missouri; Louisville, Kentucky; and Detroit, Michigan. Clement L. Vallandigham, who was the "Supreme Grand Commander" in 1864, estimated that it had eighty-four thousand members in Illinois, fifty thousand in Indiana, and forty thousand in Ohio. In several counties in Indiana it is said that practically every Democrat was a Knight of the Golden Circle.[23] In its organization the society was not unlike many well known fraternal orders of the present day. The local lodges, called "temples," gave their members a "temple degree," which was only probationary. If a member was especially active in promoting the organization or in opposing the cause of the Union, he was admitted to the higher degrees, when the real purposes of the society were fully explained to him.[24] In some of the later societies which were formed in imitation of the "Knights," the local clubs were organized into brigades and regiments, in which the higher officers bore military titles. Some of the lodges held military drills after a fashion, and it was supposed that all the organizations were a compact mili-

[23] "The Peace Democrats," p. 26-30.
[24] I. Winslow Ayer, *The Great North-western Conspiracy*, pp. 16-18.

tary unit, needing only arms to make them a formidable danger to the United States. Their activities, aside from those which were merely political and social, were directed toward the discouragement of enlistments, the protection of deserters from capture, and the interference with provost marshals in the discharge of their duties.

Naturally the organizations caused resentment, and then fear, among those who supported the government. Their secret character gave them far greater importance than the actual number of their members justified. It was commonly supposed that they had thousands more enrolled than the figures given even in the exaggerated estimates of Vallandigham. The officers were thought to be in treasonable correspondence with the Confederates. Late in the war rumors were current that arrangements had been made for a Southern army to invade the Ohio Valley, bringing arms for the secret organizations who would then rise *en masse* and create havoc in the cities of the North or attack the Federal armies in the rear.[25] Nothing, apparently, was beyond popular belief as to their purposes or their power. In order to counteract their activities, the Union men began the formation of "Loyal Leagues" in the summer of 1862, which rendered service of immense importance, though, lacking the mysterious character of their rivals, they failed to have as much effect.[26]

If the Knights of the Golden Circle, or the members of any other organization had been summoned by their leaders to join a Confederate force, they would not have responded. With the war at their doors, they would have rushed to the defense of the Union. The great

[25] Consult pages 246-250 of the article by Cochran, cited *supra*.
[26] "The Peace Democrats," p. 27.

number of Union enlistments in southern Illinois, and
the sacrifices of the citizens along the Ohio River in
Indiana in repelling guerrilla raids from Kentucky, show
that proximity to danger had a deterrent effect on
activities against the Union.[27] The Knights of the Golden
Circle obtained relatively slight support in the counties
on the Ohio River. Their principal strength was in the
interior. The greatest importance of the organization
lay in the fact that it afforded means for the swift dis-
semination of propaganda, and thus made it easy for the
Democratic party to conduct its political campaigns.

To all the opponents of the war, in whatever degree,
the Union men applied the opprobrious epithets of
"Copperhead" and "Butternut." The copperhead was
a venomous snake which struck from concealment without warning. A "Butternut" was originally a poor farmer
whose outer garments were dyed with the bark or roots
of the butternut tree. In spite of the accusations of
treason which were hurled at members of the party, the
Peace Democrats did not regard it as a disgrace to be
called a Butternut or a Copperhead. Like the Metho-
dists and the Tories—to mention only two out of a great
number—they adopted the opprobrious epithets as
names for their party; and then they devised emblems to
fit them besides. In cutting a butternut transversely
and removing the kernel, there were found the outlines
of two perfect hearts joined together. Wearing the
butternut badges, they explained that they represented
the Northern heart and the Southern heart which could
not be torn asunder by war. Others cut the head of
Liberty from an old copper cent and wore it on the

[27] Comparatively few outrages against the United States occurred
in the section along the Ohio River.

lapels of their coats to show that they stood for liberty and the Constitution, both of which they charged the Republicans with having subverted.[28]

During the year 1862 the course of events had much to do with the increased dissatisfaction with the administration. In the early months the Union armies gained a series of brilliant victories in Arkansas, Kentucky, Tennessee, North Carolina and Louisiana. But they were unable to obtain any further signal successes. McClellan's campaign against Richmond failed miserably. Pope was decisively defeated at the second battle of Bull Run. In the West, Buell wasted the greater part of the summer in an ill-advised campaign against Chattanooga, only to be recalled to Kentucky to repel an invasion by Bragg's army. He succeeded in driving the Confederates out of the State, and McClellan was able to turn back a similar offensive movement of Lee in Maryland. But after the splendid promise of the earlier campaigns, the mere repulse of the Confederates was a disappointment to the people, and led to fresh criticism of the way in which the war was being conducted.

In Ohio Governor Tod aroused a great deal of discontent by adopting a policy of rigorous repression in combating activities against the administration. Several instances occurred of the arbitrary suppression of the right of free speech. The most noteworthy of them was the arrest and imprisonment, under the suspension of the privilege of habeas corpus, of Dr. Edson B. Olds of Lancaster on the charge of treasonable utterances and the prevention of enlistments. The case aroused much sym-

[28] Albert Matthews, "Origin of Butternut and Copperhead," in the *Publications* of the Colonial Society of Massachusetts, vol. xx, pp. 205-237.

pathy for him among nearly all classes, for he was an aged man, and had been prominently identified with state and national politics for several years.[29] The arrest of prominent Democratic editors followed. From points as widely separated as Brown County on the Ohio River and Ashtabula County on Lake Erie, mass meetings protested against these arbitrary acts.

A third cause of dissatisfaction was the preliminary notice of the proclamation of emancipation. From what has already been said concerning the attitude of the Borderland toward slavery, it should be apparent that there was little disposition for the people to favor emancipation as an issue of the war. They were fighting only for the restoration of the Union without regard to the question of freeing the slaves. President Lincoln truly expressed their feeling when he wrote: "I think that we already have an important principle to rally and unite the people, in the fact that constitutional government is at stake. This is the fundamental idea, going down about as deep as anything." [30] In spite of his disinclination to act, he was forced by the pressure exerted by the abolitionists to take more advanced ground. The result was most unfortunate for the Union party in the Borderland. Instead of helping to bring the war to a speedy close, it seemed to many people that it would delay the restoration of peace; for with the greater part of the property in the South confiscated, it seemed certain that offers of concession would be refused by the Confederates. Coupled with the suspension of the privilege of habeas corpus, the emancipation proclamation seemed to indicate the adoption of a policy under which the constitu-

[29] Rhodes, vol. iv, p. 165.
[30] *Complete Works,* vol. viii, p. 33.

tional rights of citizens would be further interfered with.

For all of these reasons, there was no more inauspicious time for an election, from the standpoint of the Union party, than the fall of 1862. The Republicans were apathetic. The War Democrats showed less enthusiasm than at any other time for allying themselves with the Republicans. The regular Democrats, on the other hand, were thoroughly aroused. Their candidates, taking advantage of every false step of their opponents, conducted a vigorous campaign. In their statements of principles they were able to advance farther than in the preceding year, and to occupy a valuable strategic position which had just been vacated by the Republicans. This was on the question of maintaining the Union. By denouncing a war for the emancipation of the negroes and the subjugation of the South, they won the support of doubtful voters. At the same time, by impressing upon the people their approval of a war waged for the preservation of the Union, they suffered little from the accusations of disloyalty made by their opponents.[31]

The result of the election was an overwhelming victory for the Democrats. Their candidates for the House of Representatives were successful in fourteen of the nineteen districts of Ohio, in seven of the eleven districts of Indiana, and in eight of the thirteen districts of Illinois. The large proportion of Democratic congressmen elected in Ohio was partly the result of a gerrymander perpetrated by the Republican majority in the preceding legislature. In attempting to rearrange the districts so that they could elect seventeen congressmen, they made

[31] For a statement of the Democratic principles in Indiana consult Woodburn's article in the *Annual Report* of the American Historical Association, 1902, vol. i, p. 244.

the Republican majorities in most districts much below the margin of safety. An especially noteworthy example occurred in Cincinnati where, in trying to assure the defeat of George H. Pendleton, they lost the Republican district.[32] They succeeded, however, in defeating Clement L. Vallandigham through the addition of a strongly Republican county to his district. In the original counties he received greatly increased majorities.[33] The Democratic state tickets were swept into office by majorities of eight thousand in Ohio, of nine thousand in Indiana, and of fourteen thousand in Illinois. In the last named State the party elected fifty-four of the eighty-six members of the lower house, and secured control of the Senate by a majority of one. In Indiana they obtained large majorities in both houses. The Union party in these two States had henceforth only the executive department to depend upon for the effective prosecution of the war.

The assembling of the legislatures was awaited with anxiety by the Union authorities, for it was plain that the leaders of the Peace Democrats were bent on making trouble. Morton wrote before the session that it was contemplated in both Indiana and Illinois to pass resolutions recognizing the Southern Confederacy.[34] Though the action did not go to such an extreme application of the doctrine of state sovereignty, it nevertheless was of such a nature as to afford much comfort to the enemies of the United States. The legislature of Indiana refused to receive the message of Governor Morton,

[32] G. M. D. Bloss, *Life and Speeches of George H. Pendleton*, pp. 47-48.
[33] James L. Vallandigham, *A Life of Clement L. Vallandigham*, p. 215.
[34] *O. R.*, Series I, vol. xx, part ii, p. 297.

basing its work instead partly upon the message of the Democratic governor of New York. Him they thanked for his "clear, forceful and patriotic" recommendations. Throughout the session they questioned the financial administration of the Republican officials, subjecting it to the closest scrutiny. They appointed a committee to investigate the military arrests ordered by Morton, which in its report is said to have gone to "the verge of treason." [35] In the lower house, resolutions were passed requesting the withdrawal of the emancipation proclamation, and recommending a convention of all the States. These failed, by only a few votes, to obtain consideration in the Senate. Other resolutions denounced the arming of negroes, and declared that the plan of compensated emancipation which the President had proposed was a wicked defiance of the rights of the people. One of the members presented a resolution declaring the national conscription act subversive of state sovereignty and counseling resistance to it;[36] but this extreme measure went a little too far even for the Democrats of Indiana in 1863. Twice in the course of the session the Republican members absented themselves in order to break a quorum. The first time they did so, their object was the purely partisan one of preventing the election of two Democratic United States Senators. They were soon forced to give way and return in order to secure the consideration of measures of the highest importance to the State, especially the biennial appropriations. But in this matter, also, the Democrats held

[35] Russel M. Seeds, *History of the Republican Party in Indiana*, p. 89.
[36] Foulke, vol. i, pp. 229-230.

their position steadfastly. They gave precedence in the order of business to a military bill which would have taken the control of enlistments and the supply of the army out of the hands of the governor and placed it under the control of a commission composed of certain of the Democratic state officials. Until this bill was passed, they served notice that they would not consider any other measures. The Republican members of the lower house then withdrew to Madison and peremptorily refused to return until the conditions were changed. The legislature adjourned without having made any appropriations.[37]

It was the expectation of the Democratic majority that Morton would be forced to call the legislature into special session. Had he done so, there is little doubt that they would have carried their point and secured the control of the military establishment. But they had underestimated the qualities of their governor. He was not like Magoffin. Week followed week, and month followed month, and there was no call for a special session. Rather than endanger the cause of the Union, as he thought, by giving up his authority, Morton cut himself adrift from his constitutional moorings, and for the following two years carried on the government of Indiana on his own personal responsibility. For the first time since the reign of James II, the government of an Anglo-Saxon community was in the hands of a despot, uncontrolled by the necessity of securing legislative approval of revenues and appropriations. Morton raised funds for the necessary expenses of the State without resort to taxation, and disbursed them without the assistance of

[37] Seeds, p. 90.

the Democratic treasurer of the State. He continued to
enlist and equip regiments without any authorization
from the legislature. And all these things he did for the
preservation of constitutional government!

The funds which Morton provided came from a variety of sources. Those most easily available were the
profits, amounting to some $75,000, from the operation
of the arsenal which he had established on his own
responsibility, but which the legislature had refused to
confirm as a state institution. Since it still remained a
private concern under Morton, a demand from the treasurer that the profits should be placed in his hands could
not legally be enforced. Further funds were obtained on
appropriations of local officials in those counties in which
the Union party was in control. These sources together
being insufficient, Morton went to Washington to see if
he could not obtain advances from the national government for the equipment of Indiana regiments. His request was refused by the Secretary of the Treasury on
the ground that it was plainly illegal to pay out national
funds to a State. He then appealed to the President;
but Lincoln felt that he could not stretch his war powers
to the extent of disregarding the laws. He advised him,
however, to confer with Stanton. In the Secretary of
War, Morton found a kindred spirit. His department
had then on hand a considerable fund to aid States
threatened with rebellion, which had been appropriated
without mention of any specific object, and which was
to be expended at the discretion of the secretary. Stanton threw questions of constitutionality to the winds,
and issued orders for the payment of $250,000 out of this
fund. "If the cause fails," said Morton, "we shall both
be covered with prosecutions;" to which Stanton replied:

"If the cause fails, I do not wish to live." [38] For the
remainder of the necessary expenditures Morton raised
small sums on his own personal credit, following the
example of Pierpont in Virginia. By the exercise of the
most rigid economy, paring down the expenses of the
State to the absolute necessities of clothing, arms and
other military equipment, Morton managed to make
these sources sufficient to last until the new legislature
began its sessions in 1865.

In disbursing the funds Morton was obliged to organize an authority independent of the state treasurer, since,
if he paid them into the treasury, he could not hope to
have them paid out again except on an appropriation by
the legislature. He therefore placed them in a safe in
his own office, and disbursed them through a "bureau of
finance." At the outset he was faced by the demands of
bondholders for the payment of interest on the public
debt—demands which Morton was anxious to meet in
order to maintain the credit of the State. There was
precedent for calling the payment of interest a fixed
charge to be paid out by the treasurer without specific
appropriation; and Morton asked that he do so. But the
Democratic attorney-general thwarted his plans by declaring that such payments were unconstitutional. The
Democratic treasurer had a suit brought in order to
obtain a judicial interpretation of the question. And the
Democratic supreme court judges sustained the attorney-
general's ruling. There was then nothing for Morton to
do but to arrange for the payments himself. Owing to
the action of the Democratic financial agent of the State
in New York City, who refused to furnish him with a
list of the bondholders, he was unable to issue warrants

[38] Foulke, vol. i, p. 261.

for a long time. When he obtained the list, he began paying interest.[39] The total amount of Morton's disbursements was $457,000. By economical management, he not only guarded the credit of the State, but he also maintained the same high standard of equipment for his regiments as he had established in 1861.

In Illinois the majority of the legislature took a stand only a little less unpatriotic than that of the Democrats in Indiana. In recognition of their attitude, Governor Yates tempered his annual message somewhat, especially concerning the proclamation of emancipation and the arrests of citizens under the military laws. At the same time, he asked for united support in the war, declaring that there could be no peace worth having until the rebellion should be crushed.[40] The message was practically ignored, the majority party taking their cue instead from a Democratic meeting held in Springfield at the beginning of the session, which condemned unsparingly the policies of the administration. One of the first acts of the legislature was to elect Congressman Richardson, a bitter opponent of the war, to the United States Senate. Next, a series of resolutions passed the lower house, which recommended an armistice in order that a convention of the States might be held in Louisville. "Further prosecution of the present war," according to one of them, "cannot result in the restoration of the Union and the preservation of the constitution as our fathers made it, unless the President's emancipation proclamation is withdrawn." These resolutions failed to pass the Senate by reason of the sudden death of a Dem-

[39] Foulke, vol. i, pp. 254-268.
[40] *Message of Governor Richard Yates,* 1863, pp. 48-49.

ocratic member, which left the body evenly divided.[1] In the whole course of the session every effort of the Democratic party seemed to be directed toward obstruction and factious interference with the conduct of the war. Scarcely a constructive measure was passed, and there seemed to be little prospect that any good could come out of the session. At length, weary of their tactics, Yates seized an opportunity to get rid of them. The constitution provided that the governor should have the power to adjourn the legislature in case the two houses could not agree on the period of an adjournment. Such an occasion fortuitously occurred, whereupon Yates set the date for the next meeting of the legislature on the last day of their terms, which was the Saturday before the first Monday in January, 1865.[2] In reply, the Democratic members of the lower house met in informal session for two weeks longer and passed resolutions of protest against the action of the governor. But they could do nothing further, except to appeal individually to the people.

The expressions of public opinion concerning the prorogation were of extremely diverse character. A Democratic mass meeting in Springfield, which is said to have been attended by forty thousand citizens, protested against it as a usurpation, and reiterated the resolutions passed by the lower house on the conduct of the war.[3] On the other hand, the Douglas Democrats published resolutions declaring their devotion to the Union. "The errors of the administration," they said, "form no excuse

[1] Davidson and Stuvé, pp. 880-884.
[2] Davidson and Stuvé, p. 897.
[3] Cole, pp. 299-300.

for any loyal citizen to withhold his support from the government." Most of the regiments in the field expressed their abhorrence at the "fire in the rear." Among the leading Democrats who had accepted commissions, McClernand and Logan left the party in consequence of the attitude of the legislature.⁴⁴ On the whole the occurrence seems to have redounded to the benefit of the Union.

With the example of members of the legislature and other leaders before them, it is little wonder that private citizens adopted an attitude of bitter hostility toward the government. Many persons encouraged insubordinate and unmilitary conduct among their relatives and friends in the army. And these activities had a serious effect. The 128th regiment, which was stationed at Cairo, suffered so heavily from desertions that only thirty-five men were left in the ranks in March, 1863. In the 109th regiment, which had been recruited from southern Illinois, desertions and fraternization with the enemy became so serious that it was necessary to disarm the men in Mississippi. In many counties of southern and western Illinois armed resistance to the arrest of deserters was offered, the worst disorders occurring in Scott and Greene counties to the north of St. Louis. The enrollment of citizens for the draft was accompanied by disturbances in many parts of the State. A mob of five hundred persons besieged the village of Olney for three days, threatening to burn it unless the enrollment lists were surrendered. In the counties along the Mississippi north of St. Louis, the citizens protected and harbored bushwhackers who had crossed over from Missouri. Guerrilla bands spread terror through the rural regions of southern

⁴⁴ Davidson and Stuvé, pp. 889-890.

Illinois, whipping men who had been active in the cause of the Union, and even shooting them down in their homes.[45] In part, these disorders were in retaliation for the activities of Union vigilance committees which had previously meted out summary, and in some cases undeserved, punishment to those who sympathized with the South.

In Indiana similar outrages occurred in many sections, particularly in the district just south of Indianapolis. In Warren County a riot occurred between furloughed soldiers and citizens. In Bartholomew County resistance was offered to the enrollment of citizens and to the draft. In Rush, Putnam and Monroe counties enrolling officers were murdered in cold blood. And in Parke County the Union men suffered from an invasion of "Butternuts" from the neighboring county of Fountain.[46] Morton's aggressive companies of the Indiana Legion no doubt prevented much greater disturbances. At public meetings, cheers for Jefferson Davis and curses for the abolitionists were sometimes heard. The citizens of Shelby County asked for an armistice for such a time as necessary for "the people of the North and the South to express through a national Convention, their desire for peace and the maintenance of the Union as it was and the constitution as it is." [47] In Brown County, fifty miles south of Indianapolis, the Democrats, in a public meeting, declared that in case the Confederates were successful, their interests would demand that they withdraw from political association with New England. Similar resolutions are said to have been passed in at least fifteen

[45] Cole, pp. 305-306; Davidson and Stuvé, p. 896.
[46] *Report on Operations of the Indiana Legion and Minute Men,* 1863-1864, pp. 5-6.
[47] "The Peace Democrats," p. 24.

other counties in the first three months of the year 1863.[48]

In Ohio, according to the report of the adjutant-general, "an unusual degree of excitement, disorder and violence" prevailed during the first half of the year. An armed mob of nearly a hundred citizens of Noble County proposed that a provost guard sent to arrest a deserter should surrender and be paroled as prisoners of the Southern Confederacy. In Holmes County, following the rescue of military prisoners, a detachment of soldiers was compelled to fight citizens intrenched behind stone breastworks.[49] Other lesser disorders occurred in various parts of the State. The widespread opposition to the national authorities brought a protest from the soldiers at the battlefield of Murfreesboro. "What means this party strife at home?" they demanded, "What matters now the cause of the war? It exists!"[50]

Partly to keep down the disorders in the Northwest, partly to make a place for a defeated leader, the War Department sent General Burnside to take command of the Department of the Ohio, with headquarters at Cincinnati. Having failed to conquer Lee's army, he was probably the more anxious to suppress opposition to the war among the citizens. One of his first acts was to issue his famous "General Order No. 38," April 13, 1863, which prohibited "the habit of declaring sympathy for the enemy."[51] The subject of the order and the offensive way in which it was expressed aroused just criticism

[48] See pp. 241-242 of Cochran's article, cited *supra*.

[49] Reid, *op. cit.*, vol. i, pp. 125-128.

[50] "Address of the Ohio Soldiers in the Army of the Cumberland to the Citizens of Ohio."

[51] *O. R.*, Series I, vol. xxiii, part ii, p. 237.

among many conservative citizens. George E. Pugh is said to have "spit upon, and trampled it under foot." [52] In its enforcement, the means used were so foreign to the conceptions of law held by the people that they provoked indignation against the authorities and sympathy for those who were prosecuted under it. The leading case was that of Vallandigham.

Among all the Democratic leaders, Clement L. Vallandigham had stood out in his bitterly partisan activities during the war. Unlike his colleagues in the Congress, Pugh and S. S. Cox and Pendleton, who had carried on a constructive opposition to the acts of the administration, his course had been marked by a vindictive partisanship. In the summer of 1861 he had called a conference of Democratic leaders at Chillicothe to concert measures "to rescue the Republic from an impending military despotism"; but the conference was not held because the party had not yet begun its factious opposition to the war. [53] In the House of Representatives his efforts had been directed toward impeding the preparations for war. Smarting under his defeat for reëlection, he was now engaged in a campaign to secure the nomination for governor. His earnest manner and the intensity of his utterances carried conviction, and won for him not merely a political, but a personal following of large dimensions, which apparently was not deserved. He was selfish, egotistical and demagogic in his appeals for support. In his private life "he accepted favors of pecuniary and other character, and when the chance came to return them which a gentleman of ordinary sense of

---

[52] Cincinnati *Enquirer*, July 20, 1876.
[53] Randall and Ryan, *op. cit.*, vol. iv, p. 164.

gratitude would eagerly have embraced, he turned the cold shoulder." [54] Only this much can be said in extenuation for his public course: he had married into a slaveholding family, and had spent some time on a plantation in Maryland, where he had seen slavery at its best.[55] On May 1st he was the principal speaker at a Democratic rally at Mount Vernon. His address was undoubtedly a passionate denunciation of the war. If it had been quoted in the South, as many other addresses and resolutions of the Copperheads were, it would have gone a long way toward giving aid and comfort to the enemies of the United States. Two members of Burnside's staff were present in citizen's clothing, taking notes of all that was said. On their report to their chief, it appeared that General Order No. 38 had been flagrantly violated. An aide, with a company of soldiers, was at once sent to arrest Vallandigham. Arriving at Dayton in the dead of night, they went without delay to his home, broke into his bedchamber and placed him under arrest. He was at once conveyed to Cincinnati, where he was confined in a military prison. On May 6th he was brought before a military commission for trial. Denying its jurisdiction, his attorney appealed to a United States court for a writ of habeas corpus, which was refused. The commission then proceeded with his case, found him guilty, and sentenced him to close confinement for the remainder of the war.[56]

When the record of the trial came before President Lincoln for approval or disapproval, he faced a difficult problem. "The President," wrote Gideon Welles, "—and

[54] Rhodes, vol. iv, p. 245.
[55] "The Peace Democrats," p. 25.
[56] Rhodes, vol. iv, pp. 247-248.

I think every member of the cabinet—regrets what has been done. . . . The constitutional rights of the parties injured are undoubtedly infringed upon." [57]　But the proceedings having been carried so far as to make Vallandigham a martyr before his party, a disapproval of the sentence would probably have encouraged the Copperheads to resort to more dangerous activities.　On the other hand, the approval of the sentence would probably have caused great dissatisfaction among conservative citizens, since it appeared to be a violation of the constitutional right of free speech.　Faced with these disagreeable alternatives, Lincoln chose a middle course which was not justified either by the laws or by executive precedents, but which was justified by considerations of political expediency.　This was nothing less than banishment from the existing jurisdiction of the United States. An order was issued that Vallandigham should be sent across the Union lines into the Confederate States. [58] The action appears to have received the approval of Union men, since few criticisms of it were made from among them.　But it was not relished either by the subject of it or by the Confederate authorities.　They soon assisted Vallandigham to escape to Canada, where he was in a position to communicate with his friends in Ohio.　From his point of vantage he issued addresses which received much more attention than their character warranted.

Among the Peace Democrats the evident sympathy for Vallandigham increased greatly his "availability" for the gubernatorial nomination.　He was a candidate of whom everyone had heard as the victim of Federal

[57] *Diary*, vol. i, p. 321.
[58] Nicolay and Hay, vol. vii, p. 339.

repressive measures. No other man could so well stand
for the issues of the campaign. In the party convention
held at Columbus on June 11th, his nomination was
almost unopposed. His friends at once began a vigorous
campaign in his behalf, which showed so much strength
that his election was at first generally expected. The
prospect alarmed the Union leaders, who, in the beginning, had great difficulty in finding a candidate who
could successfully oppose him. It was felt that Governor Tod could not, since he had been forceful and outspoken in the administration of his office, and had himself been responsible for some of the earlier arbitrary
arrests. As in 1861, also, there was no Republican who
could obtain sufficient support among doubtful Democrats to give promise of success. Finally the leaders in
the southern part of the State put forward John Brough,
a Democrat who had been out of politics for fifteen years
until the outbreak of the war, when he had taken an
uncompromising stand in favor of the Union.[59]

The visible evidence of the number of Vallandigham's
open supporters and the knowledge of the invisible
membership of the Knights of the Golden Circle and
other like organizations spurred on the Republicans to
conduct an active canvass. Some officers of the national
government, feeling that the existence of the Union was
at stake in this campaign quite as much as on the battlefield, took an active part in it. Public opinion became
thoroughly aroused. On election day it is said that more
citizens went to the polls than in any other election in
the history of the State up to that time. The returns

[59] George B. Wright, "The Honorable David Tod," in the *Publications* of the Ohio Archeological and Historical Society, vol. viii, pp.
122-123.

showed that the Peace Democrats had overreached themselves. The Union party had a majority of sixty-one
thousand at the polling places within the State, which
was increased by forty thousand when the votes from
the soldiers in the field were received. In the aggregate
number, and in the sectional distribution of the vote,
the Democratic party succeeded only in holding its own
since the election of the preceding year. The overwhelming majority for Brough therefore represented a clear
gain for the Union party. The result was doubtless due
in part to the victories at Gettysburg and Vicksburg,
which gave promise for an early completion of the war;
but it was mostly due to the rallying of the people to
avert a threatened catastrophe to the cause of the
Union.°° The year 1863 marked the turning point of
the war, not only on the battlefield, but in politics as
well.

During the remainder of the conflict the Peace Democrats continued their factious opposition. It was a less
effective opposition than before, however, for as time
passed the military successes of the Federal armies and
the approaching restoration of the Union, which the people wished above all else, deprived the party of their
best campaign arguments. Moreover, the national and
state authorities were able to adopt more thorough means
of curbing sedition, as the people, gradually becoming
accustomed to the exercise of the war powers of the
executive, accepted the repressive measures as necessary.
One by one, the disloyal secret societies were exposed by
detectives who worked their way into prominent positions in their councils. A dangerous plot to arm mem-

°° I cannot agree with Rhodes that "it was the victories of Meade
and Grant that accomplished his overthrow." (vol. iv, p. 252.)

bers of the Sons of Liberty, in order that they might rise and free Confederate prisoners, was foiled by the vigilant efforts of Governor Morton.[61] Several Democratic candidates were found to have been members of the organization, and their exposure completed the temporary ruin of the party, whose influence had already been greatly impaired through a popular reaction against sedition, and by the successful prosecution of the war which they had tried so hard to cripple. In all three of the free States of the Borderland, the Republican party was successful in the campaign of 1864. Lincoln received all of their electoral votes, and Republican governors and legislatures were elected who would work in harmony for the completion of the program which the national administration had outlined. Thereafter no occasion for alarm existed among the friends of the Union.

[61] Seeds, pp. 35, 91.

CHAPTER XI

PROBLEMS OF THE BORDER SLAVE STATES

In the three slave States of the Borderland the variations in public opinion from the beginning to the end of the war were apparently less than in the free States. Those who espoused the cause of the Union in 1861 remained loyal, with few exceptions, in 1865; and nearly all of those who were secessionists stood by their opinions until after the South was subjugated. Many difficult problems were, however, left unsolved when the three States definitely took their stand with the Union. Missouri had no government. The Restored Government of Virginia was unable to exercise much authority over the southern half of the present State of West Virginia. And many people in Kentucky felt that the legislature had been unfaithful to its trust when it abandoned the principle of neutrality. In all three States there were defiant sympathizers with the South who, being denied freedom of expression by the strong arm of the military, resorted to violent clandestine methods to hinder the prosecution of the war and to spread terror among the adherents to the Union. There were also many nominally Union men of lawless dispositions who took advantage of the confusion to wreak vengeance upon their private enemies and to enrich themselves. Furthermore, the loyalty of some of the Union men was endangered by the ever present question of emancipation and by the repressive measures adopted by the national and state authorities to combat the activities of the disloyal. On the whole this period is one of the most interesting and one of the most disagreeable in American history.

Of the three States, Missouri had been the scene of the most acrimonious party struggle, and it now suffered —at least for the first year or two of the war—from the greatest amount of internal disorder. It will be recalled that Governor Jackson left Jefferson City early in June, 1861, retiring into the extreme southwestern corner of the State. For nearly two months afterward there was no state government which was recognized either by the majority of the people or by the national government. Most of the local officials continued individually and in a haphazard manner to exercise their authority and attempt to maintain order; but many of them were secessionists who had been elected before the outbreak of the war caused the overturning of the dominant political organizations. The commanders of the Union forces, who assumed the responsibility for curbing disorder and disloyalty, often worked at cross purposes with even the loyal civil officers. Such a condition could not, of course, be tolerated long. In order to remedy it, the Union men of the State demanded the establishment of a government to take the place of the one which Governor Jackson was attempting to carry into the Southern Confederacy. Some of them are said to have proposed that the President appoint Francis P. Blair, Jr., as military governor. But this proposal seems to have been generally unsatisfactory, and Blair himself was wise enough to give it no encouragement.[1] It was then suggested that

[1] Peckham, op. cit., p. 286.

the convention, which represented the most recent expression of the will of the people, should again be called into session to make provision for the emergency. On the whole this proposal seemed best, since it would present no danger to the Union and little or no opportunity for anyone to object to it on the ground of illegality. The great majority of the members continued to be loyal to the Union, only twenty of the ninety-nine delegates having joined the party of Governor Jackson. Furthermore, the means of calling it into extraordinary session had been regularly provided by the convention itself in the appointment of a committee for the purpose. This committee now acted, fixing July 22nd as the date for reassembling.

Upon its meeting the convention at once assumed complete control over all departments of the state government, justifying its action from the fact that it had been authorized to consider the relations of the people to the United States and to "adopt such measures for vindicating the sovereignty of the State and for the protection of its institutions as shall appear by them to be demanded." [2] In pursuance of these objects, it declared vacant the offices of the governor, lieutenant-governor, secretary of state, and members of the legislature, and filled the executive offices with men of its own choosing, who were to serve until their successors were elected in October. It further declared void and repealed the military bill which had been passed by the legislature in May. At a later session called by the governor, it postponed the election of officers for a year, abolished many state offices, ordered the salaries of others to be reduced by twenty per cent, and provided that all civil officers

[2] *Journal* of the Convention, July session, 1861, p. 20.

must take an oath not to take up arms against the United States.[3] In the following three years it met at intervals and passed many other ordinances under the assumed powers of a sovereign constituent body.

The action of the "Long Convention," as it is often called, has frequently been criticized as unconstitutional. It was convoked, it is said, in order to pass an ordinance of secession; and any other action should at least have been submitted to a popular referendum. These criticisms appear to be unsound. The exact nature of a constitutional convention was then a matter of doubt. There was precedent, at least in other States, for such bodies to reorganize the offices of the government and to exercise ordinary legislative powers during the continuance of the sessions. Some of them had even promulgated new constitutions, embodying extremely important changes in the fundamental law, without a submittal to a popular referendum. In the present case the act calling the convention into existence had, indeed, contemplated that its action should not be referred to the people But even granting that its proceedings were somewhat irregular, they were justified by the fact that only in this way could a civil government have been created by the people which would have been recognized by the national authorities. If there had not been a regularly elected convention subject to call, it would have behooved the people to establish one, as the people of western Virginia had already done. The results justified the action of the convention better than its members realized at the time; for it not only reëstablished civil government, but it saved the State from a military despotism during the war

[3] Violette, *op. cit.*, pp. 393-398.

and from the greater subsequent evils of Federal reconstruction.[4]

The governor elected by the convention was Hamilton R. Gamble, a conservative Union man who had worked to secure the restoration of the Union by compromises, and who had given his support to Harney in his controversy with Blair and Lyon. His selection for the difficult position of governor was extremely wise, for conservative leadership was needed more than anything else to unite the Union men and to give the lie to widespread reports that President Lincoln had promised to give the whole State to the Germans if they would only furnish enough men to conquer it.[5] Few other Union men could have secured the confidence of the people as Gamble did. If his administration did not cause many Confederate sympathizers to return to their allegiance, it at least prevented defections from the ranks of the Union men.

Although a believer in peace, Gamble was not averse to warlike measures when the occasion demanded them. One of his first acts was to issue a call for forty-two thousand volunteers to defend the State and to assist in restoring internal tranquillity. At the outset, however, his activities received the disapproval of the arrogant, selfish and incapable Fremont. On account of the discouragements placed in the way of recruiting by Federal officers, who declared that the state troops would never be paid, only six thousand volunteers were actually raised. Fremont, unable to perceive the value of this force both in assisting in the restoration of order and in

---

[4] Carr, *op. cit.*, p. 322.
[5] William Monks, *History of Southern Missouri and Northern Arkansas,* p. 44.

furnishing a recruiting ground for the United States armies, refused to supply them with arms.⁶ Instead of coöperating with the state authorities, he arrogated their whole work to himself, proclaiming that "circumstances . . . render it necessary that the commanding general of this department should assume the administrative power of the State." He declared martial law, which was to be enforced by the most thoroughgoing military acts. "All persons," Fremont threatened, "who shall be taken with arms in their hands within these lines shall be tried by court-martial, and if found guilty will be shot." ⁷ As soon as the proclamation was brought to Lincoln's attention he asked Fremont to modify it, and when that was not done, he modified it himself, fearing Confederate retaliation. After some further experiences had convinced the lordly general that he could not restore order alone, he reverted to the methods used by Harney, though without equal justification. On November 1st he entered into an agreement with General Price, which provided that no person should be arrested merely for entertaining political opinions; that peaceably disposed citizens should be allowed to return to their homes; and that all armed bands not in the service of either of the belligerents should at once cease their activities.⁸ The agreement was extremely objectionable because it failed to recognize Gamble's authority—indeed, under its terms the State Guard must have been disbanded. Furthermore, its execution would have annulled the confiscation act passed by the Congress. Fortunately Fremont's period of usefulness was at an end, and he was removed

⁶ *Journal* of the Convention, June, 1862, pp. 4-5.
⁷ *O. R.*, Series I, vol. iii, pp. 466-467.
⁸ *O. R.*, Series I, vol. iii, pp. 563-564.

before the agreement went into effect. His successor repudiated it at once.

With Fremont out of the way, Gamble was able to accomplish a great deal toward the restoration of order. A personal appeal to President Lincoln had secured arms for the state troops and, in addition, the sum of $200,000 to assist in maintaining them. Another conference resulted in much closer coöperation between national and state authorities. It was agreed that the United States would in the future support the troops of Missouri; and in return, Gamble promised to appoint as their commander the major-general in charge of the Department of Missouri, and to allow them to be used at his discretion.[9] In the existing condition of the state treasury, this was the best arrangement that could have been made. It placed the problem of restoring order under the nominal control of the state authorities, where it belonged, and gave at least the appearance of local self-government.

The action of the convention aroused the ire of Governor Jackson who at the time was in the Confederate States arranging for closer coöperation between them and his own government. Arriving at New Madrid, he issued a provisional declaration of the independence of Missouri on August 5th.[10] After Price's successful campaign which took the state armies to the Missouri River, he called the legislature to meet in special session at Neosho to complete the work of severing Missouri from the Union and to make a provisional alliance with the Confederate States, pending full admission. The response of the

[9] *Journal* of the Convention, June, 1862, pp. 5-6.
[10] The proclamation is quoted in *Senate Document No. 412*, 57th Congress, 1st session, 1902, pp. 240-241.

members must have been disappointing to Jackson. Only ten senators and thirty-nine members of the lower house were present, lacking much of the constitutional requirement for a quorum in either house. In spite of this defect, the governor presented his recommendations and the legislature acted upon them as if they represented the sole legal authority in the State. There were no roll calls in this extraordinary session: all the business which the governor had recommended was enacted under a suspension of the rules. Among the measures passed were the authorization of bonds to the amount of $10,000,000; the dissolution of the relations existing between the United States and Missouri; and the ratification of the Confederate constitution as a necessary prerequisite to admission to statehood in the Southern Confederacy.[11] An enabling act had previously been passed by the Congress at Richmond, and upon compliance with its terms, Missouri was admitted as the twelfth State on November 28th.[12] The government was able to exercise jurisdiction over only a small part of the State for a short time. The chief reason for its existence was that it furnished a justification for the position of those citizens who fought in the armies and supported the government of the Confederate States.

In Kentucky a somewhat similar movement took place at about the same time. The soldiers who had enlisted in the Confederate army, resenting the accusation that they were at war with their own State, determined to set up a state government that would recognize them. Accordingly two hundred of them, with some civilians, repre-

[11] *Journal* of the Missouri Senate, extra session of the "Rebel Legislature," October, 1861, pp. 1-43, *passim*.
[12] *O. R.*, Series IV, vol. i, p. 576; Series I, vol. liii, p. 757.

senting in all about seventy counties, met in a convention at Russellville on November 18th. Claiming to be a "sovereignty" convention with full power to determine the destinies of the State, this highly irregular body adopted a declaration of independence, drew up a constitution, and appointed commissioners to enter into negotiations with the Confederate States for the admission of Kentucky. It further established a provisional government, appointing a governor and council of ten members to exercise all the executive authority of the State until Governor Magoffin should be released from his "virtual imprisonment." As far as possible the convention sought to preserve the existing constitution and laws of the State. It declared void only the laws which were contrary to those of the Confederate States. And it relieved the people from the obligation to pay taxes both to the national government and to the state authorities at Frankfort.[13]

As a justification for their action, the leaders of the movement appealed to the right of revolution, "a natural right resting upon the law of God."[14] This might also have been the justification of the people of western Virginia in the formation of their Restored Government if they had not appealed to the authority of the Constitution of the United States. The two cases were, however, vastly different. In western Virginia practically all the people over a considerable section of the State were in full sympathy with the movement. The delegates, though irregularly elected, represented both territory and population, whereas, in Kentucky, the dele-

[13] "Declaration of Independence and Constitution of the Provisional Government of Kentucky," p. 5.
[14] O. R., Series IV, vol. i, pp. 741-743.

gates represented only the soldiers who had left their homes and who voted at a distance from them. Though the government attempted to exercise jurisdiction over about one-third of the State for two months, it was opposed by the great majority of the people even there. There is perhaps greater legal justification for the irregular proceedings of Governor Jackson and the "rump" legislature of Missouri, granting the correctness of the theory of the States' Rights party. But they, also, represented a minority in practically every section of the State.

The Confederate authorities gave full recognition to the irregular governments of Kentucky and Missouri because of the widespread belief in the South that they represented the true sentiments of the people of their States. President Davis, in recommending the admission of Kentucky, said: "In every form in which the question has been presented to the people . . . we have sufficient evidence to assure us that by a large majority their will has been manifested to unite their destinies with the Southern States whenever, despairing of the preservation of the Union, they should be required to choose between association with the North or the South. . . . There is enough of merit in the application to warrant a disregard of its irregularity." [15]   Acting upon this recommendation, the Congress admitted Kentucky as the thirteenth State of the Southern Confederacy on December 10th, in full expectation that the people would rise in support of the new government. When they failed to respond to the appeals of Buckner and Johnston, the belief of the Southerners remained unshaken. Even when Bragg, in 1862, establishing the provisional government at Frank-

[15] O. R., Series I, vol. i, pp. 755-756.

fort for a brief hour, was obliged to retreat from the State without sufficient recruits to replace his casualties, the Confederates refused to relinquish their feeling that the people of Kentucky were with them in spirit. As a matter of fact, neither Kentucky nor Missouri showed a preference for the South at any time in the course of the war. Neither of the secessionist governments ever exercised jurisdiction in their States after the first few weeks of 1862.

In the meantime a movement toward the formation of a new State had been progressing among the people of western Virginia. It will be recalled that the advocates of immediate separation from Virginia had been induced only with considerable difficulty to postpone their demands until after the interests of the Union had been safeguarded by the restoration of the state government. When this end had been accomplished, they made it plain that their silence had been only temporary and that their acceptance of the Restored Government had been in part due to the feeling that its existence would aid them. As soon as possible thereafter they set such machinery as they had in motion to create a new State. Having the people almost unanimously on their side, they were able to proceed, not in the revolutionary haste of a single day, but with circumspection and a due regard for constitutional forms, as befitted people engaged in the serious business of setting up a new government.

Before the adjournment of the second Wheeling convention they demanded that it set a date for reassembling; and upon its meeting on August 6, 1861, they proposed an ordinance for the division of Virginia. Such a measure, to be effective, would have to be approved by the legislature of the State and by the Congress of the

United States. It was strongly opposed by some members on the grounds that it was illegal and unwise, and by others on the ground that it was unfair to take advantage of the fiction that the Restored Government was the State of Virginia, when, as everyone knew, it was supported by much less than half the people of the whole State. They cited a letter from the Attorney-General of the United States which declared that the proposal was revolutionary.[16] But all these considerations were brushed aside after a long series of debates, an ordinance of separation being adopted by a vote of fifty to twenty-eight. It provided that thirty-nine counties in the western part of the State should be formed into the "State of Kanawha" if the people should so decide at a special election to be held on October 24th; and that certain other counties to the east and south should be included if a majority of their citizens expressed themselves favorably. At the same time the voters were asked to choose delegates to a constitutional convention.[17]

The election resulted in favor of the creation of a new State, the total vote being 18,408 for, and 781 against the question. The overwhelming majority and the fact that few or no unfavorable votes were recorded in the southern counties indicated that many people who opposed the proposition either did not care to vote upon it or were kept away from the polls by military interference. Nearly all the votes against it were cast in the northwestern counties where the election appears to have been free. The total vote was a little more than two-fifths of that which would normally have been cast in a presidential election, where important personalities, as

[16] Willey, op. cit., p. 81.
[17] Lewis, History of West Virginia, pp. 373-374.

well as important issues, were involved. But it represented a much greater proportion of the vote which would have been cast on a constitutional question, especially when the result was a foregone conclusion. Add to this consideration the fact that about ten thousand voters were absent in the Union army, and it is evident that a majority of the people approved the proposal. In all

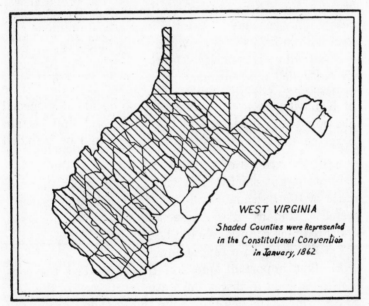

WEST VIRGINIA

Shaded Counties were Represented in the Constitutional Convention in January, 1862

but two of the counties to be included in "Kanawha," and in four other counties for the possible inclusion of which provision had been made, delegates to the constitutional convention were elected. In several other counties informal elections for delegates were held at a later date. By the middle of the session nearly every county west of the Alleghanies was represented.

The constitutional convention, like the second convention at Wheeling, assumed itself to be a sovereign body. Refusing to consider itself bound by the provisions of the ordinance which set forth the geographical limits of the new State, it reopened the whole question. Several propositions were advanced for the inclusion of the Shenandoah Valley and of southwestern Virginia; but after a long series of debates they were rejected because the delegates wished the new State to be as nearly homogeneous as possible in political opinions and economic interests. They voted to include five counties —Pocahontas, Greenbrier, Monroe, Mercer and McDowell—in which the sentiment favorable to the Union was negligible, but whose addition was considered necessary in order to gain the crest of the Alleghanies as a military frontier. They added three counties along the upper Potomac, partly in order to satisfy the demands of determined groups of people who wanted to be in the new State, but chiefly, it is suspected, in order that the route of the Baltimore and Ohio Railroad might be protected.[18] Finally, it was agreed that Berkeley, Jefferson and Frederick counties should be admitted if their people voted favorably in a referendum.

Another important question that disturbed the convention a great deal was the status of slavery in the new State. One of the delegates from the Panhandle proposed that a provision for gradual emancipation after July 4, 1865, be adopted. The resolution was supported by many members who believed in it both as a measure of abstract justice to the slaves and as essential to securing favorable action from the Congress. It was opposed by others who asserted that it would injure the property rights of many loyal citizens and would diminish the

[18] Hall, *op. cit.*, p. 407.

popular support which the movement for a new State could hope to receive. When the proposal came to a vote, it was laid on the table by a majority of one. Later, a provision was incorporated which prohibited the immigration of slaves or free negroes, thus indicating that the people of western Virginia had as great aversion to a negro population as the people of Kentucky.

In dealing with other matters the convention reflected the popular dissatisfaction with the inequalities and ineptitudes of the existing constitution of Virginia, which had been, in some measure, responsible for the popular rising against the state authorities. In order to do away with the preferred position of slave property on the tax books, it inserted a provision that all taxes were to be equal and uniform. As a protest against the internal improvement policy which had built up the eastern part of the State at the expense of the western part, it provided that the credit of the State should never be granted to corporations and that no debt should be contracted except for carrying on war and for paying the public debts. As measures of administrative reform, it abolished the county court system, substituting the township system in use in several Northern States, and it reorganized the judicial system. Finally, it remedied the ancient grievance that the people had been allowed to grow up in ignorance by making provision, on a large scale, for a system of free public education.[19] The name of the proposed new State was changed to West Virginia on account of sentimental attachments.

The draft constitution, on being submitted to the people at an election held late in April, 1862, was approved by a vote of 20,622 for and 440 against ratification. As

[19] Willey, pp. 90-91.

in the former election, the returns from the counties indicated that many adherents of the government at Richmond did not care to vote upon it. In May, the legislature of the Restored Government, which then exercised jurisdiction over only six counties outside the boundaries of the proposed new State, gave its consent to the formation of West Virginia.[20] Immediately afterward bills were introduced in both houses of the Congress for its admission into the Union. Though many members expressed grave doubts as to the constitutionality and expediency of the measure, a bill for admission was finally passed by both houses, with the proviso that the constitution of West Virginia should be amended so as to insure gradual emancipation. When the bill came before President Lincoln for his signature, he at first was doubtful of the wisdom of the measure. Later he signed it, having become satisfied that the action was constitutional and that it would aid the national government by securing additional support from the people of the section.[21] After they had willingly acceded to the proviso, he issued a proclamation for the admission of West Virginia, to take effect on June 20, 1863.

The admission of West Virginia has often been criticized, first, because it is said that it was accomplished without the consent of the State of Virginia and against the will of two-thirds of the people; and secondly, because it is said that it did not even have the approval of the people of West Virginia, or at least of many of the eastern and southern counties which were included. The answer to the first objection is that the action was accomplished with the full consent of the lawful government

[20] Lewis, *History of West Virginia*, p. 381.
[21] Nicolay and Hay, vol. vi, p. 311.

of Virginia, the only government that was competent to act under the Constitution of the United States. It would be a new and startling principle to recognize that the *de jure* government is limited in the exercise of its powers over territory and subjects under its jurisdiction by the existence of a *de facto* government controlling other portions of its territory. Nor can the people of eastern Virginia be said to have been denied their rights under the Constitution, since, by engaging in open rebellion against it, they had forfeited its protection. In answer to the second objection, it is only necessary to review the facts that the people of the northwestern counties rose almost unanimously against the state authorities; that they were later joined by the people of other populous sections; that they established a government which exercised jurisdiction, with the consent of the people, over nearly all the settled territory west of the Alleghanies; and that in two popular elections, they voted by large majorities in favor of the creation of the new State. The inclusion of some western and southern counties cannot, of course, be justified by the principle of popular consent; but it can be justified by the principle that it is sometimes necessary for the majority to deny the wishes of the minority when the safety of the State demands such action. Furthermore, if the majority of the people had not desired to live in a separate State from Virginia, they could afterward have petitioned to be reunited with the mother State. No movement of the sort ever took place—not even when, in 1872, a constitutional convention was in session, presided over by the former lieutenant-governor of the Confederate state administration, and having in its membership sixty-six Democrats out of a total of seventy-eight.

Let us turn from a discussion of constitutions and forms of public organization to a consideration of the more immediately important problems of preserving order and administering justice in time of civil war. In the confused state of affairs, with men of the same families fighting in opposing armies and with different neighborhoods taking opposite sides, it was extremely difficult for the public authorities to carry on their functions justly and effectively. And the more conflicting jurisdictions there were, the greater became the difficulties. The struggle for supremacy between different governments begat lawlessness; the state of civil conflict encouraged its growth; and the combination of the two brought about a condition of affairs but little removed from anarchy, as far as the civil authorities were concerned.

During the war most sections of northwestern Virginia appear to have been nearly free from civil disturbances. But in the whole of a broad zone extending from the Alleghanies westward through the Kanawha Valley, Kentucky and Missouri to the Kansas border, armed bands roamed, committing depredations upon peaceable citizens. Outside the larger towns and the districts in which troops were stationed, no man's life or property was safe. Murders in cold blood, acts of rapine, and the incendiary burning of farmhouses and villages were of frequent occurrence. In the Kanawha Valley, all that remained of several county seats at the close of the war were heaps of charred ruins. The condition of Kentucky in 1864 has been compared to that of Germany during the Thirty Years' War. In Missouri, which seems to have suffered most of all, whole counties were depopulated and made desolate. It became almost impossible for the people to carry on their ordinary pursuits. The condition of society reverted to that in the time of the Indian wars, and "men again tilled their fields with their muskets by their sides, and slept in expectation of combat." [22] In spite of all that military commanders, home guards and civil authorities could do, the disorders increased in numbers and violence until the close of the war.

The presence of armed bands in all of the border slave States dates almost from the beginning of hostilities. When Union or Confederate troops appeared in unfriendly districts the able-bodied men, in many instances, retired to the woods and, with the object of expelling the invaders, ambushed, or "bushwhacked," couriers, scouts and small detached parties. In the vicinity of military camps they mercilessly shot down stragglers wherever they appeared. Along the North Missouri Railroad they burned bridges, destroyed tracks, and fired into trains so often that the crews refused to make their regular runs. [23] These measures, of course, brought swift retaliation from the military authorities, who hunted down their hidden assailants like wolves, and punished them—and probably many innocent persons as well—summarily when they captured them. The bushwhackers thus became outlaws. Not daring to return to their homes except under cover of darkness, they roamed about the country, supporting themselves by forced contributions upon citizens whose opinions were known to be different from their own. When they discovered how easy it was to obtain a livelihood by these means, they swiftly degenerated into mere robbers, plunderers and murderers. Others who had a grudge to settle against someone adopted their methods. "The war," says Champ Clark, "was the evening-up time [of the feuds], and many a

[22] Shaler, p. 325.   [23] O. R., Series, I, vol. iii, pp. 423, 460.

man became a violent Unionist because the ancient enemies of his house were Southern sympathizers and *vice versa*."[24] Still others became guerrillas from no other motive than the desire for plunder. As the varying positions of the regularly organized forces made it seem advisable, they pretended to favor now one side, now the other. Many of the worst of their class plundered friends and foes without distinction. The war furnished a golden opportunity for the lowest order of society to prey upon the more provident classes. And the opportunity was used to the fullest extent.

The attitude of the military authorities toward the people of the border slave States tended to increase, rather than to diminish, the civil commotion which existed. Throughout most of the war the Federal authorities employed as "scouts," and the Confederates, as "partisan rangers," some bands of men whose character was little better than that of the marauders whom they were supposed to hunt down. Many outrages were perpetrated by them. Even the regularly organized forces often failed to behave themselves properly. In the beginning of the war, especially, the enlisted men were lacking in discipline, and the officers, having been appointed from civil life and being ignorant of the laws of war, often either ordered cruel and unnecessary reprisals upon communities or winked at the outrages committed by their men. In western Virginia, the village of Barboursville was burned, in November, 1861, by two hundred men of the Fifth Virginia regiment in retaliation for the murder of several men belonging to another regiment.[25] In Missouri, complaints were con-

[24] *My Quarter Century of American Politics*, vol. i, p. 79.
[25] Wheeling *Intelligencer*, Nov. 14, 1861.

stantly being made during the first year of the war concerning the actions of Federal soldiers. "Our State," said Governor Gamble, "has been visited by a class of troops who came with feelings of hostility to our people . . . and who, under the guise of supporting the Union, perpetrated enormous outrages." [26]   A railroad official declared that soldiers, without any provocation, had fired upon peaceable citizens, sometimes from trains.[27] It seems to have been a not infrequent occurrence for soldiers to enter and search private houses, taking from them everything they wanted. General Halleck declared that strongly Union men in southwestern Missouri had begged him not to permit Sigel's command to return, since they had robbed friends and foes alike.[28] Schofield complained that he could not trust his cavalry out of his sight for a moment, on account of their propensity to plunder. He had found it necessary to arrest two officers and to place five men in irons.[29] Much worse outrages occurred along the Kansas border where Senator "Jim" Lane and his army of volunteers were operating in the summer of 1861. When the Missouri troops retired southward from Lexington, he entered the State and began pillaging everywhere. His men sacked the town of Osceola, killing a score of citizens, and afterward looted Butler and Parksville. The spoils are said to have been sold openly at auction in Lawrence, Kansas.[30]

All of these excesses naturally resulted in increasing the internal disorder that existed. Each arbitrary act created new enemies of the government and caused other

[26] Message quoted in the *Journal* of the Convention, June, 1862, p. 7.
[27] *O. R.*, Series I, vol. iii, p. 459.
[28] *O. R.*, Series I, vol. viii, p. 502.
[29] *O. R.*, Series I, vol. viii, p. 482.
[30] Violette, pp. 381-382.

citizens to remain silent as to the whereabouts of those who committed acts of violence against it. Members of the secessionist party were roused to vengeance. Since they could not well retaliate upon the Federal troops, they increased the number and extent of their depredations upon the avowed friends of the Union. When the army of Fremont fell back from Springfield in the fall of 1861, the Union men who fled from their homes to avoid secessionist outrages were so many that the private charity of St. Louis was insufficient to care for them.[31] Those who remained behind were robbed and pillaged without mercy. Thousands of residents felt obliged to flee from their homes to the Far West, where, with only Indian depredations to fear, life was less burdensome.

The situation became so critical in 1862 that both national and state authorities took desperate measures to combat the guerrillas, whose numbers were now augmented by many deserters from both armies. Governor Gamble issued a proclamation for the enrollment of every citizen of military age in regiments and companies, who were to act under General Schofield's orders in suppressing marauders. Far from accepting it at its face value, the Southern sympathizers regarded it as only a trick to enlist them against the Confederacy. They resisted enrollment, and established many recruiting camps for the Southern armies, the dispersal of which presented a serious problem for the military authorities. In Kentucky a provost marshal system was established to unify and direct the work of suppressing internal disorder. It acted in a thoroughgoing manner, hanging guerrillas in retaliation for the murders of citizens by other guerrillas

[31] Anderson, *op. cit.*, p. 242.

and dealing severely with persons who were suspected of harboring them. In both States the military authorities for a time levied assessments upon secessionists who held property, in order to compensate loyal citizens for their losses. But this device was effective only in so far as it caused the guerrillas to desist from their outrages out of pity for the sufferings of citizens;—that is to say, it was scarcely effective at all.[32] In western Missouri, in reprisal for Quantrell's raid on Lawrence, Kansas, in 1863, the Federal commander took the extreme measure of ordering all the citizens of three counties and part of a fourth to leave their homes. He caused all grain and hay to be confiscated, and the whole countryside to be made a desert in which guerrillas could not sustain themselves.[33] Yet even this act of barbarity failed to diminish the number and ferocity of the swiftly moving bands that prowled about the district. In counties where the people were almost wholly loyal to the Union, the home guards and the troops were able to maintain order; but in other sections the outrages of guerrillas continued unabated until the restoration of peace.

The arbitrary conduct of the military commanders in attempting to suppress guerrillas is fairly indicative of the whole attitude of most of them. With the exceptions of Anderson, Buell, Sherman, Schofield and one or two others, the generals in command in Kentucky and Missouri were men of little common sense and great personal vanity who, forgetting that the majority of the people had freely espoused the cause of the Union, acted as if these States were conquered provinces. The despotic character of Fremont's rule has already been noticed.

[32] Shaler, p. 334.
[33] Violette, pp. 382-383.

Other leaders distinguished themselves by constant interference with the civil authorities, flagrant disregard for
private rights, and acts of ruthless proscription. For
four years their conduct proved the truth of the maxim,
inter arma silent leges.

In the first year of the war the subordinate commanders began a series of arbitrary arrests of citizens on trivial
grounds. Former Speaker McAfee, of the Missouri
House of Representatives, who had been living quietly
at his home, was arrested without cause by General Hurl-
but and compelled to dig trenches all day with the mer-
cury at a hundred degrees.[34] The detention of other
prominent men, against whom no charge could be sustained, followed in short order. In Kentucky so many
persons were imprisoned that General Anderson was
prompted to issue an order expressly forbidding military
arrests "except where the parties are attempting to join
the rebels or are engaged in giving aid or information to
them; and in all cases the evidence must be such as will
convict them before a court of justice." He desired that
those who had formerly sympathized with the rebels and
who now wished to change their minds should be allowed
to do so.[35] There can scarcely be any doubt that his
policy was wise, and that it would greatly have strengthened the cause of the Union. Unfortunately he was
forced to relinquish his command on account of illness,
and the provost marshal general who succeeded to a part
of his duties went to the other extreme. So many arrests were made under his authority that the prisons
were soon crowded. Many persons, in addition, were
removed to the Northern States. Among the causes for

[34] *O. R.*, Series I, vol. iii, p. 459.
[35] *O. R.*, Series I, vol. iv, p. 296.

arrest was "anything said or done to excite to rebellion." All persons who had joined the Confederate army or had given it aid were required to report to certain provost marshals, take an oath of allegiance, and give bond for future good behavior, or be sent to prison.[36] Among the persons arrested were ministers of the gospel, judges of circuit courts, and women who had relatives in the Confederate armies. Most of the last named class of prisoners were sent into the South. In order, probably, that the people might not know the extent of the system, the newspapers of Louisville were forbidden to publish the names of those arrested. There is little doubt that many innocent persons were imprisoned at the instigation of their personal enemies on evidence that would not have borne the light of day.

The people who were left at large had many minute details of their conduct regulated. It was impossible for anyone to purchase or ship goods for retail trading without having taken an oath of allegiance. Similar oaths were required preliminary to the accomplishment of many simple acts. It is said that a person could hardly go through his ordinary day's work without having taken an oath once or twice. In consequence the oath became degraded.[37] The provost marshals determined what books and religious journals the people should be allowed to read, what preachers they might listen to, what sheet music they might possess, and last, but by no means least, for whom they might vote.

The arbitrary interference of the military in elections began in Kentucky with General Boyle's "Order No. 5," July 21, 1862. "No person hostile in opinion to the gov-

[36] Collins, vol. i, p. 102.
[37] Shaler, p. 322.

ernment and desiring its overthrow," he declared, "will be allowed to stand for office in the district of Ky. The attempt of such a person to stand for office will be regarded as in itself sufficient evidence of his treasonable intent to warrant his arrest. . . . In seeking office he becomes an active traitor, if he has never become one otherwise." [38] In consequence of this monstrous order several Democratic candidates were compelled to withdraw. The system reached its climax in the following year. It was apparent to the Union leaders and the military authorities that the control of the regular Democratic party was in the hands of a group allied to the Copperheads in the northern part of the Ohio Valley. When their convention met at Frankfort, February 18, 1863, the House of Representatives therefore refused it the use of its hall, and the commander of the troops in the town, having drawn up his men with fixed bayonets outside the hall in which it met, compelled the dispersal of the members before they had a chance to organize. Against this high-handed act the Senate protested, declaring: "Such interference on the part of the military is dangerous in its tendencies, and should not pass unrebuked." [39] A month later the convention met at Louisville and nominated a state ticket. The choice being unsatisfactory to the central committee of the Union Democrats, it placed General Thomas E. Bramlette in nomination for governor. At the election in August, Federal troops were stationed at many of the polling places, who probably intimidated many persons from voting. The names of certain candidates were erased from the polling books in several counties, includ-

---

[38] Quoted by Collins, vol. i, p. 104.
[39] Quoted by Collins, vol. i, p. 120.

ing the name of the regular Democratic candidate for governor in his own district. Some persons voting for him in other districts were immediately arrested for disloyalty.

The results of the election showed the uselessness of the repressive measures. General Bramlette received over sixty-seven thousand votes, many more than a majority of those that could have been cast in the election, owing to the absence of many voters in the armies and to the legislative requirement of a preliminary oath of loyalty. His opponent received less than eighteen thousand votes. If the election had been free from military interference, it is estimated that his total vote would not have exceeded twenty thousand. The action of the provost marshals could not, therefore, have changed the result. It did, however, dampen the enthusiasm of those who were making constant sacrifices in order to maintain the Constitution and laws of the United States.[40] Thenceforth it may be said that, although the people continued to be loyal to the United States, they had little use for the administration at Washington, whose officers had perpetrated the outrages against popular liberty.

An important contributing factor to their attitude was the policy of the Federal authorities with regard to slavery. Many detachments of troops from Northern States, in an excess of abolitionist zeal, harbored runaway negroes belonging to loyal owners, and refused to surrender them even to the local civil authorities. Several commanders impressed the labor of other slaves for the construction of roads and other military works. These actions naturally caused considerable resentment. But

[40] Shaler, p. 336.

this was mild in comparison with the storm of protest that gathered when some of the States began the enlistment of negroes as soldiers. Though the people of Kentucky were anxious to save the Union and to bring the war to a close as quickly as possible, they did not want their sons and brothers to fight in the same armies with negroes. In December, 1861, the legislature adopted a resolution requesting the President to dismiss Secretary Cameron because he had recommended the arming of slaves.[41] The newspapers of the State denounced the policy in bitter terms, and many Kentucky regiments became disaffected on account of it.[42] The resignation of Cameron shortly afterward brought about a better feeling. But when, later in the war, the Federal government attempted to enroll negroes preparatory to their enlistment as soldiers, a tremendous storm of popular opposition gathered. Men who had staunchly supported the cause of the Union talked openly of armed resistance.

On the question of emancipation, their feelings were as decided and definite as on the enlistment of negroes. They regarded the proposition to free the slaves with abhorrence, on account of their fear of a free negro population. President Lincoln, who sympathized with their objection to making the question of slavery an issue of the war, strove as long as he could to resist the pressure for emancipation that was brought to bear upon him by the abolitionists. Realizing, however, that the forces arrayed against slavery would probably have their way sooner or later, he attempted to prepare the border slave States for the result. Apparently he failed to understand the real basis for their opposition, since his first measures

[41] Collins, vol. i, p. 98.
[42] W. Preston to Davis, Dec. 28, 1861, O. R., Series I, vol. vii, p. 801.

against slavery were directed toward securing to the loyal slaveholders the protection of their property rights. In his message to the Congress in December, 1861, he proposed the emancipation of the slaves in the border States, with compensation to their owners. No attention having been paid by the Congress to the recommendation, he sent a special message, March 6, 1862, asking for the passage of a resolution that the United States "ought to coöperate with any State which may adopt gradual abolishment of slavery, giving to such State pecuniary aid, to be used by such State in its discretion." He estimated that the payment of four hundred dollars for each slave in Delaware, Maryland, the District of Columbia, Kentucky and Missouri would equal only the cost of waging the war for eighty-seven days; and he thought the war would be shortened by such a policy by at least that time.[48] A few days later he summoned the members of the Congress from the border slave States and requested that they use their influence to secure the adoption of gradual emancipation by their States. After they had indicated their opposition to the proposal by taking no action, he again held a conference with them on July 12th. He argued that as long as the border States refused to abolish slavery, the people of the South would continue to cherish the delusion that these States were with them in spirit. "Beat them at elections, as you have overwhelmingly done," he said, "and, nothing daunted, they still claim you as their own." But if they were made to see that on no account would the border States ever join them, he thought they could not maintain the contest much longer. In order to overcome the aversion of the representatives to a free negro population, he pro-

[48] Nicolay and Hay, vol. v, pp. 209-210.

posed the scheme of colonizing the negroes in South America. Then, appealing again to their supposed desire to protect the property rights of their constituents, he reminded them of the pressure for emancipation to which he was subjected and to the practical impossibility of holding the slaves in bondage in the confused state of affairs. "If the war continues long," he said, "the institution in your States will be extinguished by mere friction and abrasion—by the mere incidents of the war. It will be gone, and you will have nothing valuable in lieu of it." [44]

To all of these appeals no attention was paid by the Restored Government of Virginia or by Kentucky. In Missouri, the convention considered an ordinance which would have freed all slaves born after January 1, 1865, when they reached the age of twenty-five. But it failed to pass it, apparently because doubts were expressed as to the power of the convention to act. [45] In November, 1862, the result of an election seemed to indicate that the people were in favor of gradual emancipation. Following it, the representatives from Missouri succeeded in having bills passed in both houses of the Congress which would have compensated the slaveholders. Owing to a filibuster, however, they failed to agree upon any one measure. [46] The subject was not brought up again. Meanwhile President Lincoln, after delaying the action as long as he could out of regard for the feelings of the Borderland, issued his proclamation freeing the slaves in the districts which were in revolt against the United States. It in no way disturbed the position of slavery in the loyal

[44] Nicolay and Hay, vol. vi, pp. 109-110.
[45] *Journal*, June, 1862, pp. 19-20.
[46] Rhodes, vol. iv, pp. 216-217.

slave States, yet the people received it sullenly. It seemed to them a violation of the Constitution by the national government, which deprived it of the right to appeal to them against the disregard for the Constitution by the Southern States.[47]

Owing to the conduct of the Union military leaders in Kentucky and to the policies of the national government, General Bramlette had a most trying position when he assumed the office of governor. He had been elected as a true Union man, and he strove, to the best of his ability, to promote the cause of the Union. He encouraged volunteering to fill up the quotas of Kentucky. In attempting to suppress the marauding bands, he took sterner measures even than the military authorities, ordering five of the most prominent rebel sympathizers to be arrested and held as hostages for the safe return of every Union man taken by the guerrillas.[48] But for the most part his attention was occupied in combating the arbitrary and unreasonable acts of the military commanders within the State. General Burbridge was the worst of these. He operated a system of trade orders which rewarded favorites and punished enemies, with the result that many Union men were driven out of business. In order that certain contractors in Louisville might not suffer losses, he ordered that farmers should sell their pigs only to designated agents, and at prices much below those of the markets in Cincinnati. He caused the confiscation of private property. He arrested women and sent them under a guard of negro soldiers to Canada.[49] Because many men dared to protest against these outrages he

[47] Shaler, p. 332; Carr, pp. 344-345.
[48] Collins, vol. i, p. 130.
[49] Shaler, pp. 348-353.

committed them to prison on charges that were often trumped up. Colonel Wolford of the First Kentucky Cavalry was arrested by him three times, and as many times released from confinement by orders from the War Department. But when he ventured to criticize the administration again, Burbridge arrested him a fourth time and sent him into the Confederate States. With him went Lieutenant-Governor Jacob, who had conspicuously opposed the enrollment of negroes for the draft. It is only fair to say that many of the arrests were due to a self-constituted junto of radical Union men who, in the stress of partisan excitement, attempted to proscribe all who did not agree with them.

Governor Bramlette brought all his influence to bear upon the Federal authorities to stop the outrages. Writing to President Lincoln, he especially requested that the order of banishment against Wolford and Jacob be rescinded. He suggested that the "stay-at-home patriots" who had caused their arrests be sent instead, for, he said, "they will not help us in the day of battle, and Jacob and Wolford will." [50] It is almost unnecessary to state that his appeals were effective in reversing most of Burbridge's policies. But there were other commanders almost as bad. In western Kentucky they completely interdicted the buying and selling of farm produce until the people should show friendship for the Union by driving out the guerrillas. Moreover, they instituted a system of extortions and military murders on a large scale, which were not stopped until an investigating committee caused a general officer and several subordinates of high rank to be removed from their commands. In 1864, General Ewing ordered that the county courts levy a tax

[50] Collins, vol. i, pp. 148-149.

sufficient to arm and pay fifty men in each county, who were to serve under him. Governor Bramlette immediately forbade the execution of the order; and Ewing, in revenge, then commanded that the state forces be mustered out. It was necessary for the governor and the legislature to appeal to Lincoln in order to secure a revocation of the order.[51]

All these events had the natural effect of greatly incensing the people against the national government. When the time came for the election of a judge in August, 1864, and voting for their candidate had been forbidden by the military authorities, the people quietly nominated another man, whose name was transmitted to the polling places by telegraph on the morning of the election. He was easily chosen over the candidate endorsed by the military. In November, they gave McClellan 64,301 votes to Lincoln's 27,786, as a protest against the despotic acts of the Federal commanders. Yet, notwithstanding the popular dissatisfaction, they maintained their quotas in the army, except for a few months in 1864. When a draft was ordered, it was found impossible to enforce it because most of those enrolled escaped into the South. The people, not wishing their State to have the disgrace of failing to furnish its quota, then procured the enlistment of many volunteers, including, it is said, some who had formerly served in the Confederate armies. In all, Kentucky is officially credited with having furnished 75,760 men to the Union army.[52] Besides, it is estimated that more than twenty thousand Kentucky negroes were enlisted in regiments of Northern States.

[51] Shaler, pp. 350-351.
[52] *O. R.*, Series III, vol. iv, p. 1269.

In Missouri the people fared somewhat better than in Kentucky, largely through the influence of Francis P. Blair, Jr., who became a conservative after the first few months of the war. Most of the military excesses committed there were the acts of home guards. General Schofield, who was in command during most of the war, was a man of sense, who used his great powers, on the whole, for the best interests of the Union. He allowed comparatively free expression of political opinion—a policy which resulted not in uniting the people against the national administration, as the acts of the generals in Kentucky had done, but in the continuance of the more or less normal divisions of political opinion. Southern sympathizers, conservative Union men, and radicals continued to exist as separate and distinct groups. The first party joined the Order of American Knights in such large numbers as to invite an invasion by General Price in 1864. But Schofield's policy was justified by the facts that Price was easily beaten off, and that the "Knights" did not join him. The conservatives—who came to be called "Claybanks"—loyally supported the war for the preservation of the Union, and opposed the use of negro troops and the emancipation of the slaves, because these policies appeared likely to increase the numbers of the enemies of the United States. The radicals—who came to be called "Charcoals"—demanded that all slaves be emancipated everywhere, and that no quarter be given to slaveholders.[53] They succeeded, in 1863, in having the convention pass an ordinance for the abolishment of slavery on July 4, 1870;[54] but being dissatisfied with this victory and desiring more drastic action, they appealed

[53] Anderson, *op. cit.*, pp. 276-280.
[54] Violette, p. 401.

to Lincoln, asking him to commit himself to the universal
abolition of slavery and the general use of negro troops
against the Confederate States. Complaining that Schofield had been too much under the influence of Governor
Gamble, they urged that the notorious General Benjamin
F. Butler be sent to Missouri in his place.[55] Upon Lincoln's refusal to change his policy, they worked to secure
his defeat and the accession of Fremont to the Presidency. In the autumn of 1864, when thousands of citizens were kept away from the polls by military intimidation and by test oaths, they succeeded in electing their
state ticket and in having a new convention called. This
body, on January 6, 1865, passed an ordinance abolishing
slavery immediately and without compensation.[56]

Like Kentucky, the State of Missouri loyally supported
the military forces of the Union, furnishing 109,000 men
in all, to about 30,000 who fought with the Confederates.[57] In addition, nearly every able-bodied man in the
State served with the home guards at one time or
another.

In the new State of West Virginia, the civil authorities
were left to work out their own internal problems,
unmolested by the military. Upon the admission of the
State, Governor Pierpont collected the records of the
Restored Government and moved its capital from Wheeling to Alexandria, where it remained until the capture
of Richmond. The governor of West Virginia, succeeding to his tasks, performed them well on the whole,
though he found it difficult to measure up to the standard he had set. In some counties it was impossible to

[55] W. B. Stevens in the *Missouri Historical Review*, vol. x, p. 97.
[56] Violette, p. 405.
[57] Carr, p. 357.

set up local governments which the people would recognize. The office of sheriff often remained unfilled "because of the danger incident thereto." In many of the southern counties the local officials continued to furnish men and money to the authorities at Richmond, though their course led to increasing popular dissatisfaction. In spite of the best efforts of the military authorities and of the home guards, the problem of suppressing guerrillas remained unsolved until after the war, as it did in the other two States. Throughout the war the people continued to furnish troops for the Union army, the total number being thirty thousand as against seven thousand who went with the Confederates. When it was found necessary to institute a draft in the northern counties to make up the quota of the State, it was enforced without much disorder.

CHAPTER XII

CONCLUSION

A discussion of the events following the fall of Fort Sumter in strictly chronological order would have had at least two important advantages. In the first place, it would have been possible to bring out clearly the interaction of public opinion between different sections of the Borderland. Undoubtedly Kentucky and Missouri were greatly influenced to support the Union through the determined stand taken by the people of the northern part of the Ohio Valley. Similarly, the development of the Copperhead movement received a part of its impetus from the secessionist sympathies of many people in the border slave States. The course of events in Missouri influenced Kentucky, and *vice versa*. The position taken by western Virginia had a tremendous effect on the attitude of all the other States. It is unnecessary to continue an enumeration of comparisons. In the second place, a chronological discussion would have demonstrated the unity of the Borderland on the issues of the war that were really essential, such as the maintenance of the Union, the emancipation of the slaves, and the violation of civil rights by the military authorities.

Unfortunately such a method of treatment would have been nearly impracticable. There were many secondary issues, such as States' rights and the support of the Republican administration, concerning which the people of different sections had diverse views. There were also slightly distinct social and economic interests which, in the nearly equal balancing of forces, had an influence out of proportion to their importance. Finally the policies of local leaders of both the Union and the secessionist parties varied widely from State to State. Starting from these different bases, and being greatly influenced by a succession of dissimilar local events, the progress of public opinion was naturally far from uniform. An attempt to describe the movement chronologically would therefore have resulted in much confusion.

Yet, in spite of local differences, the fact of the essential unity of the Borderland stands out. Its people lived in a compact territory having a climate and natural features which imposed barriers separating them from the surrounding sections, and at the same time promoted a community of social and economic interests among them. Even the institution of slavery, which existed in the southern half of the section, seemed of slight importance compared with the unifying influences exerted by other factors. Throughout the period of their development the people had been accustomed to act together in attempting to advance their common well-being. In the election of 1860 nearly all of them favored the same general principles, though they cast their ballots for different candidates. Afterward they were almost solidly united in their efforts to save the Union by measures of compromise and conciliation. When the war broke out, there was a natural hesitancy on the part of the people of some slave States to take the side of the North against the South; but when the issue was shown clearly to be for or against the preservation of the Union, all the States united in casting their lots with the national government. The very difference in the time of their decisions emphasizes the unity of the Borderland, since it indicates that the example set by some States profoundly influenced the others.

In reviewing the history of the period, one is impressed by the fact that when the Civil War came, it found the people of the Borderland totally unprepared. They had, of course, understood the diametrically opposed feeling of both the North and the South on the subject of slavery. They had watched with some misgivings the increasing bitterness of the controversy from the time it first arose. Yet they had always succeeded in adjusting the immediate points in dispute by means of compromises devised in the halls of the Congress. What was more natural than that they should expect future disagreements to be settled in the same way? Throughout the long continuance of the struggle they had frequently heard threats of refusal to accept the result, of nullification, and of secession unless certain demands were granted; but none of these things had come to pass. When the threats were repeated at the beginning of 1860, they regarded them simply as a means of obtaining further concessions, not as the sincere expression of a body of people who had been disillusioned by the failure of political arrangements to promote their fancied interests. The disruption of the Democratic party failed to arouse them to the true nature of the sectional struggle. In the election which followed they scattered their votes among different candidates as if they believed that the success of the parties to which they had traditionally adhered was of greater importance than the maintenance of the integrity of the nation. They even contributed the electoral votes necessary to the success of the Republican party, in the evident belief that its platform best expressed the transient needs of the day. It was only when the State of South Carolina actually seceded, and when other States were preparing to follow her example, that they awoke to the criticalness of the situation.

In this period the people of the Borderland showed unmistakably their devotion to the Union. Owing to the interior location of their section, they had always been nationalistic in sentiment, supporting internal improvements, protective tariffs and other measures which would benefit them because they would build up the prosperity of the whole country. In the controversy over slavery they had been spectators rather than participants, only interfering when it threatened to degenerate into a mere brawl conducted without regard to the rules which had been developed for the settlement of political differences. Such a condition having arisen after the election, the people bent all their efforts to restore harmony because they realized that their own future wellbeing depended upon the maintenance of the existing political structure. They proposed acts of Congress, they attempted to obtain a solution of the problem by the mediation of their States, and in every other way they strove to bring back the Southern people to their allegiance. When their efforts failed, they showed a disinclination to join either side against the other. Their position at the time of Lincoln's inauguration was practically one of neutrality.

The problem of both the Union and the Confederate governments in dealing with the Borderland was diplomatic, rather than purely political, in character. The solidarity of sentiment made advisable the adoption of a program which would appeal to the whole section; and

the considerable acceptance of the doctrine of States'
rights made necessary carefully conducted negotiations
with the authorities of the States. The prize was well
worth striving for. If the North were to conquer the
seceded States, it must secure the active coöperation of
the Borderland. If the South were to succeed in its movement for independence, it must secure its support, or at
least its continued neutrality. Each section had good
reason to be hopeful of the result. The people of the
Borderland were Southern in origin, and therefore could
be expected to maintain a sympathetic attitude toward
the South. Their trade, throughout most of their existence, had been with the port of New Orleans, and the
force of commercial habit was still influential. Their
disapproval of the purposes and methods of the extreme
abolitionists was well known. On the other hand, the
economic and social organization of the Borderland was
nearly similar to that of the North. The old barrier to
free intercourse had been broken down by the construction of the railroads, with the result that a community
of commercial interests between the two sections had
quickly developed. And the popular disapproval of the
militant pro-slavery movement in the South had just
been expressed in the election of 1860. To all appearances the forces were nearly equally balanced. The
issue depended upon the future measures taken by the
government concerning the matters in which the Borderland was peculiarly interested.

In dealing with the situation, Lincoln showed far
more acumen than Davis and other Southern leaders,
first, in estimating correctly the position of the people
of the Borderland, and secondly, in seizing upon the issue
to which, in the greatest degree, they were susceptible.

If he had based his policy upon the rights of a downtrodden race, as another Republican President might have done, he would have had the North with him, but he would have lost the Borderland and with it, all hope of reëstablishing the Union. He was extremely careful not to make this the issue. Instead, he risked having only the lukewarm support of the North by appealing, from the beginning of his administration, almost solely to the nationalist sentiments of all the people. In relieving Fort Sumter, he took the greatest possible precaution to show that he did not intend to attack any State, but only to keep possession of a fort which belonged to the national government. He made it plain that if war occurred it would have to be inaugurated by the South in firing upon the flag of the United States. The outcome won for the national government the support of all the States of the Borderland except Missouri and Kentucky; and even in Missouri, only a small faction actively aided the state authorities in their resistance. In his relations with Kentucky, he conceded points, he tacitly recognized an assumed neutrality, and he delayed important military operations, all out of deference to the feeling of States' rights which existed there. He showed such a disinclination to favor emancipation as to provoke an abolitionist gibe that "Mr. Lincoln would like to have God on his side, but he must have Kentucky." The Southern leaders, on the other hand, utterly failed to grasp the essential nature of the situation. They adopted an intractable and dictatorial policy, finally ending in a foolish invasion of the State which turned it toward the active and powerful support of the Federal government.

After the people of the Borderland had made their decisions and, on an impulse of glowing patriotism, had pledged men and money to defend the Union, the problem was by no means solved. There still remained the danger of reaction, of a sudden cooling of ardor, which would have been as calamitous as the assumption of a neutral position from the beginning. As Lincoln said, the people must have their pride enlisted, must want to beat the rebels. It was therefore necessary that the national government continue to conduct the war solely on the issue of union against disunion, and that it give the responsible leaders in each State the greatest possible latitude in the determination of purely local questions, interfering only when they went too far. This is the explanation for the freedom of action enjoyed by Dennison, Morton and Yates, by Pierpont, Garrett Davis and Blair. In pursuance of this policy the Restored Government of Virginia was recognized, and West Virginia was later admitted as a State. Through the wise advice of the leaders in Kentucky, the State was allowed to occupy a completely neutral position over a period of several months, during which secret propagandist activities gradually turned the people toward the Union. Only in Missouri was the confidence in the judgment of the leaders misplaced. Their over-aggressive policy would have been disastrous if the mass of the people had not been so strongly imbued with nationalist sentiments that they were able to overlook flagrant attacks upon the dignity of their State.

Among all the secondary problems of the war which the national government had to face, the question of slavery proved the most difficult. The North demanded immediate emancipation as a matter of justice to the slaves, as a means of bringing the war to a speedy close, and also, it is suspected, in order to punish the people of the South. If there had been only two sections, the solution of the problem would have been easy. It was difficult, because the people of the Borderland wanted the subject left alone. The slaveholders among them at no time in the course of the war formed a distinct political group against which partisan feeling could arise. Most of them heartily supported the cause of the Union, offering their lives and property freely to put down the rebellion. In spite of the outrageous treatment which they sometimes received from subordinate commanders of Northern troops, they never wavered in their loyalty. Naturally the mass of the people respected them for the attitude they had taken and wished them well. Even in the new State of West Virginia, where the feeling against slavery was more highly developed than in any other slave State, the people refused to insert a provision for emancipation in their constitution until forced to do so by the Congress. Lacking reasons to change their opinions on the subject of slavery, the people retained the ones they held at the beginning of the war. They had a distinct aversion to assisting the abolitionists in what they regarded as their meddling policy toward the South. They wanted the war to be fought solely for the preservation of the Union: they opposed its being or becoming an assault against the institution of slavery.

No one appreciated this feeling more than Lincoln. In the first months of the war he took occasion several times —and each time to the detriment of his popularity at the North—to reverse or modify the ill-advised acts of some of his subordinates in decreeing the freedom of slaves within the Union lines. Afterward for a time, he steadfastly resisted the pressure brought to bear upon him to issue a proclamation of emancipation. Whether

or not he personally desired to secure the freedom of the
slaves in this way is a debatable question, but certain it
is that he thought it necessary to delay until after he
had had an opportunity to prepare doubtful citizens for
the result. When the policy was finally forced by the
Republican leaders in the North, the war had been in
progress a sufficiently long time for the people of the
Borderland to be thoroughly enlisted in it. Despite their
almost unanimous opposition to emancipation, they generally remained willing to prosecute the war, since its
successful termination seemed to offer the only hope for
the restoration of the Union. But the popular enthusiasm was damped. Nearly everywhere throughout the
Borderland it seemed to the people that the contest had
degenerated from its previous high purpose into a mere
struggle between sections. The political discontent that
had gradually developed against the activities of the
administration was greatly increased. In the elections
of 1862 the voters generally preferred Democratic candidates. The leaders of that party, finding the people with
them, took advantage of the opportunity to promote a
factious opposition to the war, which impeded the work
of the civil and military authorities. Worse still, the
sympathizers with the South were encouraged to engage
in secret disloyal activities covering a wide range and
threatening to undermine completely the popular support of the government.

The dangers inherent in the situation led the public
authorities to adopt a rigorous system of repression.
Since most of the activities were not in contravention of
the existing laws, the measures taken were necessarily
extra-legal, perhaps extra-constitutional. They could be
justified only under the rather indefinite scope of the

war powers. Freedom of speech and of the press was curtailed. The privilege of the writ of habeas corpus was suspended in districts outside the theater of hostilities. Arbitrary arrests were frequent. Virtual banishment was added to the list of punishments to which American citizens were liable. And elections were no longer free. It is doubtful if these measures were beneficial to the government. They did not, of course, make disloyal persons loyal. They did not increase the devotion of those who were already actively engaged in supporting the war. It is probable that they did not turn doubtful people toward the Union, but rather had the effect of arousing a spirit of opposition among them. A saving feature of the situation was that the people were able to distinguish between loyalty to the Union and the support of the Republican administration.

It may be well to point out again that the course taken by the people of the Borderland exercised a decisive influence over the history of the country during the period of the Civil War. In the beginning, when many people in the North showed a disinclination to do anything toward preserving the Union, they threw their whole strength into an effort to secure a peaceful settlement of the difficulties. Though they failed, they were yet successful; for they effectually halted the secessionist movement, and they gained time for the development of nationalist sentiment everywhere except in the South. When the war was begun by the Confederate States, they devoted themselves with rare zeal to the single purpose of restoring the authority of the national government. Their voluntary enlistments were greater in proportion to population than those of other sections, and the draft was necessary among them at a later date.

Even when the issue of the war was apparently changed by the proclamation of emancipation, they were wise enough not to be turned away from the main object they had in view. They continued to support the armed forces of the Union until the military strength of the Confederacy was destroyed, and the authority of the United States was again extended over all parts of the country.

INDEX

Abolitionist movement, character, 33; attitude of the Borderland toward, 34, 37, 38; see Emancipation.

Abolitionists, in the election of 1860, 40; denounced, 79, 222; demand an emancipation proclamation, 317.

Adams, Charles Francis, would have conciliated the border States, 89.

Adams County, Ohio, in the election of 1860, 74.

Agriculture, importance, 15-17.

Alabama, economic pressure proposed by, 99.

Alexander County, Ill., in the election of 1860, 69.

American Knights, Order of, in Missouri, 382.

Anderson, Robert, at Fort Sumter, 263; commissioned to raise troops, 277; headquarters moved to Louisville, 296; forbids military arrests, 372.

Anderson County, Ky., opinion, 284.

Anti-Nebraska Democrats, 44.

Anti-slavery movement, see Abolitionist movement, Emancipation.

Arkansas, secessionist movement, 133.

Army, strength in 1860, 86.

Ashtabula County, Ohio, protest of citizens, 331.

Assessments upon secessionists, 371.

Atchison, David R., leader of proslavery movement, 34.

Baldwin, John B., conference with Lincoln, 162.

Baltimore, commercial interests, 5.

Baltimore and Ohio Railroad, construction, 20; strategic importance, 219; and the formation of West Virginia, 362.

Banks, Nathaniel P., candidate for President, 53.

Barboursville, Va., burned, 368.

Bartholomew County, Ind., resistance to the draft, 341.

Bates, Edward, candidate for President, 55-57; on the relief of Fort Sumter, 160; spokesman for Missouri conservatives, 247; declares movement to divide Virginia revolutionary, 360.

Beauregard, P. G. T., mentioned, 163.

Bell, John, nominated for President; 51; popular support, 62-75.

Bell, Major W. H., would have surrendered the St. Louis arsenal, 127.

Belleville *Democrat*, quoted, 81.

Benton, Thomas H., mentioned, 8, 54, 67; ousted from the Senate, 35; related to Fremont, 45.

Berkeley County, Va., to be included in West Virginia, 362.

Berthold mansion, riot, 150.

Blair, Francis P., Jr., Democratic leader, 54, 66; conference with Lincoln, 55; on attitude of the secessionists, 124; coöperation with other unionists, 126-127; and the removal of Major Bell, 127; friendship with Lyon, 130; secures command of the arsenal for Lyon, 155; offers troops from Missouri, 227; seeks the removal of Harney, 230; approves proposal to attack Camp Jackson, 235; on the Harney-Price agree-

341; resisted in Kentucky, 381;
necessary in West Virginia, 384.
Dred Scott case, 46.
Duke, Basil W., mission to the
South, 232.
Duncan, Blanton, enlists men for
the South, 264, 267.
Dunmore's War, influence on the
settlement of the West, 10.

Early, Jubal A., in the Virginia
convention, 112.
East Tennessee, unionist senti-
ment, 133; movement for a new
State, 287-290.
Edwards County, Ill., in the elec-
tion of 1860, 69.
Election of 1856, 45.
Election of 1860, 40-41, 48-75.
Election of 1862, 332.
Election of 1864, 348, 381.
Elections, military interference
with, 373, 381.
Emancipation, early movement
toward, 32; see Abolitionist
movement.
Emancipation, compensated, pro-
posed by Lincoln, 377-378.
Emancipation proclamation, op-
posed in Kentucky, 293; in the
border free States, 331; in the
slave States, 379; results, 392.
Everett, Edward, nominated for
Vice-President, 51.
Ewing, General Hugh, orders Ken-
tucky troops disbanded, 381.

Farrar, Ben G., on government
contracts, 247.
Filley, Oliver D., unionist leader,
125.
Fillmore, Millard, candidate of
Know-Nothings, 45.
Flatboat navigation, 18.
Floyd, General John B., in the
Kanawha Valley, 208.
Fort Donelson captured, 310.
Fort Henry captured, 310.
Fort Pickens reinforced, 161.
Fort Smith, Ark., opinion, 133.
Fort Sumter, Lincoln would re-
lieve, 159; cabinet advice, 160;
results of attack. in Virginia,

163; in the North, 167; in Indiana, 173; in Kentucky, 263.
Fountain County Ind., disorder,
341.
Franklin County, Ill., Confederate enlistments, 178.
Frederick County, Va., to be included in West Virginia, 362.
Fremont, John C., nominated for
President, 45; appointed to command in Missouri, 256; relieved
of command, 260; manumission
of slaves, 293; results of removal,
316; discourages enlistment of
state troops, 353; proclaims
martial law, 354; agreement
with Price, 354; presidential
candidacy supported by radicals,
383.
Frost, General D. M., interview
with Bell, 127; refuses to assist
Minute Men, 151; in command
of Camp Jackson, 233; offers aid
to Lyon, 234; surrenders, 237.
Fugitive slave laws, attempts to
nullify, 34; enforcement desired
in Kentucky, 84; amendments
proposed, 88, 93.

Gamble, Hamilton R., favors Crittenden compromise, 125; elected
governor of Missouri, calls for
volunteers, 353; on military excesses, 369; enrollment of citizens, 370; policy opposed by radicals, 383.
Garfield, J. A., victory in eastern
Kentucky, 310.
Garnett, General R. S., commander in northwestern Virginia,
205.
Garrard, Colonel T. T., mentioned,
309.
Garrison, William Lloyd, abolitionist leader, 47.
Gasconade County, Mo., in the
election of 1860, 68.
Georgia, sends representatives to
Virginia, 111.
Germans, distribution, 13; influence on the election of 1860, 65-
74; drilling by *Turnvereins*, 121;
volunteer to protect St. Louis

Hubbard, Chester D., opposes secession, 189.

Hunter, R. M. T., mentioned, 216.

Illinois, early settlement, 12; in the election of 1856, 45; in the election of 1860, 68; Southern sympathizers, 81; and the Peace Conference, 94; doubtful attitude of the legislature, 137; secessionist movement in, 138; response to the attack on Fort Sumter, 177; opposition in southern, 177; Douglas turns the tide, 179-181; appropriations for defense, 182; enlistments in 1861, 184; election of 1861, 320; convention in session, 320-321; in the election of 1862, 333; disloyal resolutions, 338; conflict between Yates and the legislature, 339; disorder, 340.

Indiana, early settlement, 11; in the election of 1856, 45; in the election of 1860, 69-73; and the Peace Conference, 94; Democratic resolutions, January, 1861, 136; response to the firing on Fort Sumter, 173-177; military condition at the outbreak of war, 174; enlistments in 1861, 184; criticism of the war, 323; in the election of 1862, 333; conflict between Morton and the legislature, 333-335; personal government by Morton, 335-338; disorders, 341; plot of the Sons of Liberty, 348.

Indiana Legion, organized, 176; suppresses disorder, 341.

Indianapolis, response to the attack on Fort Sumter, 173.

Irish, settle in the Borderland, 14; enlistments, 169.

Jackson, Judge Albert, unionist declaration, 222.

Jackson, Andrew, mentioned, 53; policy toward nullification, 79, 149.

Jackson, Claiborne F., pro-slavery leader, 34; candidate for governor of Missouri, supports Douglas, 66; inaugural address, 117; estimate, 118; arranges to seize the arsenal, 127; urges secession, 132; criticizes the convention, 153; refuses to furnish militia to the national government, 225; orders encampment of militia, 226; sends mission to the South, 232; organizes the state army, 242; conference with Lyon, 252; preparations to resist Lyon, 253; extent of his influence, 261-262; proclaims the independence of Missouri, 355.

Jackson, Congressman James S., raises troops for the Union, 308.

Jackson, General John J., opposes movement for a new State, 197.

Jackson, "Stonewall," mentioned, 129.

Jacob, Lieutenant-Governor R. T., banished to the South, 380.

Janney, John, president of the Virginia convention, 110; interpretation of powers, 112.

Jay, John, on the importance of the Mississippi River, 97.

Jayhawkers invade Missouri, 222.

Jefferson City, Mo., opinion, 131, 223.

Jefferson County, Va., to be included in West Virginia, 362.

Johnson, Andrew, supports compromises, 87; unionist leader, 288.

Johnson, George W., secessionist leader, 286.

Johnson, Herschel V., candidate for Vice-President, 51.

Johnson, Joseph, favors secession, 200.

Johnston, General Albert Sidney, opposes Confederate withdrawal from Kentucky, 301; evacuates Bowling Green and Columbus, 310.

Kanawha Valley, division of Methodist church, 33; in the election of 1860, 62; military operations, 207; opinion toward Union, 209; guerrilla warfare, 366.